DATE DUE

DEMCO 38-296

THE FIRST ATLANTIC LINERS

Seamanship in the Age of Paddle Wheel, Sail and Screw

The PS British Queen *was built of wood by Messrs. Curling and Young of Limehouse, London, for the British and American Steam Navigation Co, and launched on 24 May 1838. She was fitted with side-lever engines of 500 nominal hp constructed by Robert Napier. Gross register 1862 tons; length overall 275ft; breadth of hull 40.5ft; draught 17ft.*

THE FIRST ATLANTIC LINERS

Seamanship in the Age of Paddle Wheel, Sail and Screw

Peter Allington Master Mariner (HT)

Basil Greenhill BA, PhD, D.Litt, FSA, FR Hist S

CONWAY
MARITIME PRESS

Dedicated to Ewan Corlett
who initiated the saving of SS *The Great Britain*

© Basil Greenhill, Peter Allington, 1997

First published in Great Britain in 1997 by
Conway Maritime Press,
an imprint of Brassey's (UK) Ltd,
33 John Street,
London WC1N 2AT

British Library Cataloguing in Publication Data

Allington, Peter
    The first Atlantic Liners: seamanship in the age of paddle wheel, sail and screw
    1. Paddle steamers – Atlantic Ocean – History
    2. Steam-navigation – Atlantic Ocean – History
    I. Title II. Greenhill, Basil, 1920-
    623.8'8'2432'09163

ISBN 0–85177–668–X

Designed and typeset in Caslon 540 by M Rules.
Printed and bound by The Bath Press, Bath.

Contents

Acknowledgements

More than a passing interest has been taken in the writing of this book not only by historians, but also by people who have at some time been connected with the sea and ships. We are indebted to them for their comments and advice, and for the greater involvement of those who have taken the time and trouble to pursue points raised in discussion. We are most grateful to those who have made available illustrations for the book. We are also grateful for the friendly and professional help given by John Underwood and other members of staff at the Science Museum Library, and in like manner, the service offered by the Patents and Hydrographic Offices.

A few more individuals deserve a special mention – Mike Stammers, Director of the Merseyside Maritime Museum, for his help with the illustration of the *Sirius*; Campbell McMurray, Director of the Royal Naval Museum, Portsmouth for permission to quote from his work on the conditions and employment of merchant seaman; Captain Karl Kåhre of Mariehamn, Finland and Captain Søren Thirslund of the Handels og Sjøfartsmuseet at Helsingør, Denmark, for his thoughts on 'sail-assist' rigs; Captain Herbert Karting for a great deal of first hand information on the Vinnen Schooners; Adrian Reed of the Devon and Exeter Institute for making available publications; David Proctor who went out of his way to research information in the *Mariners Mirror* concerning the use of sails on fully powered vessels in the early part of this century and Denis Stonham who took time and trouble to provide us with the illustration of the *Reliant*. On the practical side, Tony Rickard of The National Trust at Cotehele, although a very busy man, always found time to enlarge or reduce the drawings on his photocopying machine, saving much time and travelling. Ann Giffard meticulously corrected the proofs.

Finally, and not least, we owe Sarah Allington our heartfelt thanks, for without her help on the computer, unstintingly and tirelessly given, this book would have taken much longer to complete, if indeed, it would ever have been completed at all.

Peter Allington
Basil Greenhill

CHAPTER 1

The Riddle of the Day

The First Ocean Steamships. A New Study

This book, as its title indicates, is about the beginnings of trans-ocean voyaging made with the continuous use of steam power. It seeks to examine the problems involved in operating deep water paddle steamers; for the resolution of these problems was critical to the commercial success of ocean passenger carrying under steam. We look also from time to time at those problems met in common with the development of the paddle propelled warship. The navy had additional complications to overcome peculiar to the function of a man-of-war which have been examined in a number of late twentieth-century publications,[1] but none of these touch in any depth on the main subject of this book: the handling of sail and paddle wheel, an understanding of which is fundamental to the study of the history of the steamship – with the steam railway locomotive probably the most important vehicle in the development of the world as we know it.

This is economic history and part of the cultural history of seafaring at the same time. Our approach to the subject injects into the economic, business, and social early history of the steamship the realities of the ship and the seaman and the marine engineer on which successful operation depended. The book is the result of collaboration between a merchant seaman of very wide experience and an academic writer much concerned with the history of ships and shipping. It suggests some of the limitations which partly conditioned the steamers' slow development. It is deliberately written in the language of the seaman of the times. It is about his life and work. It is about vessels designed and built to operate constantly under power, but still dependent on the multi-purpose assistance of sails.

This book, by showing the imperfections of the ocean going paddle steamer and the limitations on her earning power imposed by these difficulties, indicates also the great commercial possibilities inherent in solving this part of the 'Riddle of the Age'.[2]

The *Great Western* demonstrated that steam power worked in the limited application of ocean passenger trades, but it had to be made to work much better to attain a reasonable return on investment. These were the pressures which, in a world of enterprise and venture capital, led to the formation of the Screw Propeller Company and, as a result, in due course to the almost simultaneous building of the world's first screw propelled warship, the *Rattler*, and the world's first modern screw propelled merchant steamship, *The Great Britain*, at present under restoration at Bristol in the dock in which she was built.[3] It is impossible to imagine a more important survivor of our 'heritage', in terms of her significance to the industrial, economic and social development of Britain.

Advent of Steam

In its broadest sense, the word 'seamanship' means the skilled handling and safe management, particularly in unfavourable circumstances, of any craft that moves upon the water. It is difficult to define precisely as, among other considerations, the vessel's size, usage and means of propulsion all have a bearing. Before the advent of steam, 'seamanship' was a very complex matter as the main source of energy, the wind, is ever changing, often adverse and, in higher latitudes, unpredictable as to strength and direction for more than a day or so at best; and of course, periods of calm were of no use at all. Tidal streams along the coast or ocean currents could be used, but any advantage gained from tidal assistance lasted for only short periods. However, compared to the wind, it was at least a more predictable source of motive power; and, if the circumstances allowed, the vessel could be kept under control by 'dredging', a technique that involved dragging the anchor along the bottom. Human muscle, used either for kedging, warping or rowing, in its broadest sense, was the most dependable method for moving a craft in harbour; the Mediterranean and Baltic oared fighting ships were a specialised example of this form of manpower. Most of the seaman's problems would be solved if a system were devised that could provide a constant, powerful, easily controllable, economic and reliable means of propulsion, totally independent of the wind, tide or human muscle.

Steam power, already well established ashore by the end of the eighteenth century, was to prove to be the answer, but there were many technical and practical difficulties to overcome and a long period of development in service before all of these points, particularly the question of commercial profitability, were satisfactorily dealt with.

Despite early failures experiments continued until an engine and boiler worked with sufficient reliability to be considered successful. Propulsion was obtained by paddle wheels, either mounted on each side or as a single wheel at the stern, the power supplied in most cases by an engine with only one cylinder. Steam's first application commercially, and also its last for paddle wheel equipped vessels, was in river boats, harbour tugs

Figure 1:1 *Tide, wind, muscle power, paddle and screw with sail assist. This photograph was taken on the tidal River Tamar in southwest Britain about 1900. The local sailing barge* William and Thomas *making her way up river on the last of the flood is going through the wind onto the port tack, the staysail is aback and the crew of two are helping her round with poles pushed against the river bed. A 'market boat', a paddle steamer in regular service, is also making her way up stream to Calstock Quay. The screw steamer* Albion *has jib headed sails or fore and main (stowed on booms swung outboard during the loading by steam crane of her cargo of granite blocks for Dover Harbour) and a staysail made up at the foot of the forestay as her 'sail assist'. Up stream lie two schooners, a brigantine and another Tamar sailing barge. (Postcard)*

Figure 1:2 *Coal burning, hand fired, paddle steamers with two cylinder compound engines were still in use as cargo and passenger carriers on the great rivers of Bangladesh in the 1960s. (Basil Greenhill)*

Figure 1:3 Privateer, *iron paddle tug, built 1883 by T & W Toward at Newcastle, 104 tons gross, fitted with a single cylinder engine by G P Hepple of North Shields of 65hp. She was wrecked near Boulogne in 1916 when on war duties. Shown alongside Bideford Quay when engaged as a summer excursion vessel working the Bristol Channel, her port of registry throughout her career was Swansea. (Basil Greenhill Collection)*

Figure 1:4 *Bristol Hotwells on the Avon with steam packets. The two steamers are the* George IV *of Bristol (left), built there in 1822, and the* Saint Patrick *of Liverpool, also built in 1822. This contemporary engraving probably dates from 1823 when these two steamers briefly ran in competition on the Bristol – Cork service. Both vessels are schooner-rigged with standing gaffs and sails brailing to the throat, with yards on the fore, cockbilled and partly lowered, from which flying square sails could be set. The tall thin funnels provided natural draught for low pressure boilers and took the heat and smoke clear of the sails. (Private Collection)*

and ferries working in sheltered waters. One or two sails were retained aboard these small, short range vessels for steadying purposes, and on occasions could be set in a fair wind to assist progress, but they should be considered as primarily, if not entirely, power-driven.

The next stage was the building of larger vessels that were seaworthy enough for coastal passages and cross-channel routes. They now had two cylinders, which in fact were separate engines, working the same paddle shaft. The sail area was increased, mainly with fore and aft canvas, though the total amount was still small compared with the pure sailing ship of equivalent tonnage. By the 1820s many of the difficulties had been overcome; engines were relatively powerful, some vessels capable of 10 knots, reliability and control had also improved, but coal consumption was still extremely high, thus limiting the range and economic viability of the vessels. Fierce competition developed between the various steam packet companies and,

Figure 1:5 *The* Severn *of Dublin, 201 tons, was built at Liverpool by John Wilson in 1825 and equipped with two sidelever engines of 60hp each. She ran between Cork and Bristol for some years, where she is shown coaling from Severn trows with the Prince Edward Island built, Bristol registered, full rigged ship* Cambridge *in the background. The* Severn *appears to have been rigged as a three-masted schooner with standing gaffs and, allowing for errors of scale and perspective, to have resembled in many respects the Swedish steamer* Eric Nordevall *(see Figure 5:2). Note the cargo gaff-rigged on the fore side of the foremast similar to the* Iris *(Figures 7:10, 7:11 and 7:21), and the fore staysail made up in stops and hoisted on the stay. (Watercolour by T S Rowbotham, 1826, in the Bristol Museum and Art Gallery)*

as speed was all important in attracting passengers, the engines were run non-stop even if the wind was fair. It also became evident that paddle wheel propulsion, which up to a point had been ideal in harbour, had its drawbacks once the vessel started to pitch and roll heavily at sea, and its now more important combination with sail was not without problems.

Further Development to 1838

Extending the voyages down to Spain and the Mediterranean required not only a further increase in the size of vessels with even more powerful machinery, but a larger sail area as the help derived from the wind was now of greater importance; for the amount of fuel carried was not sufficient to complete the passage non-stop under steam, or at least, not with any reserve capacity. Calling in for bunkers would increase times and running costs, so whenever the wind allowed, the sails would be used and the engine either stopped altogether, or continued to

run at reduced power. More specialised rigs were developed with a high proportion of fore and aft canvas, the total amount increased to approximately two-thirds that of a sailing vessel of the same tonnage. Thus a new facet of 'seamanship', the handling of a vessel propelled by wind or steam, or both at the same time, was established, and it is this new skill that forms the main subject of this book.

The history of the beginning and subsequent development of steam propulsion up to the late 1830s has been reassessed and well published in recent years: *The Advent of Steam* (London, 1993) and *Steam, Steel and Shellfire* (London, 1992) cover the story comprehensively and incorporated much new research. It is not the purpose of this book to cover the same ground. We are concerned primarily with the problems met within the operation of the first ocean going merchant steamships in regular service. However, the subject cannot be examined in isolation, so a brief review of progress up to 1838 has been included in Chapter 2. This review is in the words of a contemporary of the period.

Demise of the Paddle Wheel

The history of the steamship is often treated as a continuity of slow development. This is a misleading approach; a more accurate portrayal of events would be that of a 'punctuated evolution', dividing the progress into four or five distinct but overlapping periods, each, after the first, marked by a major technical innovation which determined the use of the steamship for the ensuing era. For all practical purposes the first phase of the ocean going paddle steamer began in the early 1820s with the voyages of the Admiralty paddle steamers *Lightning* and *African* to North Africa and to Sierra Leone and reached its fruition with the establishment of a regular transatlantic service by the *Great Western* in 1838. This phase continued until the 1860s; when, for a number of reasons, principally the introduction of an alternative and more efficient means of propulsion, the screw, and the newly developed compound engine, it came to an end. Because of the many early technical problems and hence financial uncertainty, the screw was not adopted in merchant ships as quickly as it was accepted in the Royal Navy where its advantages over the paddle wheel made it the obvious choice. Nevertheless there were still instances when the paddle wheel was superior, even into recent times; for vessels working in shallow water, some specialist harbour tugs, and passenger ferries operating in relatively sheltered waters, exactly the same situation as at the very start of steam propulsion.

The Compatibility of Sail and Steam

The use of sail and paddle wheel were not completely compatible and herein lies one part of the 'Riddle of the Age', which posed the question: how best to make these two sources of motive power, wind and steam, complement each other?

This book will examine these problems in detail and see how the shipbuilder, seamen, and marine engineer attempted to overcome them, particularly in the period of fruition in the early North Atlantic steam packets. The conclusions reached are based principally on evidence from contemporary sources including the log books of early steamships. There is also an analysis of the various types of sailing rig that evolved, dependent, in the first instance, on the operational requirements of the vessel, and secondly, the relative power of the engines. For example, to take two extremes, a coastal packet on short haul routes capable of over 10 knots under steam had a sail plan of limited area, mostly fore and aft canvas which would be described in modern terminology as 'sail assist'. The much larger man-of-war, required to maintain a global capability independent of regular refuelling, carried nearly a full sailing ship's

Figure 1:6 *The* Lightning *was launched at Deptford in 1823. She was the second naval steam vessel to be built and the first to appear, in January 1828, in the quarterly naval list under the command of Lieutenant George Evans RN (later Admiral). She is here seen leading units of the steam battle fleet through the Ångö Sund in the Åland Islands of Finland during the war with Russia, 1854–6. The lithograph is from a drawing by Oswald Brierly who was on board her at the time. (Private Collection)*

square rig, and except in a few cases where the vessel was equipped with powerful engines, had propulsion units that were considered as auxiliary.

Sources

The technical information on hull design, engine and rig, and the seamanship and shiphandling involved, has been obtained, as the footnotes and bibliography show, in most instances from publications of the period and therefore can be considered a secondary source, but no less important for they reflect the opinions and knowledge, not of the late twentieth century but of the men who were building and sailing these vessels. Whenever possible the origin of a quotation is given; however, one of our sources has been a scrapbook of contemporary newspaper cuttings from the late 1830s to late 1840s, apparently compiled in Liverpool by a member of the family of the late Leonard Tregoning of Landue, Cornwall, who gave us the book. The family was much involved with copper ore shipments at the time and the scrapbook shows they had a strong interest in all contemporary shipping developments. Unfortunately its compiler did not always indicate the source and date of the cuttings but it can be assumed that those unattributed were contemporary with events reported.

The all important function of 'sail assist' is examined, and comparisons made with the pure sailing ship. The limitations arising from the difference between true and apparent wind on fast steamers was a crucial factor in the use of sails and is therefore looked at in depth, also the physical properties of wind power. Details of many relevant patents are given which clearly show the attempts by various engineers, inventors and seamen to improve the performance of engine, paddle wheel and rig. Some were practical, others more fanciful, but all are of historical interest as the common problems are identified.

Using the log books, principally those of the *Great Western*, we examine the techniques adopted by seamen and ships' engineers to maximise the performance of the vessel with the minimum fuel consumption by working engines and sails together. The additional thrust derived from the wind was matched by continuous adjustment of the power delivered by the engines. It was this new seaman's skill of using both sources of power to greatest advantage that kept fuel consumption down to the point at which the *Great Western*, for example, was, despite all the pioneering difficulties, probably commercially viable, operating without a subsidy.

Steam versus Sail

Merchant ships exist for one purpose only – to make a satisfactory return on invested capital, as warships exist to be instruments for the exercise of national power. The history of the development of the steamship is one of groping forward to the ultimate achievement of a vessel which could be operated with much greater efficiency but at the same time, taken overall, more economically than a sailing vessel. This situation was finally achieved only at the beginning of the 1880s with the construction of high pressure steel boilers at competitive cost and the consequent application of the marine triple expansion engine. Then the ocean going sailing vessel was finally made redundant, though her construction for limited trades remained profitable for another decade or so.

Financial, social, technical, political and managerial factors, along with development and changes in many industries ashore, all influenced in a complex network of forces the development of the steamship. All the stages involve entrepreneurial risk taking – sometimes on a very large scale, as with Alfred Holt and his fleet of pioneering compound engine screw steamers of 1866. These vessels effectively established the long distance steamer, and, placed in the China tea trade, rendered the *Cutty Sark* and her contemporaries obsolete before they were built.

On ocean voyages, the routes followed by the sail assisted steamships were different from those of the pure sailing vessel, which in most cases was forced to cover a greater distance working between the same ports. This was another fundamental advantage, for the difference in average speed through the water was, comparing the early side wheelers and the fastest packets, not much different; in fact, on the eastbound crossing of the North Atlantic, passage times were sometimes close, and on several occasions sailing vessels arrived before steamers which had left port at the same time. Many innovations, such as more formalised navigation lights, the introduction of certificates of competency, the establishment of a 'Rule of the Road' and the first use of iron for hull plating and rigging, were all due to the development of the steamship, and were as important to the progress of shipping in general as were the paddle wheel and screw.

Here, in this book, we deal with one aspect of this complex story, the birth of the ocean going sail assisted steamer, paddle wheels being the only propulsion system available at that time, and especially with the handling of her at sea and the wider operational problems she presented.

1 See for example A Lambert ed., *Steam, Steel and Shellfire* (London, 1992); B Greenhill and A Giffard, *Steam, Politics and Patronage* (London, 1994)

2 Phrase used by Swedish American gunnery officer, Rear Admiral John Adolf Dahlgren, quoted in F L Robertson, *The Evolution of Naval Armament* (London, 1921) p. 234. The 'riddle' in its entirety comprised the problem of designing a satisfactory paddle propelled warship

3 For detailed study of the developments see A Lambert op cit; B Greenhill (ed), *The Advent of Steam* (London, 1993); B Greenhill and A Giffard, op cit; E Corlett, *The Iron Ship*, 4th impression (London, 1983)

CHAPTER 2

The Early Days 1804–38

Arrival at New York

The month of April 1838 saw the first crossing of the North Atlantic by the paddle steamer *Sirius* from Cork to New York, closely followed by the *Great Western* from Bristol. Both vessels had used their engines non-stop, or as expressed at the time 'by the unceasing aid of steam'.[1] This had never been done before and the faith and commitment shown by the engineers, shipbuilders and financial backers was completely vindicated. The enterprise had received criticism and even ridicule as being impossible; no vessel, it was said, could carry enough fuel. According to a report in the *Liverpool Albion*, Dr Lardner, a respected scholar of the day, when giving a lecture on steam navigation in 1835 stated, 'the project of making a voyage directly from New York to Liverpool was perfectly chimerical; and they might as well talk of making a voyage from New York or Liverpool to the moon'.[2]

However, in his book published in the early 1850s, entitled *Steam and its Uses*, Dr Lardner denied ever having said anything of the sort. This controversy is further examined later in this chapter.

Nevertheless both vessels had arrived safely, and the doubters, if not silenced, were at least muted for the time being. It was a truly magnificent achievement and recognised as such. The following extract from the Journal of Colonel Webb, editor of the *New York Courier* and witness to the great event, is expressive of a contemporary view:[3]

> The arrival of these two steam ships in our waters, within a few hours of each other, produced an excitement in our city, which was more universal, and extended further among all classes of our population, than any event since the war of 1812; and our authorities and citizens generally, vied with each other in doing honour to the enterprising commanders, who had so successfully achieved the great work in which they had embarked. But it was not possible

Figure 2:1 *This contemporary oil painting in the Merseyside Maritime Museum is entitled* Steam Vessel *Sirius*, Lieutenant Rich. Roberts RN off New York. *(Trustees of the National Museums and Galleries on Merseyside)*

Figure 2:2 *This oil painting on canvas by Isaac Heard (1804–69) shows the* Great Western *steaming and closehauled with square fore-topsail set. It has inaccuracies of scale and detail. What appears to be* The Great Britain *is visible off the vessel's starboard quarter. (Parker Gallery)*

Figure 2:2 *This oil painting on canvas by Isaac Heard (1804–69) shows the* Great Western *steaming and closehauled with square fore-topsail set. It has inaccuracies of scale and detail. What appears to be* The Great Britain *is visible off the vessel's starboard quarter. (Parker Gallery)*

until this afternoon, justly to estimate the full extent of the excitement which existed, or properly to appreciate the universal enthusiasm which this novel event had imparted to every portion of our population. We knew that the subject was on the lips of all, and that the usual salutations of the day were always followed by congratulations upon the arrival of these thrice welcome strangers in our waters; we knew that the *Great Western* was literally run down with thousands of all classes, eager to look upon this eighth wonder of the world, this steam leviathan, which had thus realised their most sanguine anticipations in relation to the ultimate navigation of the Atlantic by steam; we knew too that the *Sirius* was very generally looked upon as a kind of interloper, chartered for the purpose of snatching honours from those to whom they justly belonged, and that the exhibition of interest at her departure was no test of what would be evinced when the *Great Western*, a ship built for the very purpose of bringing the two countries nearer together, and looked upon emphatically as 'our own', should leave our shores, yet notwithstanding all this, we did not and could not anticipate such an outpouring of public feeling as has this day been exhibited.

There were at that time over 700 steamboats in North America, almost as many as in Great Britain, the vast majority under 300 tons and employed on the rivers, lakes and inshore sounds along the coast.

A contemporary press report from 1839 states:

Whole number of steam boats, locomotives and other steam engines. The whole number of steam-engines of every kind in the United States reckoning one to each boat is ascertained and estimated to be 3,010. Of these 2,653 have been ascertained and 357 estimated, in places where the returns are either defective, or not received at all. Of this whole number about 800 are supposed to be employed in steam boats; of which 700 are ascertained and 100 estimated.

As early as 1820 the *Robert Fulton* of over 700 tons was successfully engaged in the passenger service, running from New York as far south as Havana in the Gulf of Mexico.[4]

The sight of a paddle steamer was therefore not something new to the multitude lining the shore. They were curious no doubt, but were really celebrating the safe arrival of two vessels that had achieved a tremendous advance in steam navigation which effectively brought the two continents so much closer together.

Passage Analysis

The *Sirius* was the smaller of the two and had little fuel left on arrival, and it is doubtful if she could have managed the crossing without the sails. In fact she completed only two round voyages before being withdrawn, the charterers having lost £3,500 – say very roughly a quarter of a million at mid 1990s values.[5]

The *Great Western* also made use of her canvas but still had coal on board sufficient for several days' more steaming, having covered a greater distance at a higher average speed. However, as each vessel started from a different port 200 miles apart with a time interval of four days between the commencement of the voyages, any comparison of the average speed must take these two facts into account. The calculation is usually based on the elapsed time and distance sailed or steamed between two fixed points and an ocean voyage commences at the 'departure' position and is completed when the vessel has reached the 'end of passage', a place close to the final destination. Neither the published log book of the *Great Western* nor the abstracts of the voyage of the *Sirius* contain this specific information. Some idea of the relative speed can be made by simply using the elapsed time, port to port, and the distances as given in *Brown's Nautical Almanac*, which are: Bristol to New York 3,049nm, and Cork to New York 2,851nm. For all practical purposes, this works out at 8.3 knots for the *Great Western* and 6.4 knots for the *Sirius*, which may seem considerably slower, but much of this was due to the longer period of strong to gale force head winds. In fact average speed over the ground was about half a knot more as both vessels covered a greater distance than given in the *Almanac*.

According to the notes in Joshua Field's 'Glances at Atlantic Steam Navigation 1838–1841' in the Science Museum, the *Great Western* steamed 3,223nm between Bristol and New York. The log book states she hove up her anchor at the mouth of the River Avon at 1000hrs on 8 April but was not up to full speed until 1130hrs as people were working over the bows catting the anchor. As she was under way at 1100hrs, this time can be considered as the start of the voyage which ended as she entered New York Harbour at 1400hrs on 23 April, the elapsed time being 15 days and 8 hours, if 5 hours is allowed for the difference in longitude; her average speed therefore was 8.8 knots. The total fuel consumption was reckoned to be 445 tons which left 155 tons still on board, and based on these figures, she burnt an average 29 tons of coal a day.

A report by Captain Christopher Claxton, one of the directors of the Great Western Steam Ship Company, was published in 1845 in Bristol, entitled *A Description of* The Great Britain *Steam Ship*, which contained a list of the passages made by the *Great Western* in Appendix 1. Her time for the maiden voyage, Bristol to New York, is given by chronometer as 15 days, 10 hours, the distance covered being 3,111nm. Based on these figures her average speed was 8.4 knots.

Given this data, it would seem possible for the crossing to have been made without any assistance from the sails. Under power alone, fuel consumption would have increased, probably 32 tons per day average. This estimate is based on the actual amount used on the first day when she was deep loaded, which according to the log book was 36 tons, and that required on the last full day, down to 28 tons, the vessel on a much lighter draught. On both days, although some sail was set, engines were at full power. As the assistance provided by the sail more than balanced the negative effects due to the windage of the rig, a slower speed would result from paddle propulsion alone. Provided she did not suffer a serious mechanical breakdown and the weather conditions were no worse than actually experienced, it is probable the voyage could have been completed under steam power but would have taken longer and used more fuel. If the winds had only been light and variable, force 2 or less, then the use of sails would be limited.

This view was put forward at the time by none other than Junius Smith, the Connecticut Yankee, one of the promoters of the *Sirius*, and a director in the British and American Steam Navigation Company which was to involve itself for a few years with steamers in the Atlantic trade. In his letters on steam navigation he writes:[6]

> I do not doubt that more power is lost by the resistance of the masts and rigging in steam ships, than is gained by the use of sails. I am aware that it will be said that sails relieve the engines; but upon the same principle, distress the engine in proportion to the degree of resistance and the time of its continuance. The truth is, as I apprehend it, the engines, if properly constructed, will perform their duty just as well without the aid of sails as with it.

The quotation is only part of one of Junius Smith's letters on this subject and was written before his company's *British Queen* had been put into service. Later he took passage in her to New York on her maiden voyage. According to his personal log of the crossing,[7] the winds were light for most of the time and in a letter dated 5 October 1839, he refers to this voyage:[8] 'It was a rare thing in our passage out or home to see any advantage from the wind. If the ship had been stripped of masts and sail I am perfectly satisfied from actual observation that we would have made a quicker passage.'

There seems to be no evidence that his opinions were shared by the professional seamen who served on these early steamers. Indeed, as this book will show, sails were absolutely essential to the handling and to the successful commercial operation of early ocean going paddle steamers. It was only with the introduction of the screw propeller and more efficient and reliable engines that masts and sail began to be a less important part of the seagoing capabilities of steam vessels. Even in the 1890s, some powerful ocean liners still had sails and yards crossed on two masts and as late as the 1920s, staysails were still being used. The British India Steam Navigation Company's *Cononada* set them on her run between Rangoon and the Coromandel coast in 1925 to damp down the heavy rolling.[9] Paddle

Figure 2:3 *This 'replica' of an early steam vessel gives a very good impression of the appearance of the* Sirius *under steam alone. (The late Alan Villiers)*

Figure 2:4 *The figurehead of Sirius,* the Dog Star, *is now preserved in the Hull City Museum. (Hull Museums)*

Figure 2:5 *The steel paddle steamer* Cambria *was built at Alloa in 1895 and broken up in 1946. Owned by P & A Campbell she still carried a foresail and staysail (in coats, probably little if ever used) in the 1930s. (Postcard)*

Figure 2:6 *The Estonian iron steamer* Anna, *478 tons, built 1893, completing discharge of timber cargo at Dover, August 1939. She has standing gaffs and two sails brailing to the weather. (Basil Greenhill)*

excursion steamers operating in the Bristol Channel carried sails in the 1930s, and even more recently some small steam coasters carried a sail in the 1950s.

Contemporary View of Progress

The reduction in canvas carried by steamers had started at least 40 years before the *Cononada*. In 1885 the shipowner Walter Runciman (later Baron Runciman of Shoreston) was one of the first to remove yards from steamers he purchased and according to his autobiography:

> The vessel had four square sail yards, this meant gear, sails, ropes, yards, paint, labour and retarded speed during contrary winds without obtaining anything like corresponding advantages with fair winds. All superfluity of this kind was abolished and I think I can claim to be one of the first to do away with this unnecessary and expensive furnishing. Whoever puts square sails yards on a steamer now?[10]

A brief résumé of progress up to 1840 will show how important a step forward was the ocean going, sail assisted paddle steamer, and establish its place at the beginning of the long transitional period which ended only when the carrying of sail on fully-powered deep sea commercial vessels virtually ceased.

The following extracts are from press cuttings taken from the scrapbook referred to in Chapter 1 and possibly originating from *The Times*, though the compiler did not indicate their source. They comprise a report by a Count Daru to the French Chamber of Deputies in 1839. They cover the early period, beginning slowly with just a handful of pioneering steamers up to the late 1830s and rapidly increasing development. Although the text contains errors (which have been corrected here) and the omission of a number of significant voyages, this appraisal, coming as it does from a contemporary observer outside Britain, is worth quoting. The translation is rather flowery:

> It was in 1807, that the first steam boat appeared: it was constructed by Fulton; its engine had a power of 18 horses, and accomplished the passage from New York to Albany in 33 hours. It was the lot of North America, whose streams, lakes, extensive coasts, interrupted by enormous bays and covered with islands, are so well adapted to the establishment of steamers, to enter the first in this career and cement by means of this wonderful instrument of communication, the bond of unity between the population scattered on its soil in a state of isolation and almost completely without communication with each other.
>
> The progress of steam navigation there was rapid. We see in an official report presented on the 13th of December, 1838, to the American Congress, by the

Secretary of the Treasury, that 1,300 steam-boats have been built in the United States from 1808 up to 1839. Of these 800 are still serviceable.

> In England the first steamer was launched on the Clyde in 1811. It is not uninteresting to see the progress made by Great Britain in this particular. The last statistical reports published at Liverpool give on this point the following data.
>
> There were in 1814 only two steam-boats in England, in 1816 only 15, in 1825 there were already 163; in 1835, 538; in 1839, 840.
>
> We here see in what a considerable ratio these numbers have successively increased.
>
> In France, the first attempts date scarcely sooner than from 1820, and it was only in 1826, after many fruitless attempts, that a regular service of steam-packets was established on the Saône. Our progress, therefore, has been slow in the career which other nations had thrown open. The cause of this is perhaps the bad state of our rivers. The Rhône is an impetuous stream and difficult of ascent. The Loire, extensive and changeable in its course, offers a depth of water which is frequently insufficient. The Seine has its frequent bends. Now, in every country, steam navigation was, in the first place, established on rivers, because their courses offer fewer obstacles, require less powerful engines – in short, present greater facilities for circulation than are offered by the sea. For several years, however, our advancement has been evident. In the last account given by the mining administration we see that in 1833, we had 75 steam-boats; in 1834, 82; 1835, 100; 1836, 105; 1837, 124; 1838, 160. This statement does not include Government steamers, of which there are 38, carrying engines of from 160 to 250 horse power.
>
> Thus England holds the first rank, the United States the second, and France the third. The form, dimensions, and power of steam-boats evidently depend on the service to which they are destined. They were not long merely employed in the ascent and descent of rivers, but soon the limits of steam navigation were enlarged. Increasing the power of the engines from 20 to 30, 160, 200, and 250 horses, it became possible to extend the field of their employment to venture on the sea with them. Towing boats, which had been constructed in a few ports, soon throw light on the superiority of the new system, by bringing out large vessels, weather bound and condemned to inactivity, and drawing them in their wake with a facility which seemed to defy the elements. From that day the bright days of sailnavigation, which, till then, was looked upon as the *chefd'œuvre* of human understanding, were eclipsed. Now vessels were started on every coast. Regular and rapid communication linked together every important town, such as Le Havre, London, Dover, Hamburgh, Rotterdam. This was the forerunner of more daring attempts.

In 1819 a vessel from the United States, the *Savannah*, crossed the Ocean to Liverpool, partly by wind and partly by steam. America thus had the lead again in daring to apply Fulton's machine to long voyages, and this is the more remarkable, that it has always had but few steamboats on sea service. In 1836 the English undertook the passage from Falmouth to the Cape of Good Hope; the *Atalante* using her engines continuously. The *Berenice*, the *Medea*, the *Zenobia*, performed passages of different lengths on the coast of Africa, and in the Indian sea. All these boats were English.

These numerous experiments gave rise to the idea that, by the aid of steam, it was possible to accomplish the distance between Europe and the United States. The difficulty of carrying the necessary quantity of coals for the consumption of an engine acting, without interruption, from one shore of the ocean to the other, during a space of from 15 to 20 days, was no longer an obstacle. It had been discovered that the consumption of combustibles did not

Figure 2:7 *The paddle sloop* Berenice, *664 tons, was built for the East India Company by Robert Napier on the Clyde in 1837. (India Office Library)*

Figure 2:8 *The paddle steamer* Cape Breton, *built at Blackwall, London, in 1833, made the first steam assisted crossing of the North Atlantic on her delivery passage for use in connection with coal mining operations at Sydney, Nova Scotia, in July–August 1833. In this somewhat fanciful drawing she is shown in deep trouble on a later transatlantic passage. (Maritime Museum of the Atlantic, Halifax, NS)*

increase in the same ratio with the power of the motors – that an engine of 250 horse power, for instance, was far from burning twice as much fuel as was necessary for an engine of 125 horse power; that, moreover, certain parts of the mechanism might be simplified in such a manner as to take up less room, and, consequently, leave more space at disposal for the accommodation of passengers or merchandise. From this time operations were commenced, and on the 4th of April, 1838, the first experiment was tried. You are all acquainted, Gentlemen, with the result. You all beheld the enthusiasm excited by the success of the voyage undertaken by the *Sirius*; 18 days had been sufficient for its passage. Scarcely had this vessel arrived in the port of New York when it was joined by the *Great Western*, which started from Bristol on the 8th of the same month, after a passage of 15½ days.

Henceforth the problem was solved. America was nearer the European continent by half the distance which formerly separated them. There could be no more doubt concerning it: the events which have since occurred have ratified these first expectations.

Among the notable omissions from Count Daru's report are the earlier *Charlotte Dundas*, built in Scotland in 1802 for use as a tug, and the several transatlantic voyages made by paddle steamers. Engines were used when it was advantageous but the prime mover in all cases was still the sails. These were: the *Rising Star*, which in 1821 went out to Valparaiso, the first into the Pacific; the Dutch vessel *Curaçao* in 1827; and the eastbound crossing of the *Royal William* from Canada to Liverpool in 1833, and earlier in the same year the *Cape Breton*, just over 100ft long, went the other way from England to Nova Scotia. These were all essentially delivery voyages. The Royal Navy, contrary to popular belief, was involved with steam propulsion at a very early stage, ordering the first vessel, the *Comet*, in 1821. By 1830 the navy had extended operations into the Mediterranean with a regular mail service conducted by paddle steamers. This was the first regular long distance service to be operated under steam and gave the Royal Navy unique pioneering experience. The first crossing of the Atlantic by a naval steamer was in 1833. HMSV *Rhadamanthus* refuelled in the Azores but relied on her canvas for most of the voyage. In 1825 the privately owned paddle steamer *Enterprise* went out to India via the Cape of Good Hope, a truly pioneering venture and one that will be looked at in greater detail later in this book.

The following extract from the *Liverpool Mail* gives the annual increase and tonnage of steamships up to 1836.[11] Steam tonnage is still only a small fraction of the total tonnage figure, made up predominantly of sailing vessels:

The Development of Steam

As the year 1838 will most assuredly form a remarkable epoch in the history of steam navigation, it may not be thought uninteresting to trace the advances it has made since the year 1814, when one steam-boat, of 69 tons burden, floated in solitude on the British waters.

The following authentic account of the number and tonnage of steam-vessels belonging to the British empire (including plantations), from 1814 to 1836 inclusive, has been politely supplied to us by the Secretary of the Liverpool Statistical Society:

Year	Vessels	Tonnage	Year	Vessels	Tonnage
1814	2	456	1826	248	28,958
1815	10	1,633	1827	275	32,490
1816	15	2,612	1828	293	32,032
1817	19	3,950	1829	304	32,283
1818	27	6,441	1830	315	38,444
1819	32	6,657	1831	347	37,445
1820	43	7,243	1832	380	41,669
1821	69	10,534	1833	415	45,017
1822	96	13,125	1834	462	50,736
1823	111	14,153	1835	538	60,520
1824	126	15,739	1836	600	67,969
1825	168	20,287			

The actual totals sail and steam for 1835 were 25,511 vessels with a tonnage of 2,783,000 rising in 1839 to upwards of 27,000, the tonnage now standing at 3,168,000.

Image and Reality

It would appear, from the many articles and in-depth press coverage of new vessels in the Tregoning scrapbook that during this period the public had considerable interest in steamships generally and the early transatlantic lines in particular. Glowing reports of passenger comfort made prior to the maiden voyage were not always realised in the event, and passage times claimed, and the vessels' speed, proved in most cases to be optimistic. For example, quoting from the *Liverpool Mail* under the heading 'Departure of the *Royal William* Steamer, for New York':[12]

The *Royal William*, for symmetry, strength and accommodation, is unsurpassed; and when in proper trim she averages eleven and a half knots per hour; and in a heavy head sea and gale, with fair cargo on board, she has never been known to come below nine knots.

Her actual passage time to New York was 18½ days, and on 7 July 1838 she only managed 116 miles in 24 hours, an average speed of less than 5 knots. The log abstract stated it was 'blowing hard with heavy seas'.[13]

The competition, the sailing packets (which at this stage were not unduly concerned) must have taken heart from the many stories that told of coal dust everywhere, smoke and grit, constant noise and vibration, a very uncomfortable motion when steaming into a head sea with no steadying canvas set, to say nothing of the subconscious fear of the risks of fire and boiler explosion. It appears that a large proportion of passengers were not favourably impressed, including Charles Dickens, who returned to Europe on a sailing vessel after making the outward passage in the Cunard mail steamer *Britannia*.[14]

However the one fundamental and all important advantage steamers did possess was the prospect of a shorter passage, and providing one could pay the fare, this is what most of the travelling public wanted. The competition from steam spurred on the building of larger and faster sailing packets: in fact there were thirteen American transatlantic sailing lines at the close of 1837, and this part of the shipping industry continued to thrive for many more years.[15]

Competition from Sail

Among Joshua Field's papers in the Science Museum is his collection of data on the early steamers, entitled 'Glances at Atlantic Steam Navigation 1838–1841' in which there is a newspaper cutting from the *Shipping Gazette*, January 1840, which shows the advantages of steam over sail in terms of the length of passage:

We have taken some trouble to obtain a correct return of the length of passages of the sailing vessels and steam packets of the New York lines, from the first departure of the *Great Western*, on the 8th April, 1838, to the return of the *Liverpool*, 11th January, 1840.

The withdrawing of the *Sirius* after making only two voyages, and those about the same period as the *Great Western*'s two first, justifies our omitting any notice of her passage; the more particularly as her sailing from Cork (which is just two days of her rate of going nearer New York) prevents our comparing her progress with the vessels resorting to Liverpool, London, or Bristol. We may just, however, say, that notwithstanding the place of her departure, the *Great Western* overhauled her four days on the first and seven days on the second voyage, or thereabouts.

The return before us, with few variations, details the progress of 24 sailing liners, commencing with the *South America*, on the 3rd of April, 1838, from Liverpool, and ending with the arrival of the *Independence* and *Oxford*, in company with the Liverpool steamer, on the 11th of January, 1840.

The number of voyages of each sailing liner, with the exception of those whose names we have and are still on their passages, is five, while that of the steam ships stands thus:–

Figure 2:9 *HM Steam Vessel Rhadamanthus (Commander George Evans) the first British steamer to cross the Atlantic. She was laid down at Devonport in 1831, with four guns, 220hp. The model was built by Mr T Roberts of Plymouth in 1832.* (Science Museum, London)

Great Western	11 voyages
Royal William	3 voyages
Liverpool	6 voyages
British Queen	3 voyages

The average of the sailing-liners passage from Liverpool to New York is 33 days 42 minutes, while the average of the ocean steamers during the same period (allowing an average passage of 18 days for the *Liverpool* in lieu of that in which she put back to Cork) is 17 days 18 hours. The average passage of the sailing liners from New York to Liverpool is 22 days 16 hours; while the average of the steamships, including the two long passages of the *British Queen* and *Liverpool*, is 16 days 8 hours.

The shortest passage from Liverpool to New York of the sailing liners is that of the *Roscius*, 19 days in November and December last; the shortest passages of the steamers are those of the *Great Western*, 13 days and a few hours, on two occasions. Of the sailing-liners, four appear to have been 22 days, and seventy-five range between 30 and 48 days. From New York to Liverpool, four passages of 16 days, two of 17, fourteen of 18, and five of 19, appear to have been made by the sailing-liners, the remaining seventy-five passages averaging between 20 and 36 days. The shortest home of the steamships are the *Great Western*'s on several occasions being 12½ days, and her longest home is 15 days. The average of the *Great Western*'s passages out is 16 days 2 hours; and the average of her passage home has been 13 days 18 hours.

The steamships did not have it all their own way on the North Atlantic run. Sailing packets sometimes gave them a good run for their money, with passage times very close, and on a few occasions beat them. When the *Great Western* sailed from New York early in 1839, the small sailing packet *President* departed with her, both eastbound, the latter passing Cape Clear on the southernmost coast of Ireland well ahead of the steamer. Furthermore, as it transpired later, another vessel, the smart new packet *Louis Phillippe* which had also left at the same time, was already berthed in Le Havre, a more distant port, before the *Great Western* had reached Bristol. Sometimes the steamers made a protracted voyage due to adverse conditions which either forced them to turn back, or seek a port where bunkers could be obtained, or proceed to a safe haven which was not the intended destination. Whatever the reason for delay, the press reports tended to understate any of these setbacks, ignoring the limitations of paddle wheel propulsion in heavy weather, as was the case when the steamer *Liverpool* left New York on 16 December 1839 and did not reach Liverpool until 11 January 1840, a passage of 27 days. Reporting on this voyage, the *Liverpool Albion* stated:

The gale was so severe, with such an awful sea running, that it was considered prudent to put the vessel right before it, and she scudded, under a close reefed foresail for 24 hours. On the 27th December, when in latitude 43.40 and longitude 36.30, and when within two days of Fayal, Captain Engledue ran for that island to replenish her stock of coal.

On another occasion:

The *Liverpool*, on her passage to New York, experienced so heavy a gale from the north-west, when 300 miles from Cape Clear, that her powerful machinery could not propel her beyond one and a half knots per hour . . . The result of the recent voyage of the *Liverpool* is another grand proof of the power-steam and the safety of hulls propelled by it: in hurricane, in raging sea, or in whirlwinds, the urging power of the machinery being below the deck, and not aloft attached to the mast, a steerage way is given to the hulls, under all circumstances of wind and weather, and any course can be steered according to the emergencies of the time, the loss of masts being of secondary consideration.

The last statement seems to contradict the first of these quotations.

Engine Power and Displacement

At the time, there must have been a great deal of debate as to the best size of vessel and optimum horsepower of its engines related to the length of the intended voyages, and Count Daru expresses his opinions on this subject in his report (part of the newspaper article already referred to). His conclusions are sometimes in error but his reservations on the unnamed vessel

with 1,000hp engines (*The Great Britain*) must have been shared by many in the shipping industry. A newspaper cutting in Joshua Field's papers contains the following comment on the 'Iron Ship':[16]

Much interest will doubtless be excited when the immense iron steamer now building for the Great Western Company is ready for sea, as it will then be seen what really are the advantages the screw-propeller (with which she is to be fitted) possesses over the common paddle-wheel. I know not how it may strike your readers, but it does appear to me – a disinterested person in the affair – a rather hazardous thing on the part of the Company to adopt an invention of the success of which they are not as yet fully satisfied. One voyage, however, from Bristol to New York, will be quite sufficient to decide this question.'

Count Daru's assessment of the progress in steam navigation, and in particular his views on future developments (which, as far as the French were concerned, were shared by other influential bodies, commercial, political and military, that is, the building of several steam mail packets which in time of war could easily be adapted to carry a sufficient number of guns), were to have far reaching consequences. The law as passed by the Chamber of Deputies and signed by King Louis Phillippe on 16 July 1840 contained these recommendations, including the financial resources to implement them. Although not specifically mentioned in the Articles of the Law, the most important result was the setting up of a manufacturing base and obtaining the technology required to build their own large steam engines for marine propulsion, previously relying almost entirely on British constructors.[17]

Count Daru's report continues:

We have already called your attentions to the fact, that in England, France, and America, steam-navigation was at first employed on rivers and canals with engines of very limited powers; and that the power of the engine had been gradually increased from that of three horses to 100, 200, and 250 horse power. No sooner was steam navigation applied to long voyages, than the English, committing the same mistake, increased the power of their engines: they commenced with steamers of 450 horsepower, and they are now constructing them of 500, 600, and even 1,000. Why? To obtain, doubtless, greater velocity and size. It was therefore thought that we ought to proceed on the same principles, and immediately bring ourselves on a par with them.

Gentlemen, the velocity which the steam-boat may acquire is less dependant on the absolute power of the motor than on the proper proportions kept between its shape, its size, and the effectual power of its engine. The steamers of 160 horsepower which perform the Levantine service are as rapid as the *Great Western* and the *British*

Queen: they go at the rate of 8 knots an hour. This velocity, moreover, has a limit which it is impossible to exceed, and that is 12 knots an hour, beyond which the shock of the water displaced opposes a resistance which inevitably destroys the action of the moving power. With vessels intended for the navigation of rivers and canals this extreme limit has been attained. The *Express* on the Clyde, the *Star* on the Thames, have gone at the rate of 14 English miles, equivalent to about 12 knots an hour; but this is an uncommon velocity, and which may be looked upon as unattainable at sea, without occasioning expenses immeasurably disproportionate with the result; the greater the velocity the heavier the expenses. On seeking to learn what might have been the motives which led to the gradual increase of the power of the engines, we have been able to discover one only – namely, the necessity of accomplishing distances of increasing length without renewing the provision of coal. For this only was it necessary that the new steamers should be provided with engines of 450 horsepower; when, with this power, the object was obtained where the necessity of exceeding it! It is impossible to discover.

Is it in order to increase the capacity of the vessel, to receive a greater number of passengers and of goods? The example given in the construction of sailing vessels would not justify a similar desire. After having for a considerable time employed vessels of from 300 to 500 tons, it was proposed to increase these dimensions, and to build them of a thousand tons and upwards. What ensued? It was quickly found unprofitable, because the lading was of so long a duration, that none desired to have his goods placed in the first rank of a vessel capable of receiving five or six more; it was therefore abandoned. We may consequently consider the spirit which has led the English to build steamers of 1,000 horsepower as presenting a doubtful success. The only end which it was desirable to attain is exceeded out of a vague wish to find something better, without exactly knowing what. Enormous expenses are incurred, for engines of so considerable a power are not very easy of management; their accidents are terrible, the least peg not going exactly right, the least imperfection, which in an engine of ordinary dimensions is without inconvenience, becomes, under the influence of a force equal to that of 1,000 horses, the cause of enormous damages, and may give rise to accidents of a serious character. Consequently, gentlemen, we think that it would be unwise to give our assent to a rule, the consequences of which are unknown to us, to compromise a heavier capital with a view to uncertain advantages, to have but one departure where two steamers would, with the same expense, have permitted making two, and consequently have presented more opportunities to passengers; finally, to incur without motive all the uncertain chances of experiments which have not yet been performed.

Comments and Conclusions

The comments referring to the French steamers on the Levantine service with engines of 160hp being on a par with the *Great Western*, with engines of 450hp, and the *British Queen*, 500hp, are hardly credible. While the top speed in calm water may well have equalled the Atlantic packets, and indeed achieved an average of 8 knots on these Mediterranean voyages, there can be no direct comparison. The Western Ocean run was far longer and the weather and sea conditions more severe. Furthermore, the assumption that 12 knots was the maximum a sea going paddle steamer could attain is obviously wrong, but perhaps, at that time, it was a widely held view, and Count Daru, lacking information to the contrary, repeated the fallacy in his report.

Samuel Seaward, an eminent and well respected engineer, whose firm Seaward and Capel was a great builder of marine steam engines, presented a paper[18] on 9 February 1841 to the Institute of Civil Engineers, in which he said:

> The experience of persons acquainted with steam navigation has determined, that if a vessel be propelled by the application of steam power at the rate of 8 miles an hour through the water, no multiplication of that power could double her speed; it is further a matter of great doubt whether, supposing a vessel be propelled at the rate of 8 miles an hour by an engine of 200 horses-power, an additional speed of $1\frac{1}{2}$ miles per hour could be given to her by the application of 400 horses-power.

Count Daru did, however, qualify his remark by stating that a rate of 12 knots could be achieved, but only at unjustifiable expense. Cunard's last paddler, the *Scotia* of 1862, averaged about 13.5 knots for the crossing of the Atlantic, and it was claimed 16.5 knots were attained on trials. The debate on the problem of the speed/power ratio in steam paddle vessels was characteristic of an age struggling on the brink of an entirely new technology in which there was still little knowledge of hydrodynamics. But the economics of steam propulsion at its then stage of development were fundamental.

Few of the voyages made by the early Atlantic steam packets were profitable, and when the considerable annual cost of engine and boiler overhaul was taken into account most companies made a loss. In fact (partly because of the disastrous grounding of *The Great Britain* in 1846) by the end of 1847 only Cunard survived as a passenger carrying steam packet company on the North Atlantic, primarily due to the Government subsidy provided by the Mail Contract.

According to Dr Dionysius Lardner, this matter of profitability was the point he was making when he says he was misquoted in 1836. The following extract is taken from his book:[19]

> Such was the report of the 'Times' and other periodicals

of that date of a speech in which I was afterwards, and have ever since been, represented as having declared a steam voyage across the Atlantic as *mechanical impossibility*.

What I did affirm and maintain in 1836–7 was, that the long sea voyages by steam which were contemplated, could not at that time be maintained with the regularity and certainty which are indispensable to commercial success, by any revenue which could be expected from traffic alone, and that, without a government subsidy of a considerable amount, such lines of steamers, although they might be started, could not be permanently maintained.

Seaward also came to the same conclusions in 1841 in his paper. He explains:

. . . it is evident that the attempt to perform voyages of lengthening duration by the power of steam alone must, in the present state of engineering science, be attended with an expense wholly disproportionate to the profits, when the cost of the hull and engines, the consumption of fuel, the wages of the engineers, stokers, etc, are compared with the amount of freight.

Count Daru failed to anticipate the next two important advances in shipbuilding and marine engineering, namely, the use of iron for hull construction, and the screw as a superior method of propulsion to the paddle wheel. This is understandable, for at that time, despite several iron vessels having been constructed, the long term commercial advantages had not been proved and the screw was still at the experimental stage. The vessel that would incorporate both of these innovations and provide the evidence of complete success was, in 1839, only in the earliest stages of construction, and was referred to in Count Daru's reports as having been planned with engines of 1,000hp. She had not yet been named as *The Great Britain*.

Note:
The term 'horsepower', so far mentioned, is the 'nominal horsepower' used by the manufacturers so that a direct comparison can be made between engines which, before the introduction of the compound, were single-cylinder units. Thus the *British Queen* was said to have 500hp which in fact was the sum of two separate 250nhp engines both working the same paddle wheel shaft. The formula used was as follows: the cross-sectional area of the cylinder in square inches, multiplied by the effective pressure, assumed as 7lb per square inch (7.5lb on the Clyde), and further multiplied by the piston speed in feet per minute. This depended on the length of stroke and was obtained from tables. For instance, a 4ft stroke gave a piston speed of 196ft per minute and 8ft, 240ft per minute. This sum was then divided by a contact of 33,000. The 'indicated horsepower', ihp, and the 'effective horsepower', ehp, are fully explained in chapter 5.

1 Title page of Christopher Claxton's publication of the logs of the first voyage of the *Great Western* from England to America, Bristol 1838

2 E Leroy Pond, *Junius Smith* (New York, reprint 1971), p. 9; 'Glances at Atlantic Steam Navigation 1838–1841', Joshua Field's papers, p. 14 – extract from the *Naval Chronicle*, p. 494

3 Claxton's *Logs of the Great Western*, appendix no 5; Extracts from the Journal of Col Webb, senior, pp. 73–4

4 B Greenhill (ed), *The Advent of Steam* (London, 1993) p. 73

5 Denis Griffiths, *Brunel's Great Western* (Wellingborough, 1985) p. 101

6 E Leroy Pond, *Junius Smith* (New York, reprinted 1971) Letter 1 p. 147

7 Pond, op cit, pp. 178–81

8 Leroy Pond, op cit, p. 193

9 *The Mariner's Mirror* vol 63, no 4, p. 390

10 W Runciman, *Before the Mast and After, Autobiography of a Sailor and Ship Owner*, 5th Impression (London, 1928) p. 251

11 Undated cuttings in scrapbook

12 This is the second steamer of that name, not to be confused with the earlier *Royal William* that had crossed from Canada in 1833 on a delivery voyage

13 Abstracts of the outward voyage of the *Royal William* as they appeared in contemporary press reports

14 Carl C Cutler, *Queens of the Western Ocean* (Annapolis, Maryland, 1961) p. 248

15 Cutler, op cit, p. 211

16 J Field, 'Glances at Atlantic Steam Navigation 1838–1841', the end of an article in *Mechanics Magazine*, January 1841, p. 38

17 *The Mariner's Mirror*, vol 73, no 3, p. 273; Stephen S Roberts, *The French Transatlantic Steam Packet Programme of 1840*; also contemporary press reports

18 Seaward, 'Memoir on the Practicability of Shortening the Duration of Voyages by the Adoption of Auxiliary Steam Power to Sailing Vessels', *Transaction of the Institute of Civil Engineers*, vol 3 (London, 1842) pp. 385–400

19 D Lardner, *Steam and its Uses* (London – not dated, probably early 1850s) p. 119

CHAPTER 3

Sail Assist and Steam Assist, True and Apparent Wind

Modern Definition

In the course of recent studies on wind assistance for power-driven commercial vessels, the term 'sail assist' was coined to describe the function of either fabric or wing sails to provide additional thrust to that supplied by the engine turning a screw propeller, the main and continuous motive force.[1] Figure 3:1 shows the wind propulsion spectrum between the pure sailing ship and conventional motorship.

Even though the percentage of the total propulsion derived from the sails, when measured in equivalent units of engine horsepower, may in some circumstances equal or even exceed that generated by mechanical propulsion, it will vary considerably depending on the relative direction and strength of the wind, and therefore this criterion cannot be used to establish a definite point on the spectrum. However, a close approximation can be gained by comparing the amount of fuel saved (which in modern cargo vessels is the only reason for fitting a 'sail assist' rig) with that used under engine power alone, averaged out over several voyages on the same route. This was possible in tests done aboard the Greek-owned MV *Minilace*, a conventional freighter with an average displacement loaded and in ballast of 2,905 long tons, fitted in 1981 with a single triangular cat sail rig of 3,000sq ft. After a further 18 months in service, records were compared, and it was found fuel consumption had been cut twenty-four per cent and average speed boosted by five per cent during this period.[2]

This would indicate a significant percentage of total propulsion was achieved by 'sail assist', but it is evident that a midway figure of fifty per cent, that is, half the forward thrust overall, would be almost impossible to achieve on any power-driven vessel that maintained a moderate service speed with the engine. There would of course be occasions, especially on a ballast passage, when the fuel saving would be greater than twenty-four per cent, and relatively brief periods in optimum wind and sea conditions when the sail provided more power than the engine which was rated at 1,000hp (see Figure 3:3).

The reasons for having sails on a fully-powered ocean going merchant steamer of the 1840s and those which prompted recent research into wind assistance for modern cargo-carrying vessels are not exactly the same. Both, however, include fuel saving as the prime objective. In the first case it was essential, for without the added thrust from the sails the completion of a

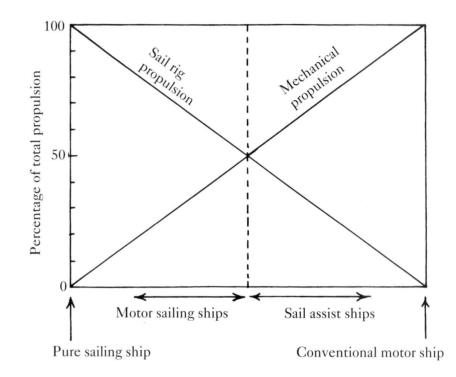

Figure 3:1 *Wind propulsion spectrum (From, Lloyd Bergeson and C Kent Greenwalt 'Sail Assist Developments 1979–1985')*

long voyage, with only marginal reserves of coal, could not be guaranteed. In the second instance the decision to develop some form of wind assistance for a modern cargo ship is optional, a purely economic consideration based on the fluctuating price of a barrel of oil, and only viable if the development, capital and running costs involved are repaid in a relatively short period. This in turn is linked to, among other considerations, a favourable wind analysis of the proposed route.

As the engines were used continuously and sail area was about half that carried by a pure sailing ship of the same tonnage, the term 'sail assist' applied to the catrig on the MV *Minilace* is equally appropriate for the rig of the *Great Western* and her contemporaries on the North Atlantic run.

Reasons for Sail Assist

The early transatlantic steamships were at the forefront of marine engineering and, operated with the continuous use of steam, there was always the possibility of a complete

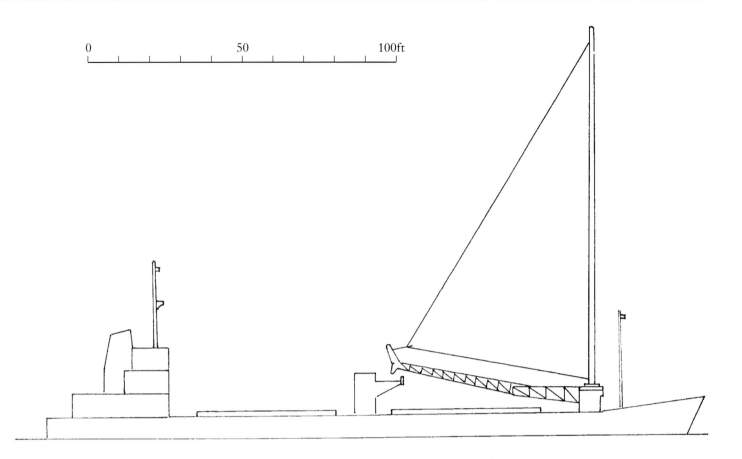

Figure 3:2 Minilace; *The unstayed mast revolves to furl reduce sail area, the outhaul line under continuous tension in conjunction with the rotation of the mast. The downhaul mechanism is mounted on the boom and connected to the clew, and travels in and out along the boom with the movement of the clew. Adjustment of tension on the outhaul and downhaul is provided by hydraulic winches and cylinders. (From, Lloyd Bergeson and C Kent Greenwalt 'Sail Assist Developments 1979–1985')*

Figure 3:3 *Rig Horsepower related to True Wind. (From, Lloyd Bergeson and C Kent Greenwalt 'Sail Assist Developments 1975–1985')*

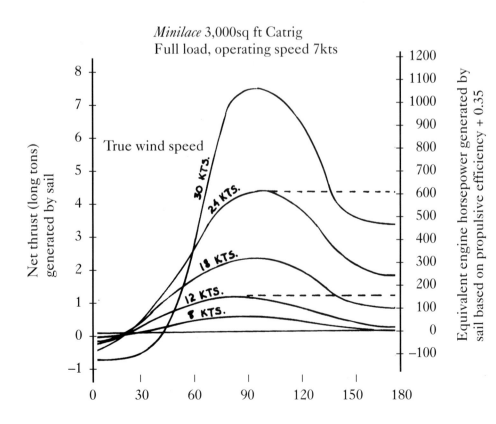

Minilace 3,000sq ft Catrig
Full load, operating speed 7kts

breakdown of the propulsion system, which although basically of robust design could be flawed due to the untested and novel equipment introduced. With communications between ships limited to line of sight, a vessel in such a predicament might have to drift for days or even weeks waiting for assistance. The likelihood of another of the handful of steamers giving a tow was extremely remote, so the carrying of sail sufficient to make port in a reasonable time was essential. However powerful the engines might have been, the deep seated traditions and centuries old reliance on the wind required vessels to have masts, spars and canvas, and the seaman trained on the pure sailing ship would not lightly abandon this expertise. These traditions lingered on into the twentieth century and with them rigging and sails.

On her second return voyage from New York to Liverpool *The Great Britain* lost all the blades from the propeller and ended up with only half an arm remaining. Her engines were stopped and she completed the passage under sail alone. Passenger confidence required this additional and well tried and tested means of propulsion: a sea going steamer without masts and sails in a maritime world still dominated by wind driven ships would seem an unnecessary risk, indeed an aberration, and as such would have been unmarketable.

Even in a light breeze the canvas reduced the motion and made life easier for crew and passengers in contrast to periods of calm when a heavy swell caused the ship to 'roll

Figure 3:4 *In 1906 the single screw steamship* Norfolk *broke her propeller shaft when 1,000 miles off the Australian coast. There was, of course, no radio communication and she was in unfrequented waters. Her master, Captain Corner, and the crew set the jib headed sails she still had on her four masts and rigged additional staysails and square sails made from tarpaulins and deck awnings, using her derricks as yards. With these the vessel successfully made Freemantle. (The late Captain F C Poyser)*

Figure 3:5 *One of the first steamers fitted with a triple expansion engine, the* Aberdeen, *built in 1881, proved conclusively that this type of machinery resulted in even greater fuel economy. Nevertheless she was rigged as a barque with a considerable amount of canvas, still of practical use on the service to Australia. It is interesting to note that even at this period, and in common with passenger steamers of more recent build, she carries the 'old fashioned' single topsails that clue up to the bunt, as do her other square sails. Most deep sea sailing ships had by then been rigged with double topsails. However, in terms of windage when the sails were furled, the two yards associated with double topsails would be at a disadvantage. Even without any sails at all she would have had three masts to work the derricks, with the fore and main heavily rigged. Photograph taken at Gravesend in 1887. (Conway Maritime Press)*

tremendously', a phrase that often appears in the log book. The movement was damped down by the slight increase in wind pressure on a large area of canvas as it was forced through the air by wave action on the hull. Both steering and propulsion, especially on a paddler, would be improved, lessening the alternate immersion of the wheels, for the deeper they rolled under water the greater the reduction in forward thrust. As we shall see later in this book, there were other and ever more powerful reasons for retaining sails on early ocean going steamers. Indeed, these vessels could not be operated without the use of sails.

Steam Assist Sailing Ships

Contemporary naval vessels fitted with engines were operated differently, the fuel capacity was limited, and cost cutting demanded they be used not continuously but only when necessary. Therefore passage making, blockading or maintaining station was done mostly under sail. Despite having, as some did, very powerful engines the function of the sails was equally if not more important, and they would later have been classed as 'steam assisted sailing ships', or 'steam auxiliaries' and, measured on the wind propulsion spectrum, be closer to the pure sailing ship than to the conventional motorship.

The following extract from John Fincham's *A History of Naval Architecture* gives an interesting contemporary view:[3]

In 1843 the *Retribution* was built of 1641 tons, having machinery of 400 horse-power; but her weight of metal thrown was only 472 pounds. Further, the quantity of sail carried has been very small in relation to the dimensions of the ship; so that, generally, the power of sail in war steamers has been merely auxiliary, and hence the constant expenditure of coals for almost all purposes of locomotion, as if there had been no such thing as wind. The quantity of sail carried by the *Retribution* is 17,192 square feet; a perfect sailing ship, of the same tonnage, would have 23,000 square feet. The error of making steam the principal power rather than the wind on the sails, has been making the cost of coals for such a ship about fifty pounds sterling per day of twenty-four hours . . . this excessive expenditure has been lately restrained by the Board of Admiralty, the use of steam being now sanctioned only when it is necessary to use it through want of wind, or on account of its being unfavourable. This general condition incident to naval steam-vessels shows the importance of making them complete sailing vessels.

Details of the *Retribution* can be found in *Paddle Warships*,[4] but only her tonnage by builder's measurement, 1,641 tons, is given, so we have estimated her load displacement as 2,650 tons. This is based on her length of 220ft with a beam of hull of 40ft 6in. Using this figure and the total sail area of 17,192sq ft

Figure 3:6 *The Grasbrook, a German steamer (built at Hamburg in 1882) in dry dock, St Johns, Newfoundland, c 1900, with damaged forefoot. She still carries two headsails, upper and lower fore topsails, standing gaff foresail, and a gaff topsail. The mainmast rigging is set up as if at one time canvas was set from that mast as well. The working derricks are separate spars not connected with sail handling. (Public Archives of Newfoundland)*

Figure 3:7 *The United States Navy's screw steam corvette* Niagara *built at New York Navy Yard in 1855 was still fully rigged as a sailing vessel. She was designed by George Steers, famous as the architect of the racing schooner yacht* America. *(Illustrated London News)*

Figure 3:8 *The* Retribution *was a wooden first-class paddle frigate with engines of 400nhp launched at Chatham in 1844 and sold out of the navy in 1864. She was rerigged as a barquentine in the late 1840s. (From an engraving in Laird Clowes,* The Royal Navy, *vol 6, London, 1901)*

she had nearly 6.5sq ft for every ton of displacement. As built she was considered undercanvased and a third fore and aft rigged mizzen was added later, the mainmast being moved forward a few feet. The amount of extra sail area and tophamper she could be given were limited to some extent by her stability.

Comparisons – Rig, Hull Shape and Displacement

In some cases, as with the sailing packet and the early transatlantic steamers, speed was considered to be of prime importance. For the wind-driven ship, the maximum amount of canvas, related to stability and displacement, contained in an easily driven hull form was the first requirement. Her speed potential was to a large extent limited by waterline length. Second in importance were the beam to length ratio and shape and area of the submerged sections, particularly those near amidships which would affect not only stability, but also how much water had to be displaced as the vessel moved forward. As the ocean steamships used both sail and steam, a comparison with the pure sailing ship of similar size using the following criteria – length to beam, area of greatest submerged cross-section, displacement and sail area – will put the 'sail assist' rigs into perspective. Table 1 compares various naval vessels, some pure sailing ships, others fitted with auxiliary or full-powered engines. It can be seen that the sailing frigates rate a higher sail area, the auxiliary slightly less, and the two full-powered vessels least in terms of their displacement. In the case of the smaller *Encounter* she would rate a proportionately higher square footage of canvas per ton because of her size. However, when comparisons are made between the amount of sail and the area of submerged midship section between those with and without engines there is much less difference, the auxiliary *Arrogant* in fact having more than the frigates *Indefatigable* and *Phaeton*.

We have been unable to locate an authentic sail plan of either the *Great Western* or *The Great Britain*, so Peter Allington

has drawn them using information from various sources. The total area of canvas including the gaff topsails, but not the stunsails, is respectively 10,985sq ft and 16,437sq ft (Figures 3:10, 3:11). In the case of the *Great Western* a comparison can be made with the clipper ship *Sir Lancelot*, (an extreme example), for she was of approximately the same loaded displacement and very similar in her dimensions. Her working sail area was 26,673sq ft but extra to this were the stunsails, totalling 6,138sq ft, making 32,811sq ft in all, plus, when it could be set to advantage, other fancy canvas totalling about 2,000sq ft.

Figure 3:12 shows the submerged loaded cross-sections at greatest waterline beam of two naval vessels with displacements similar to the *Great Western* and *The Great Britain*. The 50-gun frigate *Raleigh*, commissioned for sea in 1846, was a fast and handy vessel. Sir Thomas Herbert, rounding off his report on the vessel, referred to her as 'Taking the ship as a whole, I do not believe a more perfect man-of-war was ever built'.[5]

The *Vanguard*, which we have chosen for comparison with *The Great Britain*, was not such an outstanding vessel as the *Raleigh*, being of average all round performance for a ship of the line, and any advantage she may have had at the series of sailing trials conducted by the Royal Navy in 1846 can be put down to the new coppering on her bottom.

In calculating the cross-sectional area below the waterline, for a given shape, draught is the most important factor. According to Captain Claxton in his description of *The Great Britain* steamship,[6] her loaded draught was 16ft with a corresponding displacement of 2,984 tons. This is 2ft less than appears in Table 2, and due to the rather unorthodox shape of her submerged section, makes a significant difference to the area, reduced from 672sq ft at 18ft to 578sq ft at 16ft. The ratio of submerged section to sail area of 31.5sq ft increased from 27.1, at the deeper draught and sail area to displacement of 6.1 at 2,984 tons compared with 4.95 at 3,675 tons. Similarly, Brunel, working on a lesser draught than 16ft 8in, calculated for the *Great Western* that the submerged area of the largest section was about 462sq ft, which gives a ratio to sail area of 23.78.

Table 1

Ship name	Type	No of sq ft of sail to every ton of displacement	No of sq ft of sail to every sq ft in the area of the mid-ship section
Raleigh	Sailing frigate	9.5	36.9
Leander	Sailing frigate	10.2	38.5
Arethusa	Sailing frigate	9.9	36.7
Indefatigable	Sailing frigate	9.2	33.9
Phaeton	Sailing frigate	9.1	32.3
Thetis	Sailing frigate	10.3	37.0
Arrogant	Screw auxiliary	8.3	36.3
Dauntless	Full steam power	7.5	32.9
Encounter	Full steam power	8.2	31.4

Figure 3:9 *HMS* Arrogant, *46 guns, the first really successful steam screw frigate. Having altered course preparatory to entering Portsmouth she is shown steaming at about 5 points from the wind and taking in sail. Lithograph from a drawing by Lieut R S Thomas RN dedicated to John Fincham, Master Shipwright, Portsmouth Dockyard. (Parker Gallery)*

Table 2

	Raleigh	Great Western	The Great Britain	Vanguard
Length load waterline in feet	181.5	209.0	285.0	188.0
Maximum beam of hull waterline in feet	49.5	35.33	49.00	56.00
Main load draught in feet	21.2	16.66	18.00	22.90
Load displacement in tons	2,573	2,305	3,675	3,403
Beam to length waterline	3.66	5.91	5.81	3.36
Area of rectangle: beam waterline to keel rabbet sq ft	973.4	553.0	882.0	1,209
Area load waterline section over area rectangle	0.679	0.861	0.762	0.681
Area load waterline section in sq ft	661	476	672	823
Sail area in sq ft	24,554	10,985	18,205	28,074
Sail area to displacement sq ft	9.54	4.76	4.95	8.25
Sail area to area max section below load waterline sq ft	37.15	23.08	27.09	34.11

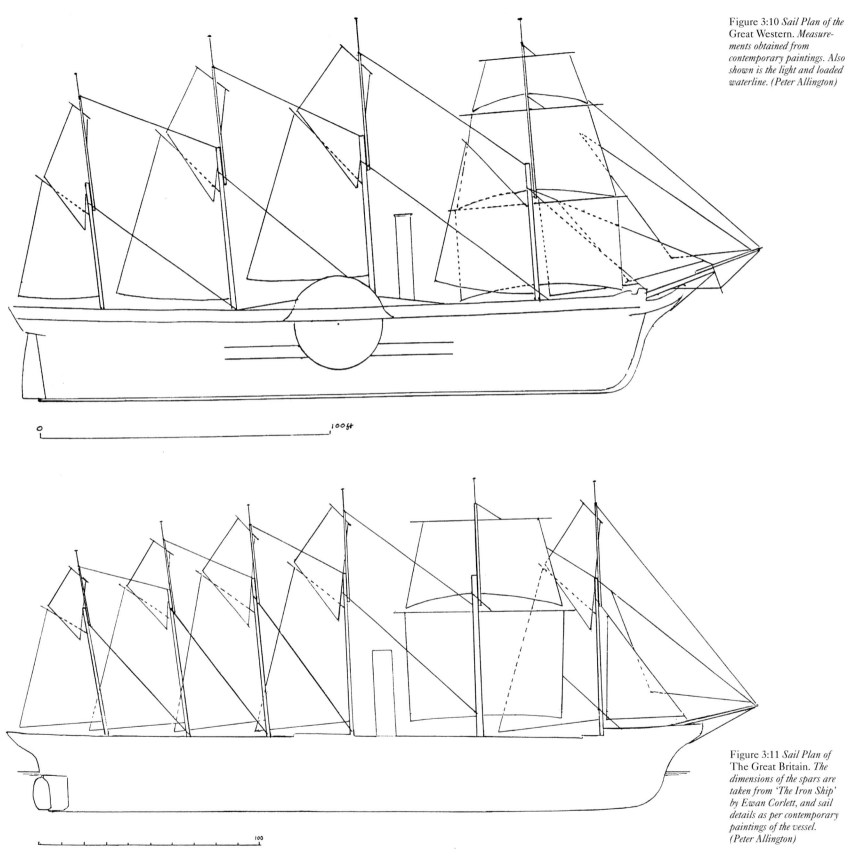

Figure 3:10 *Sail Plan of the* Great Western. *Measurements obtained from contemporary paintings. Also shown is the light and loaded waterline. (Peter Allington)*

0   100ft

Figure 3:11 *Sail Plan of* The Great Britain. *The dimensions of the spars are taken from 'The Iron Ship' by Ewan Corlett, and sail details as per contemporary paintings of the vessel. (Peter Allington)*

100

Figure 3:12 *Comparisons between sailing vessels and steamships of similar displacement. (Peter Allington)*

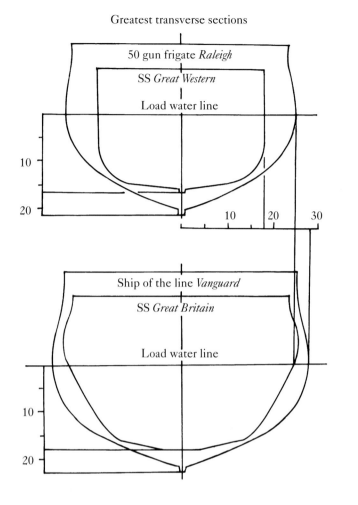

Greatest transverse sections

50 gun frigate *Raleigh*

SS *Great Western*

Load water line

Ship of the line *Vanguard*

SS *Great Britain*

Load water line

The Use of Engine and Sail Assist

Better progress to windward, especially in a rough sea, can be achieved on vessels fitted with sails and engine if both are used together rather than separately. Even if the area of canvas is relatively small, the motion will be steadied, steering improved, and engine power can be cut back if required to suit the conditions. This function of the sails, besides the obvious ones of increasing speed or maintaining speed with less engine power, is important. It is mentioned in the report 'Sail Assisted Developments', referred to earlier, on the MV *Minilace*. Subsequent to the fitting of a 'sail assist' rig, under the heading 'Service record', page 16 states:

> In addition to these performance records, there were other unexpected benefits. Use of the sail in heavy, confused Gulf Stream seas enabled the MV *Minilace* to maintain a 7 knot (in excess of her recorded actual average speed of 5.7 knots) speed when sisterships were slowed to 3 knots.

A further well-documented example of wind and steam working together is given by John Fincham. The quotation refers to information contained in a table on page 376 of his

publication, from which the necessary data has been extracted and put in brackets:

> Experiences, gained in actual service, agree with that which has been here detailed. The *Encounter*, in the experimental squadron, was subject to a trial in which the power of the screw, added to that of the wind on the sails, increased the speed of the ship by about forty percent. The ship, under sail, was going at 9.5 knots, and the steam being then got up, the speed of the engines produced seventy seven revolutions of the screw in a minute [From the table, revolutions 77.5; speed by screw 11.91; actual speed allowing for slip 10.31 knots] and increased the speed of the ship to 13.237 knots an hour (an average of several runs as such a degree of accuracy would not be possible on a single trial), hence the speed of the ship was greater than that due to the number of revolutions of the screw by 11.14 per cent.[7]

The actual wind and sea conditions during this trial are not mentioned, nor is it made clear whether the screw was retracted, freely rotating or fixed when the vessel was under sail.

Another practical example of the advantages gained is given on page 294 when Fincham gives details of the voyage out to India in 1825 by the steam paddler *Enterprize*:

> The greatest average speed of any twenty four hours, under the power of steam alone in a calm sea, was eight knots an hour; under sail alone, or without the aid of steam, it was 8.79 miles; and, with the use of sails and steam together, it was 9.36 miles.

Sail Area and Stability

The requirement for steam powered naval vessels to have a good performance under sail alone meant they had to carry a large amount of canvas, the limit being set by their reduced stability.

In this respect, paddle wheels and the type of machinery required to drive them had a higher centre of gravity in the vessel compared with an equivalent power unit using screw propulsion. It is therefore not clear why the fixed scale of masting, and hence sail area, introduced for paddle steamers of various classes was not amended upwards with the introduction of the screw so as to maximise the potential for carrying extra sail. The following extract on this subject appears in Fincham:

> The conditions of ships propelled by the screw are so dissimilar from those of ships propelled by paddle wheels, that neither as to stability nor to the circumstances in which sail should be used in screw-ships, should the quantity of their sail be inferred from the conditions of paddle-wheel steamers. A failure, as it seems, of

recognising these differences, has placed screw ships in a condition in which they cannot exhibit the full capabilities resulting from their machinery; for it is certain that their stability is sufficient to bear a higher scale of masting than that which had been officially sanctioned.[8]

True and Apparent Wind

The effective use of sails as an auxiliary means of propulsion on a power-driven vessel depends much on her service speed, for the apparent wind will become progressively finer on the bow the faster she travels. It is the direction and strength of the 'apparent' or, as it is often expressed, 'relative' wind that will determine what sails are set, if any, and how they are trimmed. It is a combination of the true winds velocity and direction, as if the observer were standing still, and that of the ship's course and speed over the ground.[9]

Figure 3:13 illustrates the change in apparent wind, both in strength and direction, on a vessel making 5, 10 and 15 knots, having a true wind of 5 knots on the beam in every case. This hypothetical situation could only occur on a power-driven vessel as no sailing ship of this period could attain a speed of 5 knots through the water with only 5 knots of true wind. It can be seen that as the steamer increases speed, the apparent wind at 45 degrees on the bow draws ahead to 27 degrees on the bow at 10 knots, and finer still at 15 knots. There is also a corresponding increase in the strength of the apparent wind, which, if any sail is set, can be used to greater advantage than is at first evident.

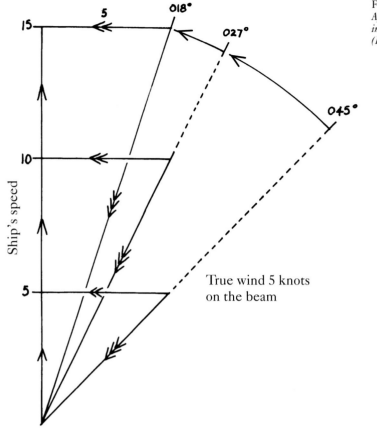

Figure 3:13 *Change in Apparent Wind due to an increase in the vessels speed. (Peter Allington)*

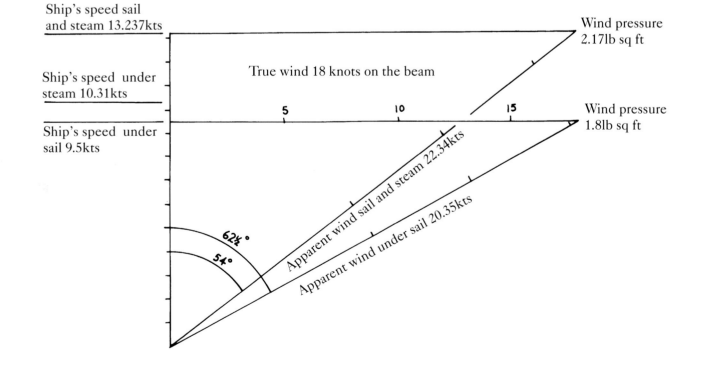

Figure 3:14 *Sail and steam trials on the naval vessel* Encounter. *The speed under sail and steam is an average of the several 'runs', hence the result to three decimal places. (Peter Allington)*

Figure 3:14 shows the situation mentioned earlier in the chapter of the naval vessel *Encounter*, which underwent special trials under sail and steam. Her speed under canvas alone was given as 9.5 knots which increased to 13.237 knots with the addition of screw propulsion. Her rate under power alone was 10.31 knots. There is no mention of the weather or sea conditions, so, for the purpose of completing a vector diagram, an assumed true wind on the beam of 18 knots has been used as this will allow her still to carry full sail. Making no allowance for leeway, the apparent wind under canvas alone is 62 degrees on the bow at 20.35 knots which shifts to 53 degrees on the bow at 22.34 knots with the addition of steam power. Using these figures she would still be able to carry her square sails. The increase in apparent wind is only 1.99 knots, or nearly a tenth, but more importantly, the wind pressure has risen from about 1.8lb per sq ft to 2.2lb per sq ft or just over a fifth. This relationship between wind speed and air pressure is shown in

the graph, Figure 3:15, and it can be seen that a doubling of wind speed will not result in twice the pressure, but in fact it will be quadrupled. For example, 20 knots on the scale indicates a pressure of nearly 1.75lb per sq ft, but an increase to 40 knots will cause the pressure to rise to just under 7lb per sq ft. Note the predicted maximum rig-hp of the *Minilace* at 12 knot wind speed, 150hp, increased to 600hp at 24 knots. Provided the greater power generated by a higher wind speed does not force the vessel to reduce sail area, the advantages are obvious. The graph actually shows the augmented wind pressure, for even in a flat calm there will always be a static atmospheric pressure acting on all surfaces of over 2,000lb to the square foot, 2,116lb being accepted as the international average standard. It can also be seen from the graph that above 16 knots or force 4, the pressure rise is very steep, doubling and redoubling.

The negative side of the wind power occurs when the wind speed rises sufficiently to cause a reduction in sail area and hence, despite the greater pressure exerted on the remaining canvas, the total propulsive force may be reduced, while at the same time the air drag created by masts, spars, rigging and hull will increase and retard the vessel if the apparent wind is forward of the beam.

Over the open sea, clear of the influence of the land, wind speed will to some extent increase with height. In other words it will be appreciably more at the top of a tall mast than at deck level. A reduction of sail area will usually commence with the highest sail, for not only is the 'lever arm' longer but area for area these sails are subjected to a relatively higher pressure per square foot; the object being to keep the centre of effort of the sail plan low enough to prevent excessive heel. It follows that a vessel with good stability, strong sails and gear will hang on to her canvas longer than one that is tender; a problem that affected the ocean going paddle steamer towards the end of the voyage. Sailing ships, or for that matter steamers equipped with square topsails, will by and large, if the apparent wind direction allows, keep these sails set in virtually any strength of wind, despite the lower or reefed single topsails being 40ft or more above the deck. At this height they are low enough in terms of stability but at the same time cannot be blanketed by large waves when the vessel is down in the trough of the sea, and hence provide forward drive at all times, a most important requirement when running downwind in heavy weather.

On a moving vessel, if the true wind direction remains constant but increases in velocity, the apparent wind will draw aft, the opposite situation to that created by a vessel which increases her speed. This has important implications, particularly for a sailing vessel working to windward, but will also have a beneficial effect on the sail assist rig of a steamer. Figure 3:16 shows a power-driven vessel making 5 knots, the true wind 55 degrees on the bow at 5 knots. If the direction does not change but the velocity increases to 10 knots, ship's course and speed remaining constant, and assuming no leeway, then the apparent wind will move aft, shifting from 27.5

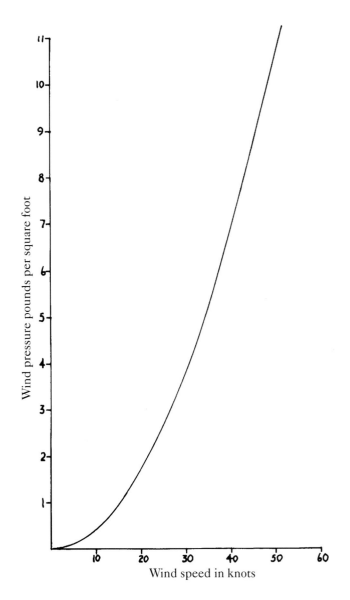

Figure 3:15 *Relationship between wind speed and air pressure. (Peter Allington)*

Wind pressure pounds per square foot

Wind speed in knots

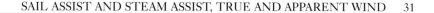

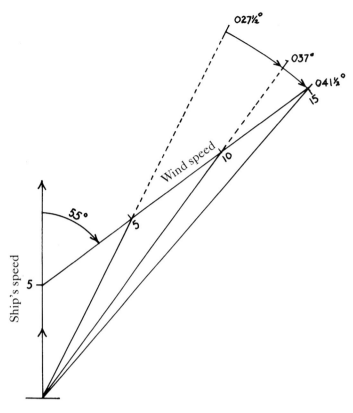

degrees on the bow to 37 degrees on the bow. A further rise to 15 knots will bring the apparent wind around to 41.5 degrees. If no sail were set then no advantage could be taken from what has become a fairer wind, and in reality the steamer would have to contend with an increased air drag. However any fore and aft canvas set would be of greater help as the breeze freshened, the advantage being limited to some extent by the increase in the vessel's speed. A sailing ship in the same circumstances, closehauled and working up to windward, would have the double benefit of the fresher breeze and a change in apparent wind direction moving aft, allowing her to lay a better course. However, as with the steamer using her 'sail assist' rig, an increase in her speed will negate this benefit to some degree. Because the apparent wind is fresher at the top of the mast its direction will be further aft than at deck level on a moving vessel, therefore the upper sails will have a 'fairer' wind in most circumstances. Hence the practice of 'fanning' the yards, clearly illustrated in Figure 3:17. This shows the *Herzogin Cecilie* with a near gale force wind fine on the port quarter judging by the sea conditions and trim of sails. Assuming her speed at the time was 15 knots and the true wind at deck level was 2 points (22.5 degrees) on the port quarter at 30 knots, then the apparent wind striking the courses, lower staysails, spanker and headsails would be about

Figure 3:16 *Effect on apparent wind by an increase in true wind velocity. (Peter Allington)*

Figure 3:17 *The four-masted barque* Herzogin Cecilie *overcanvassed in a strong wind. The practice of fanning the yards is clearly shown, the apparent wind at deck level about 4 points abaft the beam as evident from the courses, but with the increase in height, the upper sails are progressively trimmed to a direction that is from further aft. The mizzen upper topgallant and royal both have the weather leech backwinding or lifting. This is done purposely for the helmsman to steer by, a technique commonly used when a square rigger is closehauled, but in this instance, with the wind so far aft, it is more likely due to either a localised and temporary shift in wind direction or a brief lull in a turbulent air stream. (Captain J M Mattsson, taken from the four-masted barque* Olivebank *in 1933)*

Figure 3:18 *A, B and C.*
Useable Wind sectors. (Peter Allington)

A   Ship's speed 5 knots

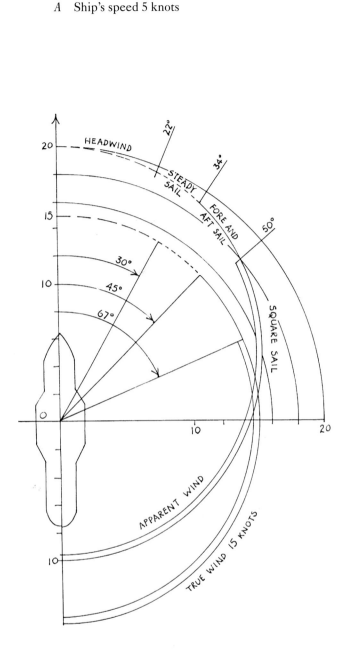

B   Ship's speed 10 knots

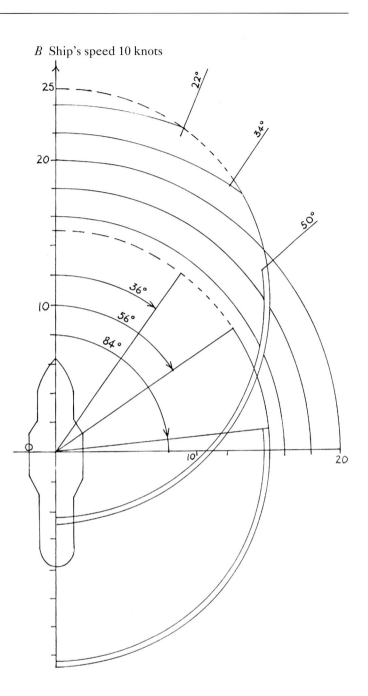

4 points (45 degrees) abaft the beam at 17 knots. However, if the surmised true wind from 2 points on the quarter were blowing at 42 knots at the masthead, the apparent wind there would be from a point further aft, or 5 points (56 degrees) abaft the beam at over 28 knots. The examples quoted and the various diagrams only serve to illustrate certain points. In fact over the open ocean the wind cannot be considered absolutely constant in either strength or direction even for a short period. Nor is the sea state taken into account.

Figures 3:18 A, B and C show the commonly accepted usable wind sectors in a true breeze of 15 knots (present global average wind speed is about 13.7 knots), ship's speed 5, 10 and 15 knots, taking no account of sea conditions or leeway. Figure A illustrates a steamer making 5 knots and a true wind on the bow of 30 degrees or less is considered a headwind; from 30 degrees to 45 degrees is only suitable for steadying canvas. At this point the fore and aft sails start to provide forward thrust in excess of the windage created by the rig, the square sails requiring the true wind about 6 points on the bow to be of any use. Using these figures, the angles have been transposed from the true wind arc to that of the apparent wind giving angles of 22 degrees, 34 degrees and 50 degrees, which are further used as

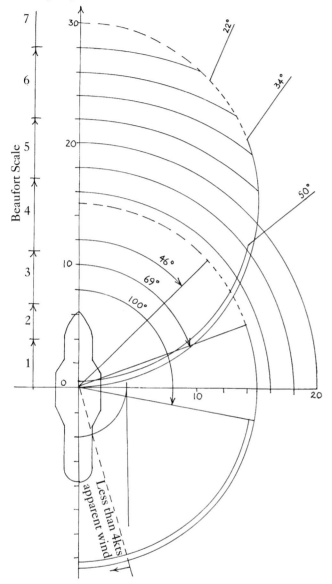

C Ship's speed 15 knots

Figure 3:18 *C*

1850s by Charles Atherton, Chief Engineer Royal Dockyard, Woolwich:[10]

The speed has been calculated with reference to steam-power alone, on which the regularity of steam-ship voyages will be mainly dependent: the influence of the wind may, in fact, be regarded as an obstruction to the regular attainment of high speed; for, a favourable wind, though helping a vessel when steaming at the speed of eight nautical miles per hour, may afford no aid, or even oppose the vessel, when steaming at twelve miles per hour; and an adverse wind will obstruct the vessel, if steaming at high speed, in a far greater ratio than it would the low speed ship.

... that extreme caution ought to attend all mercantile contracts in regard to the obligation of maintaining such a rate of speed for a long passage as exceeds the rate at which the wind may be expected to partially co-operate with the steam power.

Fore and Aft and Square Sails

It is clear from this analysis of ship's speed, true and apparent wind, that in general fore and aft canvas will be more useful on a 'sail assisted' power-driven vessel than square sails. Jibs, stay-sails and gaffsails can all provide forward thrust when the apparent wind is too fine on the bow for square sails; and, unless the wind is well aft, they will reduce rolling. Less gear is required and they can be lowered to the deck, leaving only the mast, topmast and standing rigging which creates far less air drag than a square-rigged mast with all the yards and gear aloft. There should be no need for the crew to leave the deck when setting or furling the sails, and the numbers of men required compared to a fully square-rigged vessel of the same size will be much less. For all these reasons, and because the space occupied by engines, boilers and bunkers could be more profitably used, the square-rigged auxiliary steamship was never widely adopted in general ocean trade.

However, large gaffsails which require hoisting are not easy to handle in a seaway, and compared with the square sail they tend to depress rather than lift the vessel. For a given mast height, more sail area can be spread using yards and square sails than gaffs and booms; and the centre of effort of these sails, compared with a gaffsail when the wind is aft and the boom squared off, remains closer to the centre line. There is not the worry of gybing in a rough following sea, a particular problem with paddle steamers. The corkscrew motion is given added impetus by the alternate immersion of the wheels, making steering within a point either side of the course impossible in these circumstances. Because of this a gaff-rigged paddle steamer was peculiarly liable to gybing. The danger inherent in this action was much reduced by the use of loose-footed sails brailing into the weather.

the limiting angles on the apparent wind arcs (Figures B and C). It can be seen that as ship's speed increases the usable true wind sector decreases, headwind strength increases and the wind from aft will progressively become less advantageous. If sail is carried in lighter breezes than 15 knots any benefit derived will be diminishing, while wind above 15 knots, up to a point, will be of greater use, although the limiting factor in all cases is the ship's speed.

This analysis of the sail assist on a power-driven vessel making continuous use of the engine was summed up in the

Figure 3:19 *This lithograph by J Walter is entitled* The Great Western lying at her moorings at Broad Pill. *It illustrated very well her four-masted schooner rig. It is possible that she was the first vessel ever to be registered under the British Merchant Shipping Acts as so rigged. (Bristol Museum and Art Gallery)*

1 Lloyd Bergeson and C Kent Greenwalt, 'A paper on Sail Assist Developments 1979–1985', pp. 2–3

2 Bergeson and Greenwalt, op cit, pp. 3–16

3 Fincham, *A History of Naval Architecture* (London, 1979; quotation from the first edition, 1851) p. 328

4 David K Brown, *Paddle Warships* (London, 1993) pp. 47–49.

5 J Fincham, op cit, p. 242

6 Capt Claxton RN, *A description of The Great Britain Steamship Built at Bristol*, (Bristol, 1845), page of *The Great Britain*'s dimensions

7 Fincham, op cit, p. 382

8 Fincham, op cit, p. 370

9 To illustrate this point in layman's terms consider a sports car facing straight down an airport runway with a flag on the end of its bonnet. The car is at rest and a breeze of 20mph is considered to be blowing constantly from the side. The flag is thus at 90 degrees to the centre line of the vehicle, ignoring any turbulence. The flag indicates the true wind direction and the amount it flutters gives some idea as to its strength. If the car now moves forward in a straight line the flag will start to change its direction, indicating it is subject not only to the true wind, which has remained constant, but also the 'wind' created by the car. When a road speed of 20mph has been reached the flag will be flying diagonally across the bonnet at 45 degrees to the centre line and its fluttering will be far more agitated as it is now subject to not 20mph but just under 28.3mph, which is the 'apparent' or 'relative' wind. The faster the car goes the more the flag will tend towards the centre line, until at a road speed of 100mph it is only 11.5 degrees off the fore and aft line.

10 Charles Atherton, *The Capability of Steam Ships* (London, 1853) p. 59

CHAPTER 4

Hull Shape and Stability – Some Contemporary Ideas

Proportions

In general, the hull shape required for a power-driven vessel where speed is of paramount importance must be long and lean with a fine entry forward and fine run aft to the stern. John Bourne, in his huge work on marine engineering, refers to this subject in the light of contemporary thinking:[1]

> . . . to employ such form of vessel as will disturb the water as little as possible. This will be a body of the form I have indicated with a considerable proportion of length to breadth, so that the vessel may be sharp at the ends. A length of seven times the breadth is found to be a good proportion for such speeds as 15 or 16 miles per hour. But the proportionate length that is advisable will increase with the intended speed.

However, there were limits beyond which the fineness of entry and run would, in terms of speed to power, be self-defeating on two counts. The example Bourne gives to explain this is 'extreme' when compared to the Atlantic steamers for the vessel was a man-of-war, armour-plated from stem to stern. Nonetheless his remarks hold good in principle:[2]

> Now a little reflection will show that in a ship like the *Minotaur* the ends must weigh several hundred tons more than the buoyancy which they possess, and consequently must immerse the more buoyant portion of the ship, namely, the middle portion, to a proportionate extent; and the main argument of Mr Reed (the Chief Constructor of the navy) is, that if we shorten the ships and do away with these long and heavy extremities, covered as they are with armour-plating, preserving at the same time an equal engine power, then that this power will drive the shorter ship, with its midship section and displacement both greatly reduced, at the same speed as it will drive the larger ship. No doubt a sharp bow is more conducive to speed than a blunt one. But the bow may be so elongated that the increased friction of the increased surface, and the increased immersion due to the increased weight will balance the larger hydrostatic resistance due to the diminished sharpness, while for war vessels the long bow involves special faults.

The simplest 'form' of hull with a flat bottom and vertical sides (as if cut out of a solid box-shaped rectangle, which offers the least possible hydrostatic resistance to being drawn through the water) has an entrance and run shaped as a double curve. The particles of water so displaced by the moving vessel would be forced with increasing velocity out of the way, then allowed to come progressively to rest as the largest section was reached, before moving back towards the keel line with the opposite motion. This action, Bourne deduced, could be compared with the acceleration of a heavy body under the influence of gravity which fell approximately 1ft in the first quarter of a second, 4ft in the second quarter of a second, 9ft in the third, and so on, increasing to 16ft, 25ft, 36ft, 49ft, 64ft, 81ft and 100ft. These are the squares of the ordinates used to plot this curve of least resistance in the first half of the forebody, the waterline of the second half formed by repeating the same curve, but inverted and reversed (see Figure 4:1). All the transverse sections on this hull form, with its vertical sides and a flat top and bottom, obviously do not constitute the best shape for a practical sea going vessel but the waterline curve produced by this theory is interesting when compared with previous research.

Over 30 years earlier, John Scott Russell had been carrying out experiments on hydrodynamics of waves and floating bodies, and at a meeting of the British Association held at

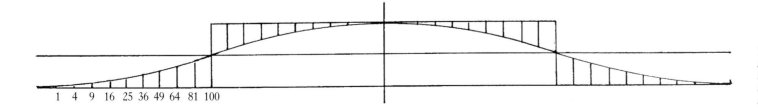

1 4 9 16 25 36 49 64 81 100

Figure 4:1 *Example of a half waterline that offers least resistance as proposed by John Bourne. (Peter Allington)*

Dublin in 1835 he presented a paper entitled, 'On the Solid of Least Resistance', often referred to as his 'Wave Line Principle'.

The idea was, in his words:

That the form of least resistance should be such as to remove the particles of water out of the way of the ship just sufficiently far to let the largest section pass and not a jot farther . . . that the ship, finding the particles in her way at rest, should leave them at rest in the new place to which they are moved . . . that the time in which this movement has to be accomplished being given, the force to accomplish that should be a constant force and the least possible.

He deduced from experiments that the bow shape on a vessel that presented least resistance would have a hollow form, the lines following the curves of a versed sine (unity minus the natural cosine) and the run aft by the curves described by a cycloid both in the horizontal and vertical plane. The length of the entrance compared with the run should be in the ratio of three to two with a mid-section of any length[3] (see Figure 4:2).

To explain this 'principle' more fully, only a single wave line has been drawn, made up of the two reverse curves of entrance and run united at the position of maximum beam. For the sake of simplicity when calculating the various points which indicate the line of entrance, the distance between the mid-line and quarter beam is assumed to be 1 unit; in this case, 1cm; which is also the value of 90 degrees. For the intermediate distances taken at every 10 degrees it is a straightforward calculation. For example, the cosine of 40 degrees is 0.76604, which subtracted from 1 gives the figure 0.23396 or 0.23396cm, measured up from the hull centre line or down from the line of half maxi-

mum beam as the case may be. The run aft is shorter in the proportion of 3 to 2 and formed by two cycloidal curves joined at the quarter beam line. These are traced out by the movement of any fixed point on the rim of a circle as it rolls along a straight line; in this case it will be the place of maximum beam located at 0 degree, the circle rolling along from C towards D until this point arrives at Y. Similarly, point X will describe the curve XY if the circle rolls from A towards B along line AB.

From this wave line principle evolved the wave form theory which stated, 'that the progression of displacement along the bow should follow the sine curve and likewise that of the stern, the cycloidal curve'.[4]

These principles were accepted almost without question, until Froude and Rankine, among others, put forward their ideas in the late 1860s.

Scott Russell also found that a hull shape built on these principles had an optimum maximum speed which he calculated as the square root of the waterline length, and to try to exceed this figure would be uneconomic as the much greater power required would be mostly absorbed in wave making. (1.25 times the square root of the waterline length was proved in practice to be closer to this optimum speed.)[5]

Most vessels built to this wave line principle had modified curves as other considerations, particularly stability and load carrying, had to be considered and any vessel built strictly to the rule would be considered 'extreme'. In fact most shipbuilders of the late 1830s were sceptical of the idea, preferring the age old methods of trial and error to produce better hull forms; a successful vessel would be taken note of, its measurements recorded and used in future construction.

However, the four sisterships built for the Royal West India Mail Company, the first launched in 1841 (the PS *Clyde* followed by the *Teviot*, *Tay* and *Tweed*, which were the founding

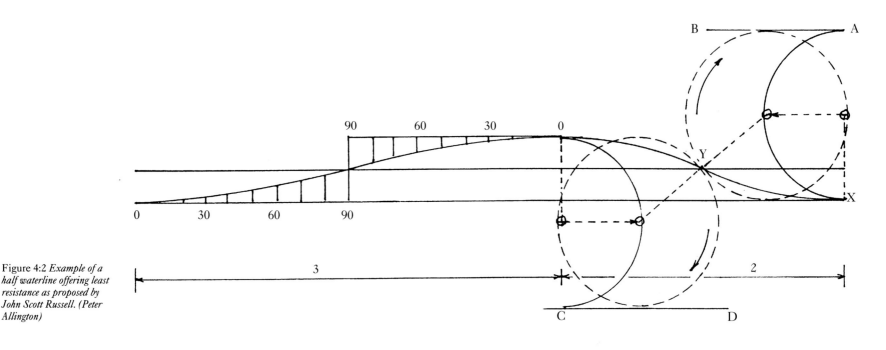

Figure 4:2 *Example of a half waterline offering least resistance as proposed by John Scott Russell. (Peter Allington)*

quartet), all embodied the wave line principle. Although not identical in hull form, they were considered among the finest class of wooden-built steamships that could, in time of war, be used to carry guns.

In terms of dimensions these vessels were very similar to the *Great Western*, the figures for which are included in brackets: length 238ft (236ft); length between perpendiculars 213ft (212ft); breadth of hull 34.5ft (35.33ft); breadth over paddle boxes about 56ft (59.66ft); depth 24.7ft (23.2ft); gross register 1,354 tons (1,340 tons).[6]

Comparison of Hull Shape – The Great Western, Coriolanus *and Others*

A study of the lines of the *Great Western* indicate she would have made a fast sailing ship without her engines and paddles, given an increased sail area. Figure 4:3 shows her drawn with much abbreviated lines for the purpose of comparison with the iron clipper *Coriolanus* at the same scale. The *Coriolanus* was built by Archibald McMillan and Son of Dumbarton, Scotland, in 1876 to the order of John Patton, Junior and Company of London and employed initially in the trade with jute cargoes from Calcutta to Scotland. Noted as a very fast vessel, according to Captain A G Course, 'her lines were so fine that her model was awarded the Gold Medal of the Worshipful Company of Shipwrights at the Exhibition held in London in 1877'.[7]

In 1887 she was purchased by John Stewart and Company who retained her until the late 1890s when she was sold to German owners. A three-masted ship of 1,053 gross tons, her measurements were: length 217.4ft, beam 35.2ft and depth 20.1ft. It will be observed that her waterline length on a draught of 16ft 8in, 207ft, is virtually identical to that of the *Great Western* (the *Coriolanus* would have been deeper when down to her

Figure 4:3 *Comparison of hull lines of the* Great Western *(above) and the* Coriolanus *(below), drawn to the same scale. (Peter Allington)*

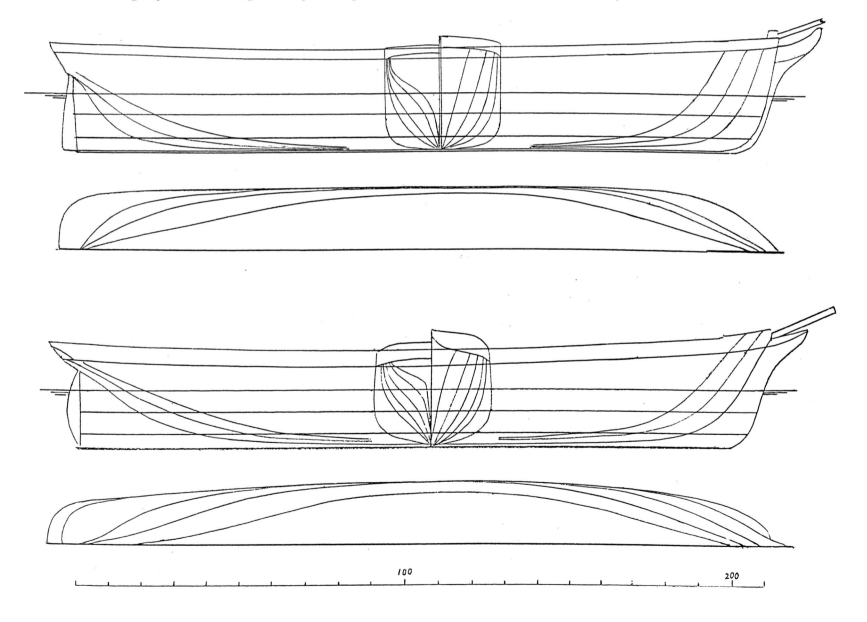

marks) and the maximum beam was only 2in different, the *Great Western*, being the broader vessel. The two other water-lines shown are 3ft and 10ft above the keel rabbet for the *Great Western* and 4ft and 10ft above the join between keel and bottom plate for the *Coriolanus*. Harold Underhill[8] describes the *Coriolanus* as one of the most perfect examples of a small iron clipper. There can be no doubt as to her speed. Captain A G Course, on page 31 of his book, quotes from her log books a passage of only 65 days from Liverpool to Calcutta. Compared to the *Great Western* she had a finer entry and run, tumble home, a greater rise of floor and slightly more sheer, though in terms of length, breadth and fore and aft position of the greatest transverse section they are very close. Nearly 40 years separate their building and this period covers the most rapid development of the pure sailing ship, making the similarities all the more remarkable. She survived well into the twentieth century. Her last passage was during the summer of 1936, rigged then as a barque and under the American flag when she was towed to the breakers in Fall River, Massachusetts, to be broken up.

William Patterson and Brunel may well have given the *Great*

Western finer lines if she had been built of iron, taking advantage of the lighter hull and greater usable internal volume. With more flare at the bows to help keep her dry in a head sea, her hull form would have been closer still to the *Coriolanus*. Even if it had been possible technically and economically to build large vessels in iron, the problem of compass error and its correction in an iron hull had not been solved in 1836,[9] and no effective antifouling had yet been produced to prevent the rapid growth of weed and barnacles, especially in warmer waters.

Hull shape depends much on the purpose for which a vessel is built and the sea conditions to be expected. To illustrate this point, and as examples of current thinking at the beginning of the 1850s John Fincham, in his *History of Naval Architecture*, included several drawings of different paddle steamers showing, for the sake of comparison, the bow and stern profile, three sections, two abbreviated waterlines and the position of the paddle wheel. Three of these are reproduced in this volume (see Figures 4:5, 4:6 and 4:7).[10]

The Gravesend Packet (Figure 4:5) built in 1846 was designed to carry passengers in relatively sheltered waters at the

Figure 4:4 Coriolanus *in dry dock (Maine Maritime Museum Collection)*

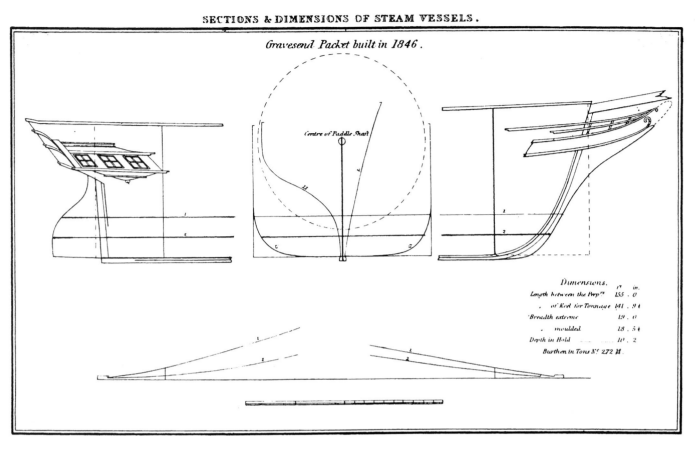

SECTIONS & DIMENSIONS OF STEAM VESSELS.

Gravesend Packet built in 1846.

Centre of Paddle Shaft

Dimensions.   f.   in.
Length between the Perp.ᵈ   155 . 0
,,   of Keel for Tonnage   141 . 9 ½
Breadth extreme   19 . 0
,,   moulded   18 . 5 ¼
Depth in Hold   10 . 2
Burthen in Tons Nᵒ 272 ½.

Figure 4:5 *Plate 39 from* A History of Naval Architecture *by John Fincham*

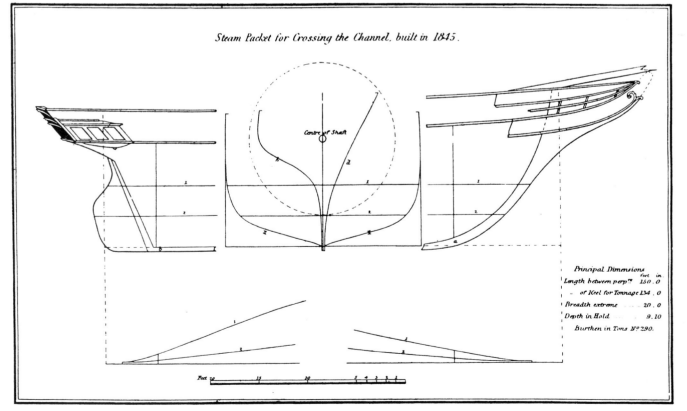

SECTIONS & DIMENSIONS OF STEAM VESSELS.

Steam Packet for Crossing the Channel, built in 1845.

Centre of Shaft

Principal Dimensions.   feet   in.
Length between perp.ᵗ   150 . 0
,,   of Keel for Tonnage   134 . 0
Breadth extreme   20 . 0
Depth in Hold   9 . 10
Burthen in Tons Nᵒ 290.

Feet

Figure 4:6 *Plate 41 from* A History of Naval Architecture *by John Fincham*

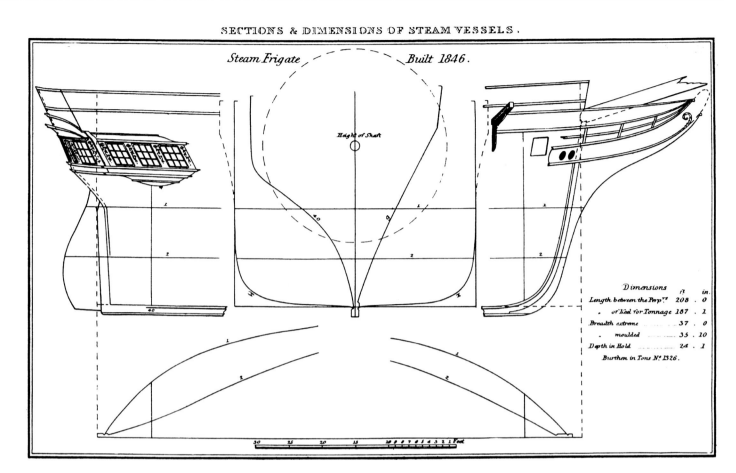

SECTIONS & DIMENSIONS OF STEAM VESSELS.

Steam Frigate   Built 1846.

Height of Shaft

Dimensions   *ft*   *in*
Length between the Perp.[rs]   208 . 0
  „ of Keel for Tonnage   167 . 1
Breadth extreme   37 . 0
  „   moulded   35 . 10
Depth in Hold   24 . 1
Burthen in Tons N.º 1326.

highest possible speed without the added stability requirements for carrying sail. She was a fairly large vessel, 155ft between perpendicular with a beam to length ratio of 8.16:1, and had a very shallow draught of only 4ft 6in, an advantage in any river craft being able to cut corners and pass over banks with little depth of water. Her submerged midship section is a compromise between a semicircle, ideal for speed, and flat floors so she could take the ground, either purposely or not, and still remain upright, thus avoiding the risk of falling over and damaging one of the wheels.

The cross-channel steam packet (Figure 4:6) built in 1845 was about the same length as the Gravesend boat. Her beam to length ratio was 7.5:1 but her stability would have to allow for a fairly good area of fore and aft canvas. The midship section is similar to the *Coriolanus* but without the tumble home, the rise of floor and soft turn of bilge characteristic of a fast sailing ship. The entry is still fine but much more flare is given to the bows to cope with the 'chops of the channel', and waterline aft is fuller, showing greater buoyancy at the stern.

The steam frigate built in 1846 (Figure 4:7) is a much larger vessel in every respect: 208ft between perpendiculars with a beam of 37ft, ratio 5.62:1, and a proportionately greater draught. Stability for the large sail area and weight of mast and spars, as well as the heavy guns, dictates a full midship section with little

rise of floor. Although the turn of bilge is not hard, the midship section, which is quite similar to that of the *Great Western*, would have been carried without much change for a distance fore and aft, a requirement of stability and carrying capacity, and then faired in with the much fuller ends, giving the required buoyancy at bow and stern. An easy motion in a seaway was important, both in rolling and pitching, for a prime function of the vessel was to carry as much armament as possible and to provide a reasonably stable firing platform, but this shape would be detrimental to speed under power.

The Relationship Between Draught and Beam

In 1845 Lieut W Gordon in his book on marine steam engines wrote:[11]

> The extreme breadth of a steam vessel should not exceed *double* her *draft of water*; if it bears a larger proportion, the vessel will be very uneasy in a sea-way, and when steaming against a head sea, will be more retarded by it. These are most important points to be attended to, and it is to be feared that their neglect in the construction of *The Great Britain*, whose breadth is about three times her draft of water, will produce very serious consequences.

By all accounts, *The Great Britain*'s 'uneasiness' was to be demonstrated once in service, although how much can be attributed to her beam to depth ratio, and how much to her peculiar midship section and huge metacentric height, is difficult to say. In all probability it was a combination of these factors.

The word 'uneasiness' is associated with a short roll period and 'jerky' action which can do more damage to the rig than strong winds especially, when the snatch loads are combined with chafe. In view of the amount of gear carried away, the entry in the log book of *The Great Britain* on 30 July 1845 when on her maiden voyage to New York, that she was 'rolling very heavily *but easily*', and repeated on several occasions, may not have been strictly true. At the time, canvas was set, wind gale force on the beam with a heavy cross sea, when both the fore peak halliard and main topmast backstays failed, loose gear about the deck had to be resecured, the jaws of the second spencer broke, and it is significant that, 'the crew showed great unwillingness to do their duty', probably having been aloft putting a double reef in the topsail when the standing rigging carried away. Reading between the lines, all these incidents point to the vessel's motion being far from 'easy', but this descriptive term may well have been added in the published form of the deck log after the usual 'ship rolling very heavily' as a public relations exercise for future passengers.

In similar circumstances but on a lighter draught Captain Crispin, who took passage in *The Great Britain* from Bristol to London on trials prior to her entering service, when reporting on her performance for the Admiralty, stated:

> At 9 when off Lundy, we found a very heavy nasty cross sea, occasioned by a spring ebb running against the Gale. I had therefore a fine opportunity of judging, both the qualities of the Ship and Screw. The former I found to have all the quickness of Motion of a vessel of 500 tons, more particularly in regard to her rolling, which certainly surpassed anything I had ever before witnessed, having timed her frequently during the passage to roll from side to side 7 times a minute, and on some occasions even as many as 9 times in the same period.[12]

Strength of Construction and Safety

The strength of the sea going paddle steamer compared with the sailing ship of the period would have to be increased significantly to cope with not only the added stress of localised weight in a long narrow hull and mechanical propulsion, but also the risk of loss by fire and, according to reports in the contemporary press, sinking as a result of collision or stranding, a not infrequent occurrence.

Judging from a letter printed in *The Times* on 4 October 1839 from Mr C W Williams, an employee of the well-established Liverpool shipbuilders Messrs William and Thomas Wilson, the boom in steamships had attracted all manner of people hoping to cash in and make a quick profit. Contracts often went to the lowest bidder, taking no account of specifications, nor the fact that the firm had no previous experience in building this type of ship. For a passenger-carrying vessel, where safety of life and limbs should be the top priority, it appeared to Mr Williams that this sort of cost cutting verged on the criminally irresponsible. Furthermore, some of those employed as 'engine-men' at sea were totally incompetent. The sad fact of the matter was, as he saw it, that a disaster was bound to occur before the necessary legislation was eventually passed by Parliament subsequent to an enquiry into the loss.

In the meantime he advocated the following improved specifications:

> . . . the adoption of copper ragged dumps or bolts, copper or composition bolts, nuts, washers, and screws, in place of wooden tree nails, which are entirely dispensed with; the substitution of oak in place of pine in many parts; the additional size and number of the 'thick stuff' pieces; additional scantlings, lengths, numbers, and boltings of the sister keelsons and sleepers; the adoption of deck beams throughout; rejecting entirely the principle of 'carlings'; iron deck and boiler beams and iron deck plates in place of timber; watertight iron plate bulkheads, with solid framing in the way of each bulkhead; the preparing of timber by Kyan's or other principle (wood preservatives). With the extra work of improved hanging knees, staple knees, garboard strake, solid flooring, and longitudinal iron bolt stays – the additional cost estimated at £3 10s per ton builder's measurement.

The letter goes on to argue the case for watertight bulkheads. He concluded that the vessel should have four:

> We come next to the division of the vessel into five sections, by means of four bulkheads. This arrangement I consider wholly unexceptional. Besides, this division fell so well in with the business of the several parts of the vessel as to give it at once precedence.

Compared with one, two or three bulkheads:

> The centre section would then be occupied by the engine, boiler, and coal bunkers, thus detaching them entirely from all other parts of the vessel. The sections Nos. 2 and 4 would be the fore and after holds, or, in case of passengers' vessels, the fore and after cabins; and the two remaining sections at the bow and the stern, need not be as high as the main deck as the water never could rise within several feet of the same.

These were more than mere proposals as Mr Williams' company had, he claimed, built for the City of Dublin Steam Packet

Company the *City of Limerick*, *Athlone* and the *Royal William* (already mentioned), all with four watertight bulkheads, and he lists in addition the following vessels also equipped: '*Royal Adelaide*, *Queen Victoria*, *Duchess of Kent*, *Prince* and *Princess*, now getting their engines on board'.

To prove the point, the *Royal Adelaide* had holes bored in the bottom and the various compartments flooded for demonstration purposes, with no other effect than an acceptable change in draught and trim. On the question of fire, his opinion was that it would not spread laterally and:

Can only make progress upwards towards the deck and which will be considerably retarded, if not altogether checked by the absence of all currents of air from either end of the vessel. Indeed, it is questionable whether the mere closing down of the hatches over the section would not at once extinguish it.

Stress and Strain

The main causes for concern were the straining of these long narrow hulls in a seaway and damage to the engines, as the following extract from the *United Services Journal* vol I (April 1840) page 534, makes clear:

The two or three winters through which the steamers on the American Station have continued to run, have brought to light prominently the advantages of the principle of Steam Navigation in making the passage of the ocean, and the defective manner in which it has been applied. It appears that both the framing of these vessels and their engines have suffered severely. The unequal wear of several parts of the machinery, and the fracture of the framework of one of the engines, may, in great measure, be attributed to the paddle wheels being keyed on the crank-shaft, by which a powerful vibratory motion, produced by the concussion of the paddles entering and leaving the water, is transmitted to the different parts of the engine.

The principal cause of the framing of the vessels on that station manifesting such weakness is to be found in the necessity of forcing them, '*end on*', against powerful headwinds and heavy seas by which it frequently happens that one-third of their length is out of the water, and left entirely without support, which the timbering of a vessel, as at present constructed, can render no support whatever, in a horizontal direction, being placed perpendicularly to the keel, and independent of each other, consequently there is nothing to resist the tendency of the vessel to droop at the ends but the strength of the planking and the keel, which is manifestly inadequate to that purpose, especially in vessels of such great length, when exposed to such heavy weather.

Although not mentioned, the bows would slam down heavily into the next advancing wave, putting an immediate but opposite strain on the fore part of the vessel.

The quotation does not say which vessels suffered in this way, nor does it name the source of the information, for there were only a handful of vessels engaged on the North Atlantic run at that time: the *Great Western*, *Liverpool*, *Royal William*, *British Queen* and *President*, and the four Cunarders, *Britannia*, *Acadia*, *Caledonia* and *Columbia*; the two voyages of the *Sirius* are discounted. Of these, the *Great Western* can be ruled out as she showed no signs of strain after her first period in service, and the others by all accounts were very strongly built, the framing virtually solid for the full length of the vessels. However, the principles on which they were built and method of construction were still the same as for the sailing ship which remained much more 'water borne' for its whole length in heavy weather.

This discussion on the construction of steam vessels continued from month to month, and is worth reproducing at some length as it reveals something of contemporary thought. The July issue of the *United Services Journal*, 1840, continues:

Having in a previous Number stated that the principal obstacle to the construction of steam vessels of sufficient size, was to be found in the absurd and unmechanical disposition of framing adopted, we will now endeavour to point out the defects inherent in the present system of naval architecture, and explain why that system is less adopted to vessels of great length than to those of but moderate dimensions.

The improvements proposed by Sir Robert Seppings, when Surveyor of the Navy, was a system of diagonal trussing laid over the internal structure, from one end of the vessel to the other. These pieces were additional to the normal framing and were called 'riders', extending from the keelson upwards to the deck beams, placed in opposite directions and firmly bolted to the timbers of the vessel.

The article continued:

Mr Scott Russell described his method of achieving a greater fore and aft strength to a meeting of the Mechanical Section of the British Association. To impart the desired inflexibility to the fabric of the vessel, he proposed a great central system of framing, or what he called the spine, from the resemblance in structure and function to that part of the skeleton of an animal, by which its principal strength is obtained. It consisted of a system of diagonal trussing of great lightness and strength, passing along the centre of the vessel from stem to stern, immediately above the keel, which was to form its lower portion and reaching as far as the lower or upper deck, and thus occupying little more room than is now required for the deck pillars and masts along the keel.

However, both methods left the framing, which was considered 'absurd', unaltered. The answer, it was stated, was for the vessel to have 'oblique framing', the invention of a naval officer, Lieut Wall, in which the ribs of the vessel are made to form an oblique angle with the keel each alternate one being inclined in the opposite direction and mutually let in to each other where they cross by one quarter the thickness and secured at these points by small copper bolts and screws. This structure is then planked over, inside and out, following the diagonal frames and filling in the spaces between them. The next stage is to let in horizontal metal bands passing right around the vessel spaced about 6ft apart between the keel and turn of bilge, through fastened to corresponding ribands of timber on the inside. Finally, the vessel is clad with the external planking laid on in the usual way; caulked and coppered in the ordinary manner.

The result is a solid structure on the same principle as modern double diagonal construction with a third laminate laid outside fore and aft. At the time, this was considered a radical proposal and opinions were reserved as to its merits or otherwise until it had been tested by practical experience.

In fact this method had already been used in the construction of the Thames steam packet *Ruby* several years before in 1836. The building of her long narrow hull, 155ft by 19ft, must have aroused considerable interest as she had no frames but partial and full bulkheads as required, her fore and aft strength relying to a great extent on the three separate layers of planking, crossing each other and nailed together with felt between each layer. Besides being the fastest vessel on the river, capable of 11.75 knots, she must have been strong enough for this service, lasting until 1845.

The September issue of 1840[13] carried on with the general theme, looking at iron as the alternative answer, for the material had many advantages. It was, strength for strength, lighter than timber, much cooler and freer from vermin. The joints in iron could be more easily secured and made watertight, it was cheaper and more abundant than timber, easily wrought to the required shape, and there was no danger from fire. However, at the time, experience in the construction of iron vessels was limited. The largest afloat was the packet *Rainbow* which ran between London and Hamburg, until her sudden and mysterious disappearance. Several question marks over its suitability were raised, although conceding that the supposed problem of the compass on an iron vessel was not, it was claimed, borne out in practice on the *Rainbow*.

First, the thinness of the plating and engine beds would not have the strength to prevent the bottom sagging or drooping downward and the metal would suffer from the reciprocating motion of the beams and piston, 'an action which sheet-iron is by no means calculated to withstand . . . if sufficient thickness be given to the metal to resist such action, all advantage in point of lightness, and indeed economy would be lost'.

Second, there was rapid oxidation of the metal. Experiments were in progress at the time by Mr Mallet of Dublin, at the instance of the British Association, who tested samples of all the major iron makers in Britain in '1st the clear water of Kingston Harbour (Dublin); 2nd, in the foul water of the same; 3rd, in the foul river Liffey water; 4th, in the clear water of the same; and 5th, in the sea-water, constantly maintained at a temperature of 120 degrees Fahrenheit, and to be examined and measured twice a year'.

Third, there was the question of expansion of the metal in a hot climate and the allowance made for it in bridges and other structures of iron. This, it was said by Lardner, writing in the *Mechanics Magazine*, 'ought not to be overlooked'.

The general conclusion of this long discussion in the pages of the *United Services Journal* of 1840 was that vessels should be constructed using a combination of timber and iron as best suited the purpose.

These deliberations mention Scott Russell in respect of the longitudinal strengthening of conventionally framed wooden vessels, but do not refer to his work in connection with the design and building of iron hulls using a totally new method. The first of these in 1836 was only a small vessel 60ft long with iron frames instead of wood, not much different in concept from the established ways of shipbuilding. However, on the second and larger vessel, *Storm*, 120ft, these transverse frames were abandoned in favour of a longitudinal system using a few transverse bulkheads but reinforcing the lap joints of each strake of plating with a 'T' bar on the inside. This was a radical new concept and the forerunner, perhaps not recognised at the time, of future iron ship construction.[14]

Stability

At least at the beginning of a long voyage, the steamer could stand up to her canvas in a strong blow, but towards the end, when most of the coal had been consumed, this was often not the case. Some, it was reported, as they neared the destination had 'coal fever', that is, stability had been reduced to such an extent that little sail, if any, could be set even in a light breeze and the rolling was very slow and heavy.

A vessel in this condition was usually described as 'cranky' or 'tender' and it is possible the term 'coal fever'[15] referred specifically to steamers arriving at the end of a long voyage, bunkers nearly exhausted, and listing over to one side as if she were a sick person, unable to stand up properly. This situation could arise quite simply by the ship having unequal weight either side of the centre line; but it may well have been caused by her centre of gravity having risen sufficiently to coincide with the 'metacentre'.[16] A state of 'neutral equilibrium' would then exist and the vessel would lay over with a considerable heel to one side, taking up an 'angle of loll'. Normally a ship is in 'stable equilibrium', that is, the vessel will return to the upright after removal of the inclining force; the metacentre is above the centre of gravity, and the further these two points are apart the greater the righting lever (see Figure 4:8). The optimum

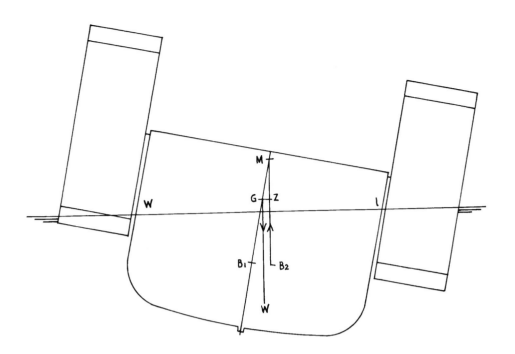

Fig 4:8 *Section of the* Great Western *at the paddle shaft with stability diagram (not to scale). The metacentric height, (the distance GM) for sailing ships was considered to be between 2.5 and 3.5 feet, allowing them to stand up to their canvas. This was also a requirement for the early ocean steamships, particularly naval vessels that carried a considerable amount of sail. (Peter Allington)*

distance is unique to each vessel and will ensure she is neither too stiff nor too tender, and in a cargo-carrying ship will depend much on where the various parcels are stowed, or the amount and distribution of any ballast. The position G is the centre of gravity where the whole weight of the ship and her contents W are conceived to act vertically downwards. B is the centre of buoyancy which acts vertically upwards, exerting a force equal to G, and when the vessel is heeled over will intersect the centre line at M, the metacentre, as B1 moves to B2. The two parallel forces, acting on the lever GZ, form a couple which tends to turn the ship upright again. The actual righting moment is the length of GZ multiplied by the displacement. This stability diagram and the foregoing principles apply to small angles of heel up to 12 degrees and is referred to as 'initial stability', and the metacentre is assumed to be a fixed point, but only inasmuch as it is related to the vessel's draught. The distance between G and M, the metacentric height, does not have to be large; for example, a 10,000 ton shelter deck type cargo liner of the 1950s, fully loaded in Far Eastern ports, with a draught of 28ft, behaved remarkably well when crossing the Indian and Atlantic Oceans, her metacentric height being 1ft 8 in.[17]

Practical Seamanship for the Merchant Service by John Todd and W B Whall states,[18] 'So far as can be judged, it would appear that metacentric heights in laden cargo vessels frequently lie between 1½ feet and 3 feet, sometimes falling to 6 or 8 inches, at other times exceed 3 feet'. However, with a hull shape as shown it will gradually rise with a decrease in draught. In other words, it will be higher above the keel when light and less when loaded. The waterline beam also has an effect on the height of the metacentre, which up to a point will tend to rise at larger angles of heel due to the increased length between w

and l. Therefore, the state of 'neutral equilibrium' that occurs when G coincides with M will result in the vessel laying over to the slightest external force and she will not recover the upright position, but in most cases, providing the cargo does not shift, will not capsize, for having reached a sufficient angle, M will rise above G due to the much increased waterline beam. It can be seen that the righting lever GZ has a direct bearing on stability and up to a point, roughly 40 degrees of heel, it will increase in a modified box section hull as shown in Figure 4:8, but from then on as heel increases it will diminish in length.

Distribution of Weight and Ballast

How does all this affect the early ocean going passenger steamer? For the first time vessels gradually lost a significant amount of their displacement as fuel was used during the voyage; the pure sailing ship once loaded or in ballast remained virtually the same throughout except for the water and stores consumed, certainly not losing much weight unless deliberately jettisoned; or she might become heavier if leaking badly or a deck cargo of timber became saturated. It was this loss of weight, particularly from low down in a vessel with a relatively narrow beam and fine ends, and carrying a lot of top weight in the form of paddle wheels and shaft, sponsons, wheel covers and propulsion machinery with a relatively high centre of gravity plus all the masts, spars and rigging, that was the root of the problem.

The *Great Western* carried 40 tons of permanent ballast and relied on a certain amount of cargo to provide additional stability. If, as occurred on the maiden voyage, part of this space was used for coal bunkers, which could, unlike the cargo, be expended at some time or other, it can be seen that in extreme circumstances when these reserves had to be used, then the rising centre of gravity could very well reach the metacentre. As it was she arrived with over 100 tons on board. Nevertheless, it is significant that an entry in the log book for 19 April, 11 days out from Bristol, mentions, 'All hands employed shifting copper into the fore part of the cargo space, trimming coals from the fore peak, filling the empty water casks with salt water below'.

This last phrase sums up the ever worsening stability situation for the total weight could not have amounted to more than 10 to 15 tons if replacing the fresh water used, and yet it was deemed necessary. Furthermore, two days later, to reduce the heeling under sail as she became more and more tender, the anchor cable was shifted over to the weather side, the wind strength according to the log book only force 3 on the beam, the ship carrying two headsails, two gaffsails, and square topsail.

Another indication was the frequent entry in the log book that the vessel was 'rolling heavily but very easily', a characteristic phrase often attributed to a small metacentric height.

Part of the problem as mentioned was the amount of top weight. Brunel, in his report on the advantages of the screw compared with the paddle wheel and recommending the change for *The Great Britain*, stated:[19]

> I have gone into some detail in calculating the weights of the parts which are not common to the two systems and I find that the difference, or actual diminution of weight in favour of the screw as applied to our new ship, is upward of 95 tons; but that a much greater weight even than this is transposed from the top of the ship to the bottom . . . no less a mass than one hundred and sixty tons is removed from the level of the paddle shaft, or from about 10 feet above the waterline and replaced by 65 tons at about 7 feet below the waterline; not only is buoyancy, and consequently proportionate space for cargo, gained to the extent of the difference, but the relief to the labouring of the vessel in bad weather from the change of position must be immense. If the reverse were under consideration, if in a vessel fitted for sea, however stiff in trim and form, it were suggested to remove 65 tons of her ballast, and to place 160 tons upon her deck, and thus navigate her across the Atlantic in all weathers, it would probably be considered, not merely as highly dangerous but as actually impossible. Although such as an opinion as that it would be incorrect, yet the extent of the beneficial change is much more striking when considered in this way.

Water Ballast Tanks

What was the solution to this problem, if any? Either top weight must be reduced or the bottom weight loss of coal replaced by ballast. The first option is limited to stowing such heavy movables as the anchor and cable as low down as possible once clear of the port, and reducing top hamper by housing the topmasts and sending down yards. The second, taking on water ballast when needed, seems an obvious remedy, and as early as 1825 the *Enterprize* was fitted with dual-purpose tanks that could be flooded once the coal had been emptied. She departed Falmouth on 16 August bound for Calcutta under the command of Lieutenant Johnston who kept a journal of the voyage. On 31 August, 15 days out, he records the following entry for the afternoon:[20]

> People employed as before moving coals from the Midship tanks which will be nearly emptied tonight. The heat in these tanks is excessive and overpowering that they can never be worked but after the fires have been a long time extinguished. The ship beginning to be crank and as I must trust entirely to the water ballast before I can consume the coals in the after hold I must endeavour to ascertain the effect of filling the Tanks or I may lighten the ship too much without the means of remedying the evils. Midnight calm.

With her engines shut down and no wind she must have been just drifting while the work was completed. It is apparent from this entry that the fitting of dual-purpose tanks was not thought through properly. Those near the boilers became so hot that no coal could be extracted when under steam, and , as they were also required to carry water, the openings or manholes must have been small, making it very difficult of access.

The next day, 1 September:

> AM. Light airs inclining to calm all hands cleaning the coal tanks. Noon ordered the fires to be lighted Lat 19.24 Long 18.25. at 2 set on the engines with calm and cloudy weather. The Paddle Boards have been shifted close out. There have been no sufficiently calm weather to ascertain the Draft of waters but I suppose it to be 12.4 and 13ft 6in. The Ship in good trim. Crew employed making up sails.

There is no specific mention of actually filling tanks but fires were lit and steam raised, she was said to be in good trim, and next day when there was a light breeze from the west the sails were set, so one can conclude she was no longer so cranky. It is interesting also to note the paddle boards must have been 'reefed' at the outset, that is, positioned closer to the axis; and now, with a lighter draught moved out towards the rim of the wheel, her mean of 15ft 1½in on departure reduced to 12ft 11in taking into account, one must assume, the additional ballast.

The log book of the *Great Western* mentions 'coal tanks' such as on 12 April 'one man trimming coals off the fore coal tanks for the use of the stoker at fore end of boilers'. The only spaces referred to that carried fuel were the fore and after tanks, the latter probably the official bunker spaces along the ship's side outboard of the boilers; the others contained the excess required for this length of voyage. It would seem these tanks were divided into sections, perhaps to keep a better record of consumption and prevent any shifting, but no mention is made of cleaning them or filling with water ballast when empty of coal.

In naval vessels the bunker spaces were called 'coal boxes' and in one vessel at least, provision was made for them to carry water ballast as well. Robert Murray, in his book on marine engines, describes the steam paddle frigate *Sidon* of 1846 as:[21]

> Carries about 700 tons of coal, with her main deck portsills 6 feet 6 inches above the water; the coal boxes being so fitted that when the coals are expended, water ballast may be taken in to prevent too great a variation in the dip of the wheels.

Hull Shape Related to Performance and Horsepower

The sluggish pitching into a head sea at the start of the voyage became ever more lively towards the destination, for not only did she float higher in the water but the peaks at either end had been relieved of a lot of deadweight. It was said that looking aft from the bowsprit of the *Great Western* 'the whole cutwater and a considerable length of keel is frequently seen out of the water'. This is probably true, but impossible from the vantage point of the bowsprit; even hanging upside down there is no way the keel could be sighted.[22]

All the early Atlantic steamers suffered to some degree from the problem of reconciling a hull form required for speed and the carrying of a large weight in fuel which had its effect on stability and seaworthiness particularly at the beginning and end of the voyage. Some fared worse than others in heavy weather. The *Liverpool*, for example, was forced to turn back to Cork on her maiden voyage due to a slow progress in adverse conditions; total fuel consumption being greater than expected, the stocks remaining on board had been reduced to a critical level. At times she was down to 2.5 knots, and it was said that had she tried to turn and head south in the hope of better weather, it would have been too dangerous with a heavy sea on the beam. Correspondence at the time refers to the *Liverpool* as being:[23]

Extremely wet, burying herself in every sea; that she rolled tremendously putting the tops of the paddle boxes under water; has two little beam for her length; and 'God help the man who attempts to get canvas on her' . . .

Despite the criticism, she was very strongly built and had engines of adequate power, provided of course there was sufficient steam. However, the hull was too extreme, her beam was only 30ft 10in with a length on deck of 223ft giving a ratio of over 7:1. Most of her contemporaries of this length had about 35ft of beam. Drastic measures were taken to improve her, a report at the time referring to the *Liverpool* after the refit:[24]

It may also be mentioned that the *Liverpool* has had 7ft more beam given her, and is now 393 tons larger than formerly, the proportion of power has, therefore, been decreased, whilst her speed and weatherly qualities have been increased.

Also the first four and best vessels, [referring to a table in the text] and which vary least in their speed in bad weather, have more beam [in proportion to their length] than the other three.

It appears to me, that more depends on the form and construction of the vessel than on having a large engine power.

The last part of this quotation could almost have been written by Samuel Seaward, who was an advocate of less power hence less weight of machinery, therefore less displacement; or given a smaller engine, there could be more room for cargo or fuel on the same draught. He makes these comments when referring to the *Liverpool* in his paper, published in 1841:[25]

The *Liverpool* constructed at the port after which she was named, in the year 1837, for Sir John Tobin, was considered to be a perfect model of an Atlantic steamer, her beam being only 29 feet* to her length of 220 feet*, whilst her sharp bows and clean run aft were calculated, it was anticipated, greatly to increase her speed. The measurement of the *Liverpool* according to the old rule, would have given her a register of 1000 tons, but this burthen was virtually diminished to 900 tons by the sharpness of her bow and stern, which lessened her stowage to the extent of 100 tons. Into the vessel, so constructed, engines of 450 horses-power were placed, thus giving her exactly one horse-power to each two tons of burthen, which was the greatest proportion of power to tonnage that had up to that period been adopted to a steam-ship. The weight of the engines, together with that of the boilers when filled with water, brought the hull of the vessel down to within two feet of the estimated water-line with her coals and cargo on board; but when 500 tons of fuel (a short supply for 18 days consumption) were added to the weight already on board, she sank so deep that her paddle-wheels became immersed 4 feet below their proper dip, and the action of the engines was very much impeded, occasioning great waste of power.

It may fairly be estimated, that had engines of 300 horses-power been placed in this vessel, instead of those of 450 horses-power, her speed would have been materially increased, as the full force of the engines could have been exerted, and the diminution of one-third in the quantity of fuel required, as also one-third in the weight of the engines, would have kept the vessel in fair trim for sea going purposes.[26]

Advances in steam propulsion commonly imply an increase in speed and improved passage times, but in the 1840s there were, with the exception of Scott Russell's wave line and wave form theories, no set formulae when designing the hull form, only the knowledge that for a given area of midship section different waterlines were best suited depending on the intended speed of the vessel. The example of the *Liverpool* showed that among other considerations a too narrow hull was a disadvantage in heavy weather and smaller vessels with proportionately greater beam employed on the same service were faster. The Cunarder *Acadia* was of virtually the same registered tonnage and had equal engine power at 2.75nhp per ton to that of the *Liverpool* but her beam to length was 6.66:1 and at the time she was considered one of the fastest steamers on the western ocean.

Other factors, besides the proportion of beam to length, played an important part in overall performance, including initial stability, windage of hull and rig, the vessel's sailing qualities, ability to maintain steam pressure and the indicated horsepower developed by the engine. The *Great Western* appears to have had a slight performance advantage over her nearest rivals; although compared to the *British Queen* she was smaller proportionately narrower with less indicated horsepower per ton, but nonetheless proved the better passage maker of the two.

1 J Bourne, *A Treatise on the Screw Propeller* (London, 1867) p. 218

2 J Bourne, op cit, p. 222

3 George S Emmerson, *John Scott Russell* (London, 1977) p. 14

4 George S Emmerson, op cit, p. 53

5 David R MacGregor, *Fast Sailing Ships* (London, 1988) p. 168

6 Information on the vessels' dimensions from H P Spratt, *Outline History of Transatlantic Steam Navigation* (London, 1950) p. 19; Denis Griffiths, *Brunel's Great Western* (Wellingborough, 1985) Appendix 4

7 A G Course, *The Wheels Kick and the Winds Song* (Newton Abbot, 1968) p. 31

8 H Underhill, *Deep Water Sail* (Glasgow, 1963) pp. 134, 141

9 B Greenhill (ed), *The Advent of Steam* (London, 1993) pp. 24–5. *The Last Century of Sail* (London, 1993) pp. 52–73

10 J Fincham, *A History of Naval Architecture* (Yorkshire, 1979) from the first edition of 1851, plates at back of book

11 Lieut W Gordon RN, *The Economy of the Marine Steam Engine with suggestions for its improvement* (London, 1845) p. 9, Introduction

12 B Greenhill and A Giffard, *Steam, Politics and Patronage* (London, 1994) pp. 157–8

13 *United Services Journal* (September, 1840) p. 94

14 George S Emmerson, *John Scott Russell* (London, 1977) pp. 12 and 13

15 Denis Griffiths, *Brunel's* Great Western (Wellingborough, 1985) p. 127

16 A term probably coined by the Frenchman M Bouguerand and already in use in 1798 when Atwood published his paper 'A Disquisition on the Stability of Ships' in which stability is dependent upon the interaction of two forces, viz weight and buoyancy, and to a slightly lesser extent on the position of what he described as the 'metacentre'. This was defined as the point where a vertical line passing through the centre of buoyancy, when the vessel is inclined, intersects her middle line

17 Captain L G Taylor, *Cargo Work* (Glasgow, 5th edition, 1959) p. 181

18 John Todd and W B Whall, *Practical Seamanship for the Merchant Service* (London, 3rd edition enlarged, 1898) p. 327

19 'Report to the Directors of the Great Western Steamship Company', October 1840, Appendix II. 'Report on the Screw Propeller', p. 553

20 Part of the Field Papers, Science Museum, London, Ref: Arch; Field 1/22 – 1/31

21 R Murray, *Marine Engine* (London, 1851) p. 155

22 'Report to the Directors of G W Steamship Company', Appendix XII, p. 550

23 Extracts from letters published in Daphne D C Pochin Mould, *Captain Roberts of the* Sirius, *Sirius* Commemoration Committee (Cork, 1988), pp. 120 and 121

24 J Fincham, *A History of Naval Architecture* (London, 1851, reprinted 1979) p. 317

25 S Seaward, 'Memoir on the Practicability of Shortening the Duration of Voyages, by the Adaption of Auxiliary Steam Power to Sailing Vessels', *Transactions of the Institute of Civil Engineers*, volume 3 (London, 1842) p. 387

26 * There is a slight difference in these dimensions from other published sources

CHAPTER 5

The Engine and Boilers

Improvements in Performance

For those steamship companies engaged in passenger carrying worldwide it was obvious they must build larger vessels to be competitive with the sailing packets and other well established lines such as the East India Company. As speed was also a crucial factor, this inevitably meant longer and proportionately narrower hulls, so that by the 1850s a ratio of 8:1 was common. Ever more powerful engines were required which, for paddle propelled merchant vessels, usually meant side lever machinery, a simple and robust design that had changed little over the years. The only

surviving example in Europe complete in the vessel it propelled, the steam tug *Reliant*, is now part of the collection at the National Maritime Museum, Greenwich, London, and being of the same genre as these early marine engines, is of great historical importance. There is also the *Eric Nordevall*, a steamer built especially for the Göta Canal in southern Sweden: brought into service in 1837, she worked successfully for nearly 20 years. In June 1856 she sank to the bottom of Lake Vattern after striking a shoal and has lain in 45m of water ever since. Reportedly in very good condition, including the side lever engines, she may be raised and restored in a similar manner to the *Wasa* or a reconstruction built.

Figure 5:1 *The paddle tug* Reliant, *formerly the* Old Trafford, *dried out at the Cory Barge Works, Charlton, in August 1969. Built at Eltringham's of South Shields in 1907 she now belongs to the National Maritime Museum. (Denis Stonham)*

Bigger engines need more steam, hence more fuel consumed, for the increase in efficiency over the years had only been marginal. These low pressure single-expansion engines could hardly better 4lb of coal per indicated horsepower per hour despite improvements in boiler steam pressure, up to 20lb per sq in, and in some cases 25lb per sq in from the modest 5lb on the *Great Western*. However, between 1838 and 1855 the indicated horsepower compared with the nominal horsepower had doubled, and in some cases trebled, that of the early machinery, mainly due to this increase in steam pressure. At the time many engineers did not see any practical reason for increasing it beyond these limits. It was the introduction of the more fuel efficient compound engine in 1854 that made it necessary to have a higher steam pressure, resulting in the much improved figure of 2lb of coal per indicated horsepower per hour.

These new compound engines often proved unreliable in service, and it was not until 1869 that the P & O company, for example, succeeded in building a steamer with high and low pressure machinery which could be considered thoroughly successful, having in previous years had to re-engine vessels with the older type low pressure single-expansion engines.

Early Experiments with Compound Engines

Fifty years before, experiments had taken place using two cylinders, and in fact, earlier still in 1781, a double cylinder engine had been constructed by Hornblower in which, according to an ongoing feature in the *United Services Journal*:[1]

Mr Hornblower's plan consisted of using steam of great elasticity [high pressure] and allowing it to actuate the piston of a small cylinder, and then permitted it to flow in and perform the same office in a larger one, in virtue of its expandability – the piston rods of both being attached to the beam of the engine. Owing to circumstances not necessary to be explained here, Hornblower's engine was laid aside but not from any defect in the principle of expansion.

In the year 1804, the principle of double-cylinder engines, with some modifications, was revived by Mr Arthur Woolfe, of Cornwall, an engineer of eminence, who, with an intuitive knowledge of the subject, perceived that the principle of expansion could be brought into the most advantageous operation by the adoption of steam of very great elasticity; he accordingly invented, and brought to perfection, a very ingenious modification of the tubular boiler, which conferred the power of producing highly elastic steam with safety. By this arrangement, a considerable saving of fuel was effected, which at the time was attributed to the adoption of the second cylinder – the smaller one of which, in Mr Woolfe's engine, was constructed of considerably less dimensions than that in Hornblower's arrangement. No doubt, a considerable saving of fuel was effected by the adoption of these engines; but that was not produced by the use of two cylinders, but resulted from the excellent arrangement of the steam generators, the employment of steam of great elasticity, and the extreme application of the principle of expansion; and if it be desired to economise the

Figure 5:2 *This side view, in her actual state, including damage, shows the paddle steamer* Eric Nordevall *built at Norrköping in Sweden in 1836. Probably the oldest surviving steam vessel, she lies intact at the bottom of Lake Vattern in southern Sweden. (Carl Olof Cederlund)*

space required for fuel on board steam-vessels, these principles ought to be applied in a greater or less degree in the management of marine engines.

The reasons why it took so long for the obvious advantage in fuel saving, due to a higher boiler pressure combined with the double expansion of steam, to be implemented are complex and include technical, operational and financial considerations.

On the first point, steam pressure was limited by the strength and properties of wrought iron and copper for boiler construction; simply making the plating thicker was not the answer. Even assuming that boilers could be built to withstand much higher pressure, the established practice of using salt water and the jet condenser which could cope very well with low pressure machinery would not be efficient enough for pressures of 60lb per sq in or more. The use of fresh water in the boiler combined with a reliable surface condenser was therefore essential. With no practical alternative, problems arose from the use of tallow as a lubricant for the piston, cylinder and valves, being unavoidably distributed throughout the internal parts of the machinery along with the steam, causing the twofold problem of blockages in the condenser tubes and corrosion of them by the fatty acid content. These complications were not mentioned by the inventor of the apparatus, Samuel Hall, when he took out another patent, number 6359, in 1833 which described a device for removing oil from the surface of the boiler water. Although not the complete answer, such an improvement must have reduced the adverse effects of tallow in the surface condenser. For the compound engine to succeed fully, all these conditions must be satisfied – much higher boiler pressure, fresh water and surface condenser, and lubricants that were non-corrosive and worked at higher temperatures.

However, slow progress had been made over the years within the limits of the materials, principally wrought iron, and this evolutionary process with little scientific research saw the ordinary boiler pressure of 5lb per sq in in the 1830s rise to 10lb in the '40s and 20lb in the '50s. During the three decades, any pressures above these figures would have been considered 'high pressure steam'.

Even in 1849, Seaward, one of the well known engineers of the day, in a paper entitled 'On the Employment of High-pressure Steam working expansively in Marine Engines' read before the Institution of Civil Engineers, stated (in brief) that

1) the highest pressure on any boiler his company built was 16lb per sq in,
2) the steam pressure of 8lb per sq in was quite adequate,
3) it was strongly recommended that 'steam employed in the navy should not be of greater pressure than 10 lb per sq in or in extreme cases 12lb per sq in. Any material increase in the latter will be attended with considerable risk without any adequate advantage'.

Scott Russell, another marine engineer at the meeting remarked that Field, Farey, A M Perkins and Rennie, all respected engineers at the time, agreed with Seaward.

Operationally, the low steam pressure combined with the jet condenser suited the majority of marine engines and paddle wheel propulsion, and by 1850 it was thought that after 40 years of development, the pinnacle had been reached. On the grounds of economy, the use of higher pressure steam had already been demonstrated in trials with existing machinery, but the Admiralty was still to be convinced of all-round benefit; and, as they were the major single purchaser of marine engines, the impetus for change did not come from them, despite strong argument in favour of high pressure steam by Lieut Gordon in 1845 (author of the book *The Economy of the Marine Steam Engine*).

After the initial excitement and speculative ventures in the North Atlantic passenger trade, which proved unprofitable except in the case of the *Great Western*, and then only with a modest return on capital, and with Cunard only surviving on its mail contract with the Government, shipowners, with one exception, were unwilling to commit funds to untried and untested schemes such as the compound engine.

It was not until the 1860s that the various technical and engineering problems were overcome and compound engines were finally adopted. Boiler pressure was at first still relatively modest. The P & O liner *Carnatic*, built in 1862, had two high and two low pressure cylinders working with steam at 26lb per sq in. By 1866 P & O had ten vessels running with compound engines, for it was the trade to the Far East that required the much improved fuel consumption of 2lb of coal per indicated horsepower per hour (4lb being the usual best figure for low pressure single-expansion condensing engines at that time, which was certainly much better than an average 6lb in the era of the *Great Western*). The Blue Funnel line, founded by the engineer Alfred Holt, made the real breakthrough. The *Agamemnon*, *Ajax* and *Achilles* were able to steam 8,500 miles without refuelling and could carry three times the cargo of the clipper ships on the China run. Furthermore, when the Suez Canal was opened in 1869, a route unsuitable for sailing ships, several thousand miles were cut from the journey to the Orient; for example, Liverpool to Shanghai via Suez 10,387 miles; via the Cape 13,717 miles.

Vessels on the North Atlantic or short sea trades around Europe where coal was easy to obtain continued to use the low pressure steam for many more years, and even Alfred Holt reserved judgement on the single-expansion condensing engine, for he saw that even with this type of machinery fuel consumption could be much improved with high pressure steam.

Increase in Performance of the Ocean Going Paddle Steamer

The *Great Western*'s daily consumption of coal when under full steam averaged out at about 32 tons per day but the later and much larger vessels required over 100 tons a day. Nevertheless,

the total amount of bunkers carried at the outset of the voyage as a percentage of displacement was less, and did not have to be stowed in the ends of the vessels. Iron hulls were increasingly employed as size for size they were much lighter than wooden ones and had a greater usable internal volume. Variation of draught between the beginning and end of the voyage was proportionately less; and therefore the paddle wheels would be working at the most efficient immersion for a greater part of the passage. The machinery was much more powerful as the indicated horsepower compared to the nominal horsepower had increased significantly, ensuring progress was still maintained in adverse conditions, and the wheels themselves being of greater diameter were more efficient.

A good example of the ultimate development of the ocean going paddle steamer, although not the last one built, was the iron Cunarder *Persia* of 1856, 398ft long with a beam of 45ft 4in, a ratio of 8.78:1, the side lever engines of 950nhp, now developing over 3,000ihp with a consumption of 3.9lb of coal for every horsepower per hour, or about 150 tons per day. At an average rate of about 13 knots for the 3,000 mile crossing to New York she would have taken just under 10 days and there-fore used 1,500 tons of coal or thereabouts. This compares with the *Great Western* built 18 years earlier with engines of 450nhp and 750ihp using 5lb of coal per indicated hp per hour, giving a maximum daily consumption of 40 tons, which at 8.5 knots would take just under 15 days using a total of 600 tons of bunkers to cover the same distance. These figures are approximate and take no account of assistance from the sails, nevertheless they illustrate the tremendous advances made in simple expansion engines in the mid nineteenth century.

The Use of Steam and Sail

The use and management of the engines is summarised by Robert Murray in his book on marine engines, published in 1851,[2] from which the following extract is taken. The first paragraph refers back to the formula and calculations used to work out fuel consumption related to speed:

Economy attending a diminished Speed in the Vessel. – These examples all show the great economy which

Figure 5:3 *The* Agamemnon's *tandem compound engines enabled her to carry 3,500 tons of cargo on a coal consumption of little more than 20 tons per day. She could steam from Britain to Mauritius without coaling en route. Thus in 1866 the economical cargo steamer was born, and placed in the China tea trade. She and her sisters rendered the* Cutty Sark *and her contemporaries obsolete before they were built. (Conway Maritime Press)*

attends a diminution of speed in the vessel; and although in the case of merchant steamers, the loss of time is generally too serious a disadvantage to admit of any permanent reduction of speed, much benefit has resulted to ships in the Royal Navy from the judicious husbanding of the fuel in this manner, whether it be to meet the requirements of an unusually long run, or merely to save coal when the vessel is employed on a service not demanding extraordinary despatch.

Use of Sails of a Steamer. —The steamer's sails, also, form a most important addition to her capabilities, as for each knot that the vessel is propelled by their aid, as much fuel is saved as may afterwards propel her the same number of knots in a calm. The sails should therefore be set upon every occasion of a fair wind, and according as it is more or less favourable, so should the steam be more or less cut off and expanded in the cylinders. By this means we avoid the unnecessary consumption of dense steam, which would otherwise be used at a disadvantage, for it is evident that however little the engines may assist in propelling the ship, they must nevertheless work very fast in order to overtake the vessel's speed generated by the sails alone, and two cylinders full of steam must always be used for each revolution.

Disconnecting the Engines. —Hence, when a moderate speed is attained by the sails alone, it is more economical (though otherwise not always to be recommended) to stop the engines entirely, and disconnect the wheels or screw when practicable, suffering them to revolve freely in their journals by the re-action of the water. When, on the other hand, the wind and sea are adverse, the full power of the engines must be applied, every knot gained being now of double value.

Thomas Tredgold's observations on this subject, made over a decade earlier when the assistance from the sails to steam power was, if anything, more important, writes in article 646 of his book:[3]

It appears to be impossible to apply so much sail as to give a steam vessel the advantage of being used as an effective sailing vessel, in the event of the engines or coals failing. The proper object of sails in a steam vessel is to save fuel when the wind can be of service,* and to do this with economy, the engines should be worked expansively; hence, the arrangement of the engines should be such as would answer to work at full pressure in a calm. This condition enables us to fix the power of the engine by the rate for still water; and if the vessel has sails sufficient to maintain the speed with about half the power of the engines, when the wind is fair, it will be as much as can be usefully employed. The greater attention should be given to keep the centre of effort of the sails as low as possible, and to arrange them so that the angle of the vessel's

inclination may be inconsiderable, that the wheels may not dip unequally.

*It is a common notion, that the sails should be used in addition to the steam power, to gain greater velocity; but this is not desirable, except for post-office packets and the like, because an immense extent of canvas affords, only a very small power when the vessel moves at a considerable velocity; hence, economy directs to saving fuel, rather than increasing speed.

The paragraphs which follow explain how the steam and vacuum cycle worked and the application of the principle of 'expansion' – to use the contemporary terminology – and it will become apparent that the economic operation of the engines depended much on the co-ordination with the use of sails, a skilled business on which the commercial success of the voyage could well depend. The fundamental requirement was to adjust the engine power to suit the wind and sea conditions and if sail was set to reduce steam consumption accordingly. The greater the assistance from the sails, the lower the fuel consumption, allowing a much greater range than would at first appear possible, thus making longer ocean routes feasible when related to bunker capacity. On this question of economy, larger ships which could carry more fuel did not have to have engines of proportionately larger power to achieve the same speed.

Furthermore, as Brunel pointed out in 1836, 'It is well known that the proportional consumption of fuel decreases as the dimensions and power of the engines are increased and consequently a large engine can be much more economical than a small one'.[4]

This argument had its limits: and critics who included Seaward, mentioned in the previous chapter in connection with the PS *Liverpool*, recommended smaller, lighter engines as being the most economic in terms of the vessel's displacement and the amount of space required for fuel.

The Engine

The low steam pressure of 5–10lb per sq in was considered sufficient for these engines, and the slow revolutions of between 15 and 20 per minute suited paddle propulsion. (This pressure is of course above atmospheric reckoned to be 14.75lb per sq in when the barometer is reading 30.00in.) These were low pressure condensing engines, that is, while steam was admitted to the cylinder on one side of the piston, a partial vacuum was established on the other by the condenser, and at the end of each stroke, the valve mechanism transposed pressure and vacuum to facilitate the opposite motion of the piston.

The up and down movement of the piston rod was transferred via a cross-head mounted on the top to side rods which connected with the sway beams or side levers at their lower end. These were mounted either side and pivoted about the centres. At the other end, the sway beams were united by a cross-tail or fork-head to which the lower end of the connecting rod was secured. Therefore the oscillating motion given to the sway beam by the piston rod and side rods was transferred to the connecting rod and hence at its top end to the crank pin and cranks, imparting a rotary motion to the paddle shaft. The complete mechanism, as described, is shown in the drawing and photograph, both the engines depicted being built by Napier of Glasgow (see Figures 5:4 and 5:5).

As already mentioned, the two engines worked as a pair, so arranged that when the crank of one was at the 'dead' point with the piston at the top or bottom of its stroke, the other was at its most effective, the piston at half stroke developing full power, and the crank on the paddle shaft being at right angles to the connecting rod, exerting maximum torque.

Figure 5:4 *Diagrammatic representation of a typical side lever engine built by Robert Napier. (from Plate 3, Commander R S Robinson RN,* The Nautical Steam Engine *(London, 1839)*

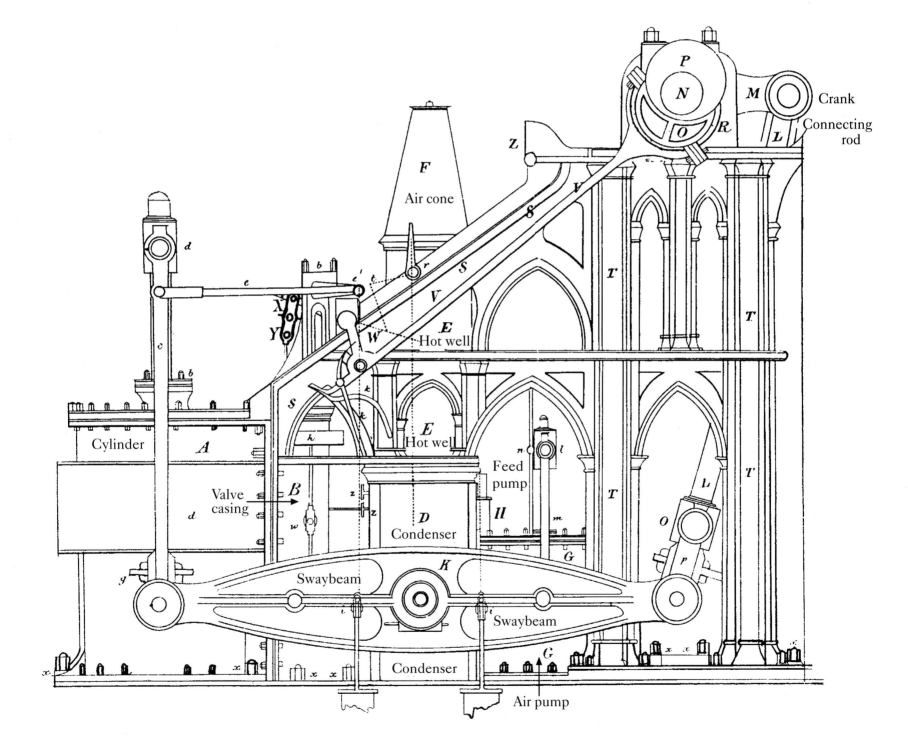

Figure 5:5 *The first marine engine built by Robert Napier in 1824 for the steamer* Leven *in service on the Clyde. It is now preserved at Dumbarton. (John R Hume)*

Other types of engine were built besides the 'side lever', and various methods devised to do away with the sway beams by making the end of the piston rod work the connecting rod directly, so this group of engines was termed 'direct acting'. The naval paddle steamer *Gorgon*, completed in 1838, was an early example. The 'oscillating' engine was another type, which also came under this heading of 'direct acting' but in this case the cylinders were not fixed to the bed plate but arranged to pivot about trunnions so that the piston rod was able to work the crank directly without an intervening connecting rod. The trunnions were designed to accommodate both the steam and eduction pipes, on opposite sides. It was the speciality of two London firms, Penn, and Miller and Ravenhill, and was much favoured for fast Post Office packets. A set of oscillating engines built by Penn in 1841 is still in operation (1996) in the German paddle steamer *Diesbar*, working on the Elbe from Dresden. Like the side lever engine of the *Reliant* until recently on exhibition at the National Maritime Museum, Greenwich, this engine is of great historical importance. The introduction of the screw required higher revolutions which led to even more variations of steam engines being developed. Although the 'side lever' engine was

heavier and more bulky by comparison, its working parts were very well balanced and little effort was required to set the engine in motion in either direction. Furthermore the long length of the connecting rod suited paddle wheel propulsion.

Steam, Vacuum and Expansion

For the purpose of explaining the working of these side lever engines, consider first the steam pressure part of the cycle. The valve admitting the steam to the cylinder opened a fraction after the piston had passed top or bottom dead centre, when the connecting rod and crank would have been in line, thus relieving the bearings and other parts of the machinery of unwarranted stress. It continued to be let in for some length of the stroke and was then cut off, the trapped steam expanding and reducing in pressure, which by the end of the stroke had reached that of the atmosphere or slightly below. This meant not only was the steam used economically, but the piston was relieved of a sudden stop at the end of the stroke. Much depended on the boiler pressure as to the point the cut off

Figure 5:6 *The engineering work of Penn & Son at Greenwich. The kind of machinery shown was replaced with the development of a machine tool industry in Britain. (Conway Maritime Press)*

occurred. For instance, the Cornish land engines working on 40lb per sq in cut off the steam after only one-sixth or even one-eighth of the stroke, the remaining seven-eighths being performed wholly by expansion.

On the other hand the early steamships with a boiler pressure of only 2lb per sq in must have admitted the steam for the full stroke or nearly so.

Robert Murray writes on the subject of 'expansion':

The limit to this principle is imposed, in practise, by the increasing size required for the cylinder, and the inequality in the speed of the piston during the stroke. It is found by calculation that if the steam be cut off at half stroke its mechanical effect is multiplied by 1.7 nearly; if at one third, by 2.1; if at one fourth, by 2.4 nearly.[5]

The vacuum part of the cycle commenced at the start of the stroke with the cylinder full of steam at atmospheric pressure or even below, which was immediately opened to the condenser, via the eduction port. The vacuum, taking some time to build up to its maximum effect, was then maintained until close to

the end of the eduction stroke when the valve was shut and the vacuum in the cylinder reduced rapidly as a consequence, building up right at the end to a slight pressure above atmospheric to 'cushion' the piston at the end of the stroke.

The Indicator

The measurement of pressure/vacuum at any time during this cycle could be obtained by an ingenious device called an 'indicator'. This instrument was connected directly to the interior of the cylinder via one of the grease cocks and consisted of a plunger working vertically up and down within a cylinder against a spring and to which a pencil was attached, the movement dependent on the amount of pressure or vacuum. The pencil was so arranged as to scribe a line on the indicator card which moved sideways the required amount each stroke by the action of one of the side rods or parallel motion gear to which it was temporarily linked.

An example of an indicator diagram, taken on board the *Commodore*, 2 January 1839, is shown in Figure 5:7, to which

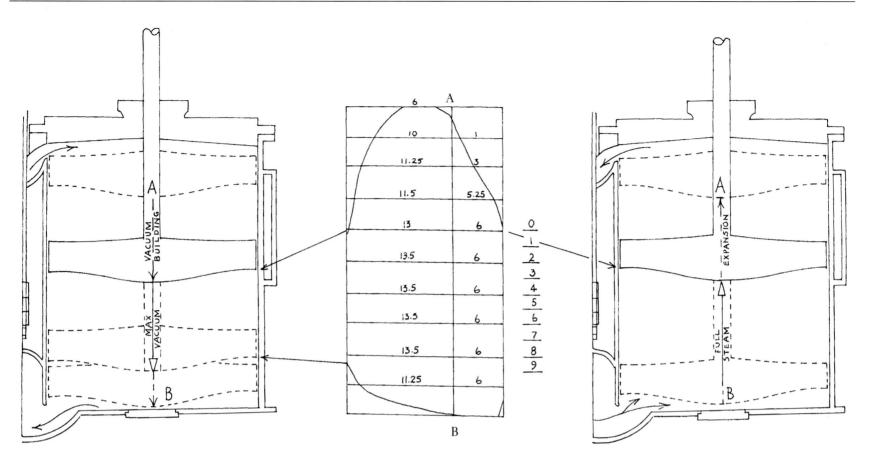

Fig 5:7 *Indicator diagram shown between two sections through the cylinder, the line AB depicts atmospheric pressure; the right hand side, steam pressure (max 6lbs per square inch); the left, vacuum (max 13.5lbs per square inch below atmosphere). (Peter Allington)*

have been added half section drawings of a cylinder and piston on each side.[6]

At the time of the experiment, boiler pressure was 7lb per sq in, and vacuum in the condenser 13.75lb below atmospheric (represented by the line AB).

The diagram shows a complete cycle on one side of the piston commencing with the admission of steam beneath the piston on the right-hand drawing at B; which, as already mentioned, occurs a fraction after the upward travel begins. From the indicator diagram, full steam pressure in the cylinder is not attained until about 5 per cent of the stroke has been completed and is maintained at 6lb per sq in until at 6/10 it is cut off. This point is 0 on the expansion scale and represented the full power cut off point on this engine. The last 40 per cent of the piston stroke is accomplished by the trapped steam at 6lb per sq in expanding and reducing in pressure, until it is actually below atmospheric by the end of the stroke.

If less power was required, it was not obtained by shutting down the main throttle valve, but by the advancement of the cut off point, thus increasing the amount of expansion. This was proved to be more economic in the use of steam.[7]

The graduations alongside the indicator diagram, 0 to 9, show the various cut off points controlled on the engine by the 'expansion valve' placed between the throttle valve and the slide valves, and arranged so as to operate both sides of the piston on the pressure stroke. If, for example, the sails were

doing all the work and the valve was set at 9, steam would only be admitted for the first 15 per cent of the stroke, the other 85 per cent accomplished by expansion. However, the expanding steam in this case would soon be less than atmospheric creating a partial vacuum which consequently retarded the stroke considerably; but, provided a sufficiently good vacuum was established on the other side of the piston by the condenser, the resultant force on the piston would be positive. The valve was operated via a rod linkage to a lever working on a cam located on the intermediate or paddle shaft, each graduation having a separate cam.

The piston has now arrived at A, the end of the upstroke, with the cylinder below having a slight vacuum. The eduction port is then opened connecting the cylinder with the condenser; the downstroke is represented in the drawing and indicator diagram on the left of the line AB. The piston travels 40 per cent of the downstroke before the full vacuum of 13.5lb per sq in below atmospheric is established and the situation is maintained until the eduction port is closed with about 20 per cent of the stroke still to be completed. It can be seen there is a rapid drop in the vacuum, the piston compressing the trapped vapour at the very end, causing a slight pressure above atmosphere, which again serves to cushion the end of the stroke at B. In terms of the average force on the piston during this cycle, the vacuum exerts 11.8lb per sq in, which is over twice as much as average steam pressure of 4.25lb per sq in. The efficiency of this particular engine, including both the boiler and condenser, is very good for this period, the combined average force on the piston being 16.32lb per sq in, comparing favourably with the maximum steam pressure and vacuum of 20.75lb per sq in.

Commander R S Robinson RN explains the physical properties of steam and why the vacuum was so important in these engines. He states:[8]

> When a cubic foot of pure fresh water is converted into steam at 212 degrees,[†] it occupies a space of 1711 feet,[*] but in condensation in a closed vessel, the 1711 feet[*] return to one foot[*] of water, leaving 1710 feet[*] with nothing in them or a vacuum.
>
> We have already seen in a perfect vacuum a moving power of nearly 15 lbs on the square inch is obtained from the pressure of the atmosphere, and the more perfect the vacuum, the greater the power. It was the chief object in all of these types of steam engines to obtain this vacuum as perfectly as possible.'
>
> [†]When produced under the average pressure of the atmosphere – 30 inches of mercury on the barometer.
> [*]Cubic feet

Thus it can be seen that these low pressure marine engines were really as much 'atmospheric' as 'steam' driven and were true heirs of the atmospheric engines with which the application of steam power had begun in the eighteenth century.

Calculating Horsepower

The average force on the piston, in this example 16.32lb per sq in would have been used to calculate the 'indicated horsepower'. If instead the 'effective horsepower' was required, then the power absorbed by the air pump, feed and bilge pump and friction of the machinery would have to be taken into account, the allowance subtracted in this instance was reckoned to be 2lb per sq in. Therefore, in this example the calculation would be 14.32 × 3,218 (area of piston in square inches – 64in cylinder) × 190 (velocity of piston in feet per minute), divided by the constant 33,000. The answer is 265.3ehp, or, using 16.32lb per sq in, the indicated horsepower works out at 302.4.

It is evident that the formula, except for piston area and the constant divisor of 33000, depends on variables, so the horsepower figures can likewise change accordingly. Lieut Gordon RN makes this point in his chapter on 'Determination of the Horsepower' when he states:[9]

> Consequently, when we speak of the power of a given engine, we can only correctly allude to the evaporative power of its boiler. The power of the engine is only relative to the strength of its various parts, and the capacity of cylinder proportional to the elasticity [pressure] of the steam.

Hence, if we apply boilers of different powers to the same engine, whose strength of material is equal to the maximum, the velocity of the piston and power of the engine will vary in like manner.

Practical Use of Expansion Valve

As the log books of the *Great Western* both deck and engine refer to these expansion valve settings and fuel consumption, it can be seen at which times the sails are of real assistance to the engine. In fact on the maiden voyage to New York the expansion valve was set at zero, that is, full power for only 29 per cent of the time. For example, the engineer's log for 11 April 1838 under the heading 'Occurrences and Remarks' states:[10]

> 6am Canvas taken off the ship, set expansion valve to 0. 8am. wind favoured us; set expansion to 4th grade. 9am. more sail; set expansion to 5th. grade. 9¾ expansion 7th grade; 10am. having measured coal for 5 hours, consumed 12,880 lbs.; 2576 lbs per hour or 23 cwt. per hour. Meridian, fine steady breeze, north easterly; canvas set; engine performing well; expansion 7th grade. 11pm. canvas reduced on ship, and rolling much; set expansion back to 5th. grade.

According to the deck log the day ended with a strong wind east by south force 7, a heavy northwest swell, ship rolling heavily, speed 10.5 knots.

Without the sails and the ship steaming into a headwind and sea, cam setting 0, coal consumption was 30cwt per hour or more, so the use of the canvas resulted in significant savings in fuel. The lowest consumption was on 22 April, a day before her arrival in New York, the sea smooth and wind favourable, cam setting 7/9, when she used only 21 tons that is, 17.5cwt per hour.

Boilers and Condensers

There were many designs of marine boiler, but in general, at least up to 1840, most were described as 'flue boilers'. They were basically a large rectangular box, usually made of wrought iron, but sometimes copper, with the plates riveted together, making the structure as steam and watertight as possible. The furnace, grate and ashpit were placed at one end and the flue constructed so as to wind back and fore as much as possible to provide the maximum amount of heat transference before reaching the uptakes and funnel placed at the top. The boiler water completely surrounded the flues and extended above the furnace and below the ashpit, leaving sufficient space on top for the steam to collect.

Figure 5:8 shows a sectional side view of this type of boiler with the sloping grate leading down to a brick firewall with the

Fig 5:8 *Side lever engine and flue boiler, drawn after Dr Lordner's* The Use of Steam, *published in the 1850s.*

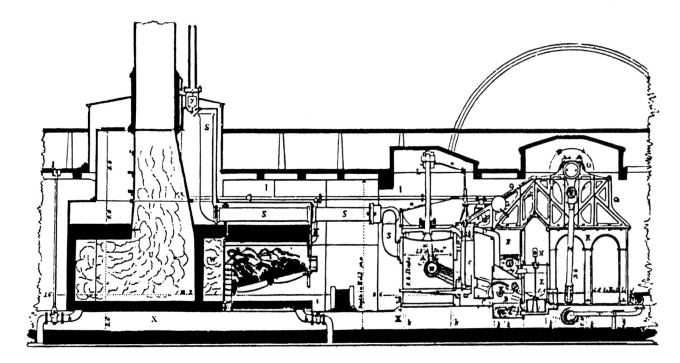

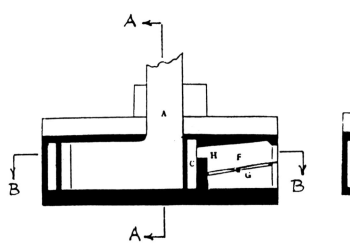

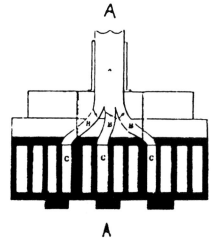

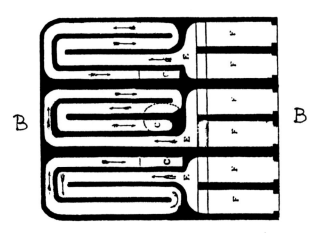

ashpit below. On the engine side of the funnel is the pressure relief valve y next to the pipe marked S which is the main steam supply to the side lever engine. The shaded area, not to be confused with the lower part of the vessel, indicates the water. Below is a simplified drawing of the boiler, the section AA illustrating the flues end on; and the sectional plan view through BB is looking down on the furnaces F and the flues from above, the arrows indicating the passage of the hot gases from the furnace to the uptakes.[11]

Despite having the advantage of less weight and bulk, the tubular boiler did not displace the flue boiler which continued to be used even in the '60s. The first naval vessels to be fitted with them in 1843 were the first-class frigate *Penelope* and the second-class frigate *Firebrand*.[12]

The main difference between the two types was the method of heat transference. The hot gases from the furnace, instead of making their way to the funnel uptakes via a long winding flue, passed through hundreds of brass or iron tubes, 2in or 3in in diameter laid close together and parallel, the open ends supported by iron plates, one mounted so as to receive the heat, the other positioned below the uptakes. As with the flue boiler, the water surrounded the tubes, which were kept submerged at all times.

A disagreeable but vital job was to keep the heat generating part of the boiler clean, as Dr Lardner explains: 'Since the flues are liable occasionally to become choked with soot and ashes, it is necessary that their magnitude shall be sufficient to allow a boy to enter them for the purpose of cleaning them'.[13]

Likewise the tubes had to be freed of any obstructions with a brush and rod.

One of the immediate problems facing the steamship once engaged on sea voyages longer than a day or two was the lack of fresh water to replenish the boilers. Some vessels were fitted with Samuel Hall's condenser which converted the exhaust steam back into fresh water by the action of the air pump drawing the steam through pipes placed in a cistern of cold sea water which was constantly being changed by a circulating pump, but as already mentioned, the apparatus suffered from blockages and corrosion. It was also suggested by some engineers that it did not establish the vacuum as quickly as the 'jet condenser'. This latter criticism may well have been unjustified as both the *Sirius* and the *British Queen* were fitted with Hall's condenser and by all accounts were a success. However most ocean going steamships, at least in the early days, had salt water in the boilers and invariably used a 'jet condenser' (see Figure 5:9). The exhaust steam was drawn into the cast iron cistern A adjacent to the cylinder where it was subjected to a spray of cold sea water, thus creating a constantly maintained partial vacuum, the resultant combination of cooling water, condensed steam and vapour drawn off by the air pump D which transferred it to the hot well B above. Here the air was separated and allowed to pass over the side along with most of the hot salt water. The salinity was less than sea water from the addition of condensed steam, hence the feed to replenish the boilers was taken from the hot well.

The jet of cold sea water was supplied by gravity, the outlet in the cistern being sufficiently below the waterline, and was regulated by a valve, the control mechanism made easy to get at, as fine adjustment was essential for the efficient running of the engine. A non-return valve was placed between the condenser and air pump so that on the down stroke as shown, the water/vapour mixture was trapped in the pump cylinder and forced upwards past a disc-shaped valve working freely on the bucket rod. On the return upward stroke this valve closed and the upper one, similar in shape opened, allowing access to the hot well above. At the same time the foot valve opened and another charge of salt water, condensed steam, vapour and air was drawn into the pump cylinder below the bucket. (The position of two valves on the upstroke are shown in dotted lines.)

The overboard discharge from the hot well was sometimes below sea level, hence the need for a large vertical pipe above so as to prevent water flooding back into the vessel if deep loaded and lurching heavily in a seaway. The cone at the top collected the air which was usually piped overboard.

This process of evaporating and replenishing the boilers with sea water could not last for more than 40 or 50 hours as the salinity would gradually rise until saturation point was reached and salt would then be deposited on the inside faces of the boiler. One answer was to 'blow off' the concentrated brine solution from the lowest point in the boilers, usually through the bottom of the vessel. This would be done at regular intervals, perhaps hourly, but the method was far from ideal as steam and heat were wasted in the operation. Before this could be done, the boiler water would have to be 'topped up' to avoid the danger of the water level being suddenly reduced too far, thus exposing the flues or tubes.

Joshua Field invented a means of changing the salt water in the boiler continuously so that the salinity remained at workable levels. Writing to Simon Goodrich who had been appointed Mechanist to the Navy Board in 1814, the letter dated 26 December 1825, he explains the principle, and information received on its use supplied by Lieut Johnston of the *Enterprize*.[14]

We have received very satisfactory accounts from Capt. Johnston of the *Enterprize* from the Cape [the vessel was on passage from Falmouth to India]. That her voyage has been longer than could be wished owing to the unusual prevalence of headwinds, it is pleasing to hear that they have not had the slightest accident, that the machinery has performed its duty well – that the difficulty of working in sea water is completely overcome by our apparatus which has succeeded in the fullest degree. He states that after working 11 days and nights without intermission the thermometer in the boiler never ran above 227½ degrees. [Sea water of average salinity boils at about 222 degrees Fahrenheit with a steam pressure of 2½lb per sq in in the boiler and Joshua Field recommended it not be allowed to rise above 230 degrees]. On opening the boiler after this

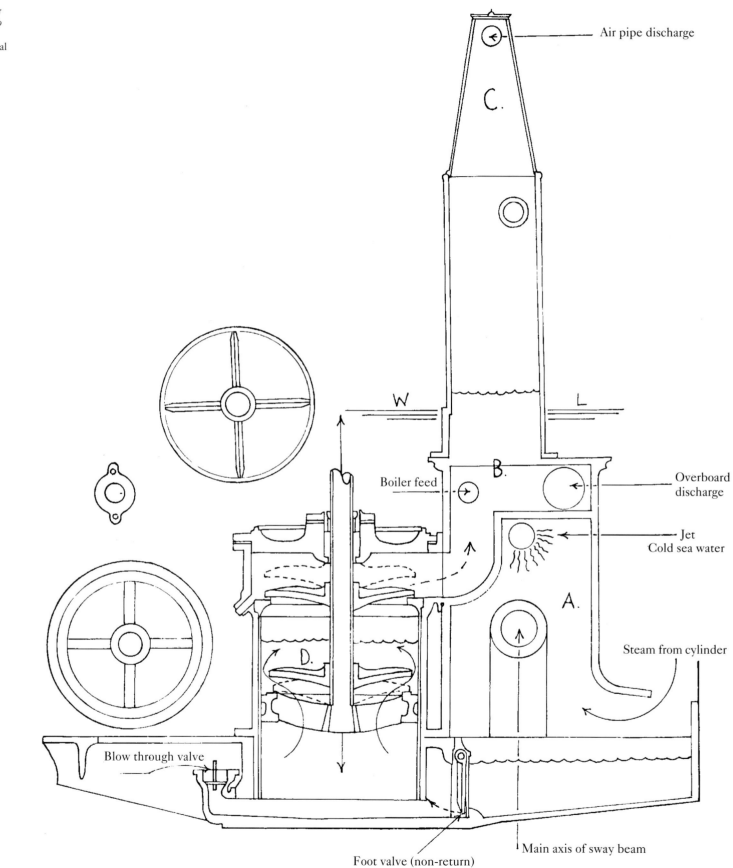

Air pipe discharge

C.

W

L

B.

Boiler feed

Overboard discharge

Jet
Cold sea water

A.

Steam from cylinder

D.

Blow through valve

Y

Foot valve (non-return)

Main axis of sway beam

no salt was to be seen, only a thin fur on the fire plates of the thickness of a wafer – in other latitudes he worked 9 days and nights, the thermometer rose to 229 degrees: on opening he found no salt but rather more deposits of fur. [The boilers had in fact been 'blown off' once, but as Lieut Johnston's journal states, 'only as a precaution'.] His fuel has averaged 11 Bushels per hour, [1 Bushel Coals variously given as 84lb or 88lb] the stoking much less arduous than he expected in hot latitudes.

This last statement contradicts Lieut Johnston's remarks in his Journal on the day the fires were extinguished, 28 August 1825:[15]

The engineers and stokers have been much fatigued and today being Sunday, as we are I trust, fairly in the Trade, I have desired every thing connected with the Engineers Department to stand over till tomorrow.

This letter followed a previous one to Goodrich dated 7 September 1825 in which Joshua Field explains the technical details of his 'water changing apparatus' as fitted to the *Lightning*. This later became the first steam vessel ever to be commissioned into the Royal Navy under the command of Lieut, later Rear Admiral, George Evans:[16]

These Engines require 16 gallons per minute to be supplied to the boiler for evaporation and we have found that 25 per cent or ¼ this quantity or 4 gallons taken constantly out per minute will keep the water in the Boiler within a degree of concentration that will avoid the evils felt in Boilers using sea water without such precaution. The water in its passage from the lowest part of the Boiler goes through a Refrigerator laying on the top of the Boiler. This Refrigerator consists of one tube within another, the rejected water between the tubes and the feed or supply water for the Boiler passing through the inner tube. This is of course ¼ more than usual, that is, 20 gallons per minute instead of 16 to make up for the 4 gallons withdrawn. The hot rejected water entering at one end and the cool water for the supply at the other. The heat of one is communicated to the other and thus carried back again into the Boiler and the foul water passing off comparatively cool. There is in the front of the Boiler a Thermometer immersed in a bowl of mercury which is immersed in the boiling water so that the heat of the water can at all times be seen and as the boiling point increases with the quantity of salt with which the water is charged, it is a constant test of the state of the water. The boiling point of clean sea water under pressure of 2½ lbs on the square inch or which the steam is blowing out of the safety valve is 222 degrees. The saltiness which accompanies the temperature from 222 degrees to 239 degrees are shown in a table sent herewith in which the

saltiness is shown after working various hours without changing and also with changing 25 per cent as above detailed. [See Figure 5:10]

The principal improvement adopted aboard the *Enterprize* is that the water is drawn through the Refrigerator from the bottom of the Boiler by a small pump working by the Engine, so proportioned that when the engine is making its proper number of strokes it shall exactly take out the 25 per cent, then whether the engine works quick or slow the discharge is exactly suited to the quantity passed out from the Boiler to the cylinder in the form of steam or in other words, as much salt is taken out of the boiler in the brine discharged by the pump every stroke as has been separated from the water which furnished the steam for that stroke. Also when the engine is stopped, this pump stops and the discharge ceases, whereas in the *Lightning* it is necessary to shut the cock in the upright pipe in front of the Boiler.

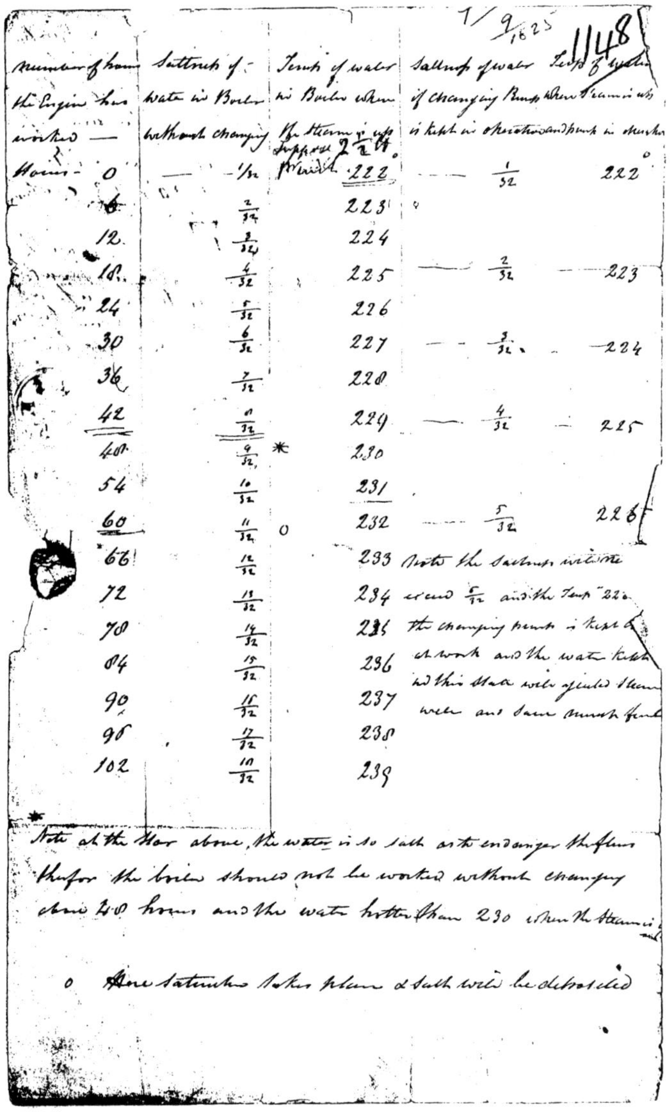

Figure 5:10 *Salinity Tables from the Field Papers.*

I took a voyage of 3 days in the *Enterprize* and made very accurate observations, taking out a bottle of water every 6 hours which I afterwards accurately examined with a hydrometer and found the apparatus completely to effect the object in view, and from the information thereby obtained formed the enclosed table.

Problems occurred on the maiden voyage of the *Great Western* when the cocks on one boiler became chocked so that the brine could not be drawn off by the pump, the engineers therefore had to resort to 'blowing off' the boiler water at intervals.

Feeding the Furnaces

The production of steam not only depended on the efficiency of the boiler, which certainly had room for improvement, but also on the quality of the coal, a point often mentioned in the log books as the reason for the low pressure and high consumption. The following figures are taken from *The Economy of the Marine Steam Engine* by Lieut W Gordon RN[17]

1lb of the Best Welsh	evaporates 9.493lb of water
Anthracite	9.014
Best small Newcastle	8.524
Average	8.074
Average Welsh	8.045
Average Newcastle	7.658
Derbyshire	6.772
Blyth Main	6.600
Staffordshire	5.600

The most common cause of reduced engine performance was the lack of steam pressure, the result of either poor coal, difficulty in stoking the furnace due to the violent motion, or seasickness, especially soon after leaving port, but primarily the result of getting insufficient fuel to the stoke hold. With only eight stokers and coal trimmers in each of two watches, which turned out to be not enough, this difficulty became so acute on the *Great Western* that the sailors were called on to help, much to their disgust. On 17 April 1838 the engine room log book states:

. . . difficulty in maintaining steam, by reason that the coal cannot be got from the ends of the ship, and brought to the furnaces fast enough for consumption; stokers and trimmers becoming languid from continued work; number of men not being adequate to the duty.

The deck log of the same day states:

watch busily employed securing boats, striking topmasts, hauling up ashes, trimming coals.

The wind was at the time southwest force 8, no sail was set

and the ship was lurching and pitching deep into a short heavy sea. This weather continued for some days, moderating at times. Entries for 19 April show things coming to a head. The engine room log states:

10am. turned all stokers and trimmers to, to get coal from the extreme ends of the ship, and promised to give them half a dollar each.

Extract from deck log:

. . . all hands busily employed trimming coals from peaks; hauling ash up; commenced using the coal in fore tanks; watch went below; much murmuring amongst the seamen respecting coal trimming.

It appears from these entries that at one stage both watches, deck and engine room, were involved.

Fuel Consumption in Adverse Conditions

It would seem reasonable to assume that a paddle steamer heading into a strong wind and heavy sea would be making much reduced headway, and with the engines at full power, cam setting 0, fuel consumption would be high. This premise is confirmed, although not conclusively proved, by the log books of the *Great Western* and also demonstrated on the first voyage of the *Liverpool*, already referred to, when she was forced to abandon her maiden voyage to New York, her bunkers being so depleted after several days of severe headwinds that she was forced to turn back to Cork. However, there was an opposite point of view expressed by the eminent engineer John Bourne, that fuel consumption would actually be reduced in these circumstances, although no figures are supplied to validate this argument.

The following passage is taken from his book and appears in the appendix, 'Screw and Paddle Vessels on the Atlantic':[18]

The main defect of screw vessels, however, is that when steaming head to wind, the screw revolves with nearly the same velocity as if no extra impediment had to be encountered; whereas, in the case of paddle vessels, the number of revolutions of the engines diminishes nearly in the same proportions as the speed of the vessel. It follows from this peculiarity that a screw vessel consumes nearly the same quantity of coals per hour in a strong adverse wind as in a calm; whereas, in a paddle vessel, there is much less steam and fuel consumed in strong headwinds, in consequence of the diminished speed of the engines on those occasions. Screw vessels must consequently carry a greater reserve of coals than paddle vessels in all cases in which strong headwinds have to be met. At the present moment I do not know of any screw vessel that is not subject to this weighty disparagement and its existence gives a superiority to paddle vessels in all cases of ocean transport, in which a large quantity of coal has to be maintained.

Theoretically speaking, the slower the engine's speed, the greater the economy of fuel, provided always that no steam escapes from the safety valve, or is otherwise wasted.

Strong winds are invariably associated with a rough sea when clear of the land so the vessel would not just be retarded by the windage of hull and rig but also the reduced efficiency of the paddle wheels. At one moment they may be clear of the water and starting to 'race', consuming steam at a rapid rate to no great effect, the next, brought to a standstill as the next wave submerged them to the level of the shaft, causing the relief valve on the boiler to lift and allow excess steam to escape. Both of these actions will no doubt slow the wheels in terms of average revolutions per hour, but at the same time consumption of coal is high as steam pressure must be maintained at the maximum, if the object is to proceed as fast as possible in the circumstances. The speeding up and slowing down of the wheels directly affects both the air pump and the efficiency of the condenser, reducing the vacuum upon which so much of the engine power depends.

One reason why the fuel consumption may have been less in adverse conditions is that steam production was cut back to protect the machinery from the violent changes in load, a point made by Thomas Tredgold:[19]

But when the force of the wind becomes considerable, and the sea rough, the wheels often revolve without touching the water in the hollow of the waves and acquire a greater increase of velocity, to be reduced, as soon as they meet the wave again, to less than ordinary speed. To lessen the abruptness of these changes, it is necessary to diminish the supply of steam, consequently the power of the engine.

1 'Notices of Steam Navigation', *United Services Journal* No 148 (March, 1841) p. 385

2 R Murray, *Marine Engines and Steam Vessels* (London, 1851) pp. 107 and 108

3 T Tredgold, *The Steam Engine* vol 1 (London, 1838) p. 310

4 E Corlett, *The Iron Ship* (Bradford-on-Avon, 1975) p. 10

5 R Murray, op cit, p. 82

6 Commander Robinson RN, Plates in *The Nautical Steam Engine* (London, 1839)

7 R Murray, op cit, p. 92

8 Commander R S Robinson, op cit, p. 26

9 Lieut W Gordon RN, *The Economy of the Marine Steam Engine* (London, 1845) p. 81

10 C Claxton, 'Logs of the First Voyage, made with Unceasing Aid of Steam between England and America, by the *Great Western* of Bristol, Lieut James Hoskens RN Commander'

11 Dr Lardner, illustration from *The Use of Steam* (London, undated 1850s)

12 B Greenhill and A Giffard, *Steam Politics and Patronage* (London, 1994) p. 166

13 D Lardner, op cit, p. 134

14 Goodrich Collection, Science Museum Library Archive Department, Ref; Arch; Good A 1001–1500

15 Lieut Johnstone, 'Journal of the *Enterprize* from August 16 1825 to October 13 1825', Field Papers: Arch; Field 1/22 – 1/31, Science Museum Library Archive Department

16 Goodrich Collection, op cit

17 Lieut W Gordon RN, op cit, p. 8

18 J Bourne, *The Screw Propeller* (London, 1867)

19 T Tredgold, *The Steam Engine* vol 1 (London, 1838) p. 310

CHAPTER 6

Paddle Wheels

Size and Position of the Wheels

The first consideration is the diameter of the wheel in relation to the vessel's size and the power of the engines. Large wheels have some advantages as, when working at the proper depth of immersion, the paddle boards strike the water in a more favourable direction and also leave it without lifting so much water; the greater weight of the wheel acting somewhat like a flywheel regulated the speed of revolution, and the boards can be made narrower. On the other hand, according to Thomas Tredgold:[1]

> There are some strong practical objections to very large wheels for sea vessels; they give the momentum of the waves a greater hold on the machinery, they are cumbersome and unsightly, and they raise the point of action too high above the waterline.

The rule for establishing the correct proportions between speed, revolutions of the engine and size of wheel was:

> The velocity of the vessel per hour multiplied by 21 is equal to the number of strokes per minute multiplied by the radius of the wheel.

Using the *Great Western* as an example with a speed of about 10 knots allowing for slip when the engines were doing 15 strokes, then the radius of the wheel would be 14ft or diameter 28ft (28ft 9ins the actual diameter).

In these particular vessels it was also essential for the paddle wheels to be positioned clear of the trough and crest of the waves created by the vessel at maximum speed; and, in practice, this was usually close to, or slightly ahead of, the mid-length. It is apparent from studying the hull lines of sea going paddle steamers, both naval and mercantile, that in most cases the position of the paddle wheel shaft coincides with, or nearly with, that of the vessel's maximum cross-section. The early examples, having a 'cod head, mackerel tail' hull form, show the wheels set well forward, but as the shape required of a power-driven vessel evolved separately from the sailing ship, the placing of the largest section and consequently the wheels was closer to the mid-load waterline length. Some of the later steamers, particularly those designs by John Scott Russell, with the largest section placed aft of the centre, had the paddle shaft similarly located as can be seen on three of the four steamer sail draughts (Figure 7:27). The *Great Eastern* was a famous exception. This vessel, huge for her time, was 690ft long, the hull lines produced by Scott Russell's design team in collaboration with Brunel, the engineer in overall charge of the project. Typically, the largest cross-section was placed 62ft aft of the mid-hull length; but in this instance the paddle shaft was located 35ft ahead of this reference point, or nearly 100ft, a sixth of the vessel's length, separating them. The proportions of the hull ahead and abaft the largest section measured along the load waterline are close to the 3:2 ratio he advocated as ideal.

Slip of the Wheel

A measure of performance can be gained by calculating the amount of 'slip', that is, the greater distance in terms of revolutions of the wheel to that actually made by the vessel through the water, and is reckoned according to Robert Murray in *Marine Engines* by using the 'effective diameter' of the wheel; arrived at by subtracting one-third of the depth of the boards from each end of the extreme diameter. In the case of the *Great Western* this 'effective diameter' was 26ft 10in, or 84ft 4in circumference; 900rph being 12.48nm. Using the figures for entering New York the vessel's speed through the water for 900 revolutions was 10.5 knots, the difference therefore being 1.98nm or a 'slip' of 16 per cent, a very good result indeed, albeit in ideal conditions.

Murray estimates the average amount of slip at about 0.2 per cent (or twenty per cent), which appears to be on the low side, and is probably based on fast passenger-carrying vessels operating in sheltered waters with the boards working close to optimum immersion. Brunel analysed the records of several crossings by the *Great Western*, comparing the mileage by paddle revolution and that by common log, the former greater by 0.27 per cent, a good result for a sea going vessel, confirming the efficiency of hull shape, propulsion system and rig. He also published figures which he attributes to Tredgold of thirteen paddle steamers, some naval or engaged in the Post Office service, which averaged out at 0.38 per cent for the group as a whole, several over 0.5 per cent.[2] This amount of slip can be attributed to heavily rigged men-of-war only using the engines in calms or when required to steam into a headwind. The combination of considerable air drag and relatively low power will inevitably result in mediocre performance figures.

The *Medea*, completed in 1833, tops the list in terms of slip at 0.595 per cent which would indicate a very inefficient propulsion system. However, she would not be judged on this criterion only, for in other respects the *Medea* was a very successful all round performer, well able to keep up with the sailing fleet without using steam. As a matter of interest she was credited with a speed of 8.25 knots, closehauled within 6 points of the wind, blowing strong, smooth water; and with the wind on the quarter in the same circumstances 11.25 knots. In both cases, the wheels were allowed to revolve freely. The principal cause for the high slip of the wheels must be attributed to the relatively low power of the engine at 220nhp related to her displacement of 1,142 tons.

Another cause of slip, besides the usual ones of strong headwind and sea or a poor power to weight ratio, was, according to Tredgold:[3]

> The velocity of sea vessels appears to average about ten miles per hour; their power to face a wind is inconsiderable, because the wind gives the surface of the water so much velocity that the paddles act with less force in proportion as the velocity of the water approaches to the difference between the velocity of the paddles and that of the vessel.

It is unlikely that this disadvantage would affect the propulsive powers of a deeply-immersed screw.

Unceasing Aid of Steam

The Atlantic paddle steamers kept the boilers working and wheels turning at all times, irrespective of the assistance gained by the sails in fair wind; for, to stop the engine in most circumstances would probably mean a slower rate of progress as well as the delay incurred while the paddle wheels were either disconnected and 'permitted to revolve in their bearings while the ship is under canvas', or have half the boards removed from the lower part and the wheels secured.

Even if the conditions were ideal, that is, winds of force 5 to 6 on or just abaft the beam with a moderate sea, so that speed under canvas alone with the wheels disconnected equalled that attained using engine and sail, the unpredictable and ever changing weather experienced in the North Atlantic meant this situation might not last for more than a few hours. A sudden change to adverse winds, requiring steam once more, would probably take an hour or so even if the fires had only been banked, in the meantime the ship hove to and the wheels reconnected causing more delay. As the prime objective was to make the passage in the shortest possible time, any hold ups of this nature would be avoided by continuous use of the engine.

Part Steam, Part Sail

Before the *Sirius* and the *Great Western* had managed to steam the whole way non-stop, the practice had been on previous crossings of the Atlantic and other deep sea voyages to use the engines for only part of the way and when no longer under steam, secure the wheels after removing half the paddle floats. This was no easy job in a seaway, the problems, if anything worse when they had to be bolted back in place. Lieut Johnston wrote in his Journal of the *Enterprize* on 27 August 1825, 11 days out from Falmouth, having had the engines in continuous use:[4]

> A.M. Extremes of G. Canary NW ½W to North, at 8 a.m. increasing N.E. Trade. I worked the Fire down. Stopped the Engines took off 7 Paddle Boards on each side and disconnected the Wheels, locked them with the cranks and shipped arms downwards, made all sail. Noon, the wind more moderate Lat 27.2 Long 15.32 P.M. Light Trade and fine weather going 3 to 5 knots, all sail set.

The paddle floats were replaced on 1 September and positioned closer to the wheel rim to compensate for the reduced draught, the sea calm with only light airs.

On 6 September, a fresh breeze having sprung up, instead of removing the floats, the paddle wheels themselves were disconnected from the engine and allowed to rotate freely. This course of action was preferable because the heavy swell running at the time would have made the job of unshipping the floats a time-consuming and difficult operation.

Two days later the wheels had to be reconnected in heavy weather with a gale blowing. It is not clear if the ship was hove to with no way on, but difficulties were experienced in holding the paddles stationary while this operation was in progress. An extract from Lieut Johnston's Journal for that day reads:

> . . . bent the storm mizzen, at 6 increasing gales, lighted the fires at 7 stopped the wheels to connect the engine. Worms most effectually prevent the wheels moving but the whole bed into which the Worm is fixed is very much strained by every pitch or roll and the whole of the Deck and Gunwale piece suffers, the play is considerable and the straining so great that I should fear many repetitions of this operation in blowing weather.

On 11 September, after the wheels had once more been disconnected, the breeze favourable, he noted:

> PM Moderate breezes ship going 6 or 7 knots under the canvas by the wind heeling about 2 strakes. The paddles revolve without appearing to impede her in the least and they make 9 or 10 revolutions per minute very regularly nor is there any differences between the revolutions of

the lee and the weather wheel, though one is considerably immersed and the other sometimes out of the water. The ship carries a weather helm and I suppose her to be about 13 ft 6 ins and 12.4 forward.

This situation of the vessel having a strong tendency to turn into the wind (when closehauled) can be helped by setting more sail in the fore part, preferably on the bowsprit or shifting weight so that she trimmed deeper aft. The entry for the following day includes, 'All hands getting coals from out of the Tanks in the Fore Hold'.

After calling at the island of Saint Thomas for stores and water the *Enterprize* continued her voyage towards Cape Town having ballasted some of her tanks while at anchor. However, stability, or the lack of it, was once again a problem and on 5 October she was down to her last reserves of coal. The entry for that day reads:

> . . . put every heavy article into the After Hold from off the Deck and stowed the booms on deck P.M. at 4 calm lighted the fires and got up steam, set all hands to work to hoist the remaining coal from the after Hold and employed them until eleven.

The coal could not be moved out of the hold before weight from the deck had been shifted below so that stability, such as it was, did not worsen. Next day, due to the light draught, it was observed that:

> . . . the Paddle Boards have scarcely sufficient hold of the water, but as I intend never to be on so light a Draft again I do not choose to notch the boards down, moving the coals from the After Hold has made a perceptible difference in her trim and stability.

On 8 October although the engines were shut down the freely rotating wheels were noted to be:

> . . . making 12½ and 13 Revolutions. The weather wheel frequently out of the water for half a minute during which time it continues to revolve by its own impetus. I feel persuaded that the wheels do not retard the Ship, I even think that they help a little being once set in motion.

It was always debatable which method to use when under sail, either to remove half the boards and lock the wheels or allow them to revolve freely after disconnecting from the engine. The arguments for and against each method, with reference to naval vessels are set out in Tredgold, *The Steam Engine*, vol 1, pages 86 and 87:

> We should however observe, with reference to this part of our subject, that the wheels with the paddle boards in place, must tend in a great degree, in light winds particu-

larly, to lessen the speed at which the vessel would attain under canvas, if the boards were displaced, besides effecting the concomitant evil of considerable wear, and consequent deterioration, more especially to the machinery of the vertical paddle [Morgan's feathering wheel] and although the experiment of this vessel [*Medea*] fully proved, that the resistance of the paddle boards afforded, did not prevent her from keeping company with the squadron, and, in some instances beating them, yet it is evident, in making long passages under sail, that it is desirable at least the lower float boards should be removed and the wheels locked.

> . . . and as steam could never be raised from cold water in so short a time as that stated by Captain Ramsey [Paddle boards could be slipped in about an hour and unshipped or detached in about half that time] to be occupied in unshipping the paddle boards, we might from this premises come to the conclusion, that in all cases when a steam vessel is required to act under sail, the paddles ought to be removed. We are, however, very doubtful, that it would be proper to establish this as a general rule under all circumstances, particularly when the service of the ship is such that she may be required, at the shortest possible notice, to resume her steaming duties. It must be quite obvious to the seaman that the case may occur in which it would be extremely difficult, if not impossible to re-attach the boards; and when the ship has any considerable motion from the waves, it must always be done at some degree of risk to the men employed on the duty; whereas, under similar circumstances, the wheels can always be connected with the engine, in less time than would be occupied in getting up steam.

Disconnecting Paddle Wheels

All the early Atlantic steamers referred to in the text appear to have used continuous paddle propulsion irrespective of wind assistance so the wheels were not disengaged from the engines unless for reasons of repair. As the *Great Western* started her return passage from New York on 7 May 1838, the log book entry states:

> At 8, larboard outside crank bearing got hot, and in the act of cooling it with water, the upper brass broke nearly in the centre; stopped and disconnected and proceeded at 11h 30m, with the starboard engine; set all drawing sails, and set the watch.

Over 3 hours were needed to complete the job, not by any patent disconnecting gear, but the removal of the port engine connecting rod from its crank pin on the main paddle shaft; the starboard engine rotating both paddle wheels on restarting. Revolutions were 10.5 per minute, speed 7 to 7.5 knots, light breeze and smooth sea. On 9 May repairs to the damaged brass bearing were completed and at 0730hrs the starboard engine was stopped and by 1000hrs the connecting rod had been re-secured to the crank pin. During this period, the vessel being under sail only in a light quartering breeze, she made 3 knots with the wheels locked which increased to 10 knots when both engines were once more at work.

Naval vessels were commonly equipped with some form of disconnecting gear that allowed the paddle wheels to rotate freely when the engines were shut down, which could be for days or weeks at a time.

Several methods were used to disconnect the wheels; Braithwaite, Field and Seaward all developed systems that operated on different principles. Braithwaite's gear relied on friction between an inner cast iron disc keyed into the inboard end of the paddle shaft and an outer hoop of wrought iron lined with brass that carried the crank pin. The method of locking them together depended on a tapered key driven through a swelling in the top of the hoop forcing down a shaped pad onto the disc. To free them and allow the paddle shaft to rotate inde-

pendent of the crank the key would be knocked back releasing the pressure on the shaped pad. Figure 6:1 illustrates the mechanism: a, the cast iron disc; b, the inboard end of the paddle shaft; c, the wrought iron hoop; d, the crank pin; e, the shaped pad; f, the tapered key.

A completely different method was advocated by Joshua Field in his patent no 8888 taken out in 1841, describing his invention as:

> . . . the mode herein – before described of moving the axis of the paddle wheel endways in the direction of its length by means of a suitable mechanism, so that the paddle wheel crank may be approached towards or removed away from the extremity of the crank pin of the engine crank with as much motion as is required in order to effect the operation of connecting and disconnecting the paddle wheel from the engine.

The mechanism suggested by Joshua Field (see Figure 6:2) controls the movement of paddle shaft and crank from the deck;

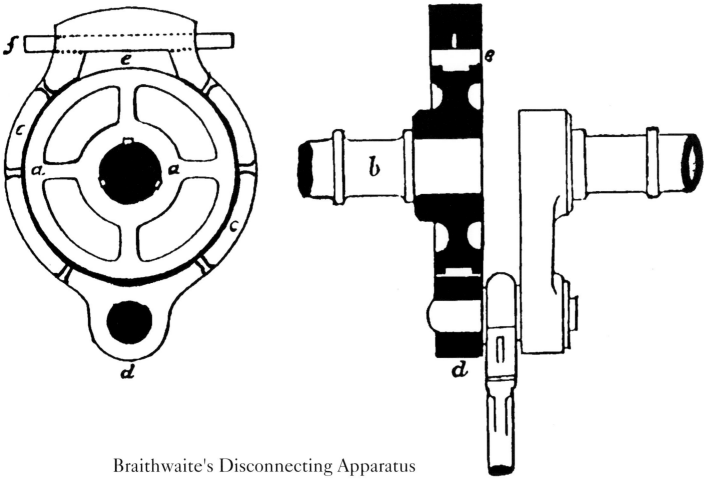

Braithwaite's Disconnecting Apparatus

Figure 6:1 *From Robert Murray's* Marine Engines and Steam Vessels *(London 1857)*

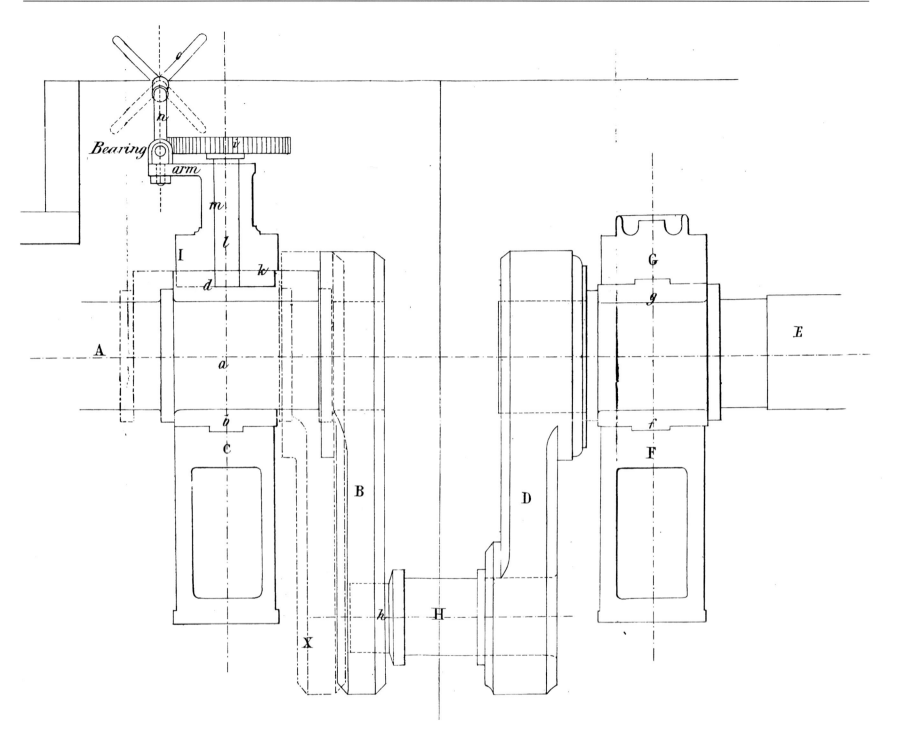

Figure 6:2 *Patent no 8888, 22 March 1841, Connecting and Disconnecting Paddle Wheels. (Joshua Field)*

it consists of an operating handle at one end of a spindle, the other having a worm engaged with a cog wheel at the point marked 'Bearing' on the drawing. By turning the handle and thus rotating the worm, a powerful but slow circular movement of the toothed wheel is carried by the vertical shaft *l* to an eccentric *k* on the lower end. This works in a specially-shaped recess machined in the top face of the upper bearing brass. As the eccentric is forced to rotate half a turn the reaction of the bearing brass, constrained by its guides, is to slide one way or the other, pushing on the inboard or outboard flange of the paddle shaft and thus imparting the required lateral movement. It follows that sufficient space must be allowed within the paddle box, plus the appropriate amount of end float in the outboard bearing on the spring beam to accommodate this action. Not shown on the drawing are two pawls that can be engaged once the paddle shaft is in the desired mode to prevent any sideways movement, as this could be disastrous should the paddles accidentally become disengaged or otherwise with the engine turning.

The connecting or disconnecting, by whatever method, requires both engine and wheels to be stopped and prevented from further rotation. If under sail, the vessel would have to be hove to so that she had little or no way on. Either a brake could be applied to the paddle shaft or, as Joshua Field describes in his patent, the following mechanism for holding or turning the paddle wheels:

And for the convenience of turning the paddle wheel round when it is disconnected, and of keeping the wheel steady after it has been properly placed, and until it is connected as aforesaid, one of the circular rims of the paddle wheel may have teeth formed around its circumference, and a long pinion or pinions may be mounted in a frame, so that they can be applied with those teeth when required, the said pinions having winch handles by which they can be turned round by men in order to turn the paddle wheel round and retain it steadily as required.

Figure 6:3 *This photograph of the portside paddle wheel of the* Great Eastern, *under construction, clearly shows the teeth on the middle rim which, engaged by a pinion, enabled the wheel to be turned by hand. (Royal Photographic Society)*

Seaward's patent no 8436, registered in 1840, contains six inventions entitled, 'Certain Improvements in the Construction of Steam Engines, and in the Application of Steam Engines to Propelling Ships and other Vessels', three of which are different types of disconnecting gear. Another one explains in general terms what would now be described as a '3 speed gearbox' with provision for 'neutral', that is, the paddle wheels able to revolve freely. The primary aim of this invention was to:

. . . vary the relative rates of the stroke of the engine and paddle-wheel, or other propeller, so as to suit the velocity of the vessel, whether lightly or heavily laden, the speed of the engine thereby maintained as near as may be possible at a proper rate, or the engine and paddle-wheel may with great facility be thrown altogether out of work whenever that may be found expedient.

Figure 6:4 from the patent specification shows the system of three spur wheels and three pinions operated by levers and mounted on parallel shafts so that either a direct drive can be engaged by sliding 6 to engage with 3, or one of two ratios can be selected providing a 'lower gear', the lowest required when:

. . . the speed of the wheels become still further reduced by greater draught of water or more adverse gales, recourse is then had to the pinion 4 and wheel 1.

Seaward estimated that the time occupied in throwing one set of pinions out of gear or another into gear need not exceed 2 or 3 minutes.

This facility of adjusting engine speed to suit the draught and heavy weather may well have been used in practice despite the additional expense and complication of the machinery, for the jet condensers commonly used on the ocean going paddle steamers did not work efficiently to supply the required vacuum if piston speed was constantly slowed or even brought to a standstill for a few seconds. Robert Murray

Fig 6:4 Part of Patent no 8436, 17 March 1840, Construction of Steam Engine. (Samuel Seaward)

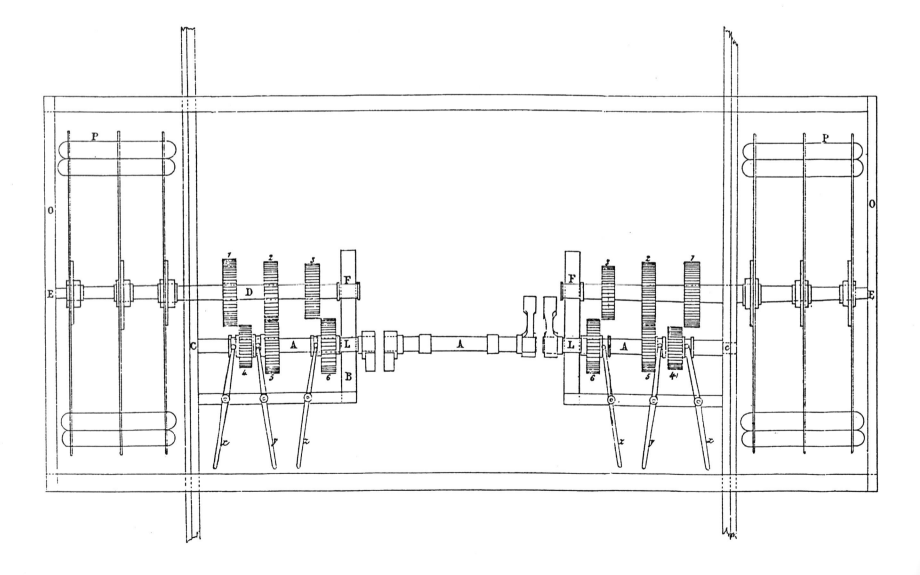

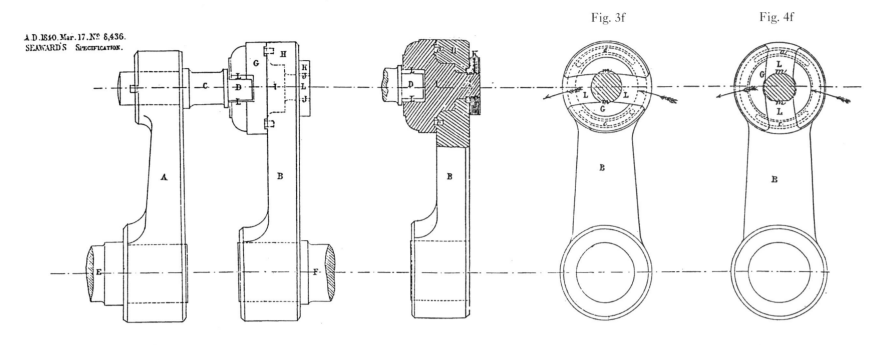

A.D. 1840. Mar. 17. N.º 8,436.
SEAWARD'S SPECIFICATION.

Fig. 3f   Fig. 4f

Fig 6:5 *Part of Patent no 8436, 17 March 1840, Construction of Steam Engine. (Samuel Seaward)*

gives the following advice on engine management which highlights a common problem and one which a 'gearbox' would overcome:[5]

When the vessel is labouring in a heavy sea, it is recommended that the supply of injection water should be diminished; for in such a case, where the speed of the engines is subject to great and constant fluctuations, depending upon the greater or less submersion of the wheels or screwpropeller, the condenser is liable to become chocked with water, thereby causing the engines to stop. The effect of working the engines with a stinted supply of condensing water is, of course, that the condensers will become hot, and the vacuum will be diminished; but this is a minor evil in comparison with endangering the machinery by subjecting it to too severe a strain.

Seaward's third method of connecting and disconnecting the paddle wheels is shown in Figure 6:5 and consists of a moveable circular head G which is inserted into the boss H at the end of the driven or paddle crank, able to rotate within the limits of the stops and held securely in position by a large nut K at the back. Figure 3f shows the crank pin end portion D in section having two flats m m in line with the shaped slot LL allowing the drive crank A to remain stationary while the paddle crank B is free to rotate. To reconnect, the back nut K would be slacked up and the head turned a quarter circle to the new position shown in Figure 4f and then retightened. The slot LL no longer coincides with the plane of rotation of crank pin D, which therefore becomes fixed in the shaped recess worked into the side of the slot, connecting both cranks. It can be seen that for this system to function, due to the small clearance between the slot sides

and the flats on the end of the crank pin, there can be no racking or movement of the hull athwartships or slack in the shaft bearing brasses.

The Cycloidal Wheel

Improvements in power output and fuel efficiency were matched by a continuous development of the paddle wheel. In August 1835 Elijah Galloway patented a system of segregated paddle floats on the 'cycloidal' principle, although two years previously Joshua Field had also experimented with divided boards, and, as both had certain similarities, Elijah Galloway wrote the following in his patent to clarify the situation:[6]

It should be remarked, that since the sealing of my said Letters Patent I have been informed that Joshua Field, Esquire, Engineer of Lambeth, some years before the date of my said Patent, made an experiment of a paddle wheel on a small vessel belonging to him or his partners, called the *Endeavour*, the floats of which were divided into portions, but they are not fixed according to the principle the application of which constitutes the object of my invention; and which experiment I have been informed, and, from the nature of the construction of the wheel, I verily believe was declared by him to be a failure. And I have only thus noticed this experiment in order to state that I do not claim the exclusive use of divided floats or paddles unless they be applied and affixed to paddle wheels according to the principle herein described. And in order to point out more accurately the difference of a wheel constructed according to my invention and that experimented on by the said Joshua Field, I have annexed a drawing of a portion of the said wheel so used in the *Endeavour* sufficient to show the principle there of; but on inspecting the same drawing at Fig 4, it will be evident that the portions of the floats are not fixed according to the method described and claimed by me.

For a comparison see Figure 6:6, Diagram 4 showing a portion of Joshua Field's wheel, and Diagram 1, Elijah Galloway's 'cycloidal' principle. The idea of dividing the single board into several bars and arranging them as shown in Figure 6:7 is to reduce the shock of entering the water and avoid lifting too much water on leaving it, both actions absorbing power from the engine. If the inner rim BB (as shown in Diagram 1, Figure 6:6) just touching the waterline were to revolve at such a speed in relation to that of the vessel that in effect it was rolling along the surface, the point on the radial line d e where it intersects this circle would describe a cycloidal curve GGGG to position F,

Fig 6:6 *Diagrams 1 and 4 from Patent no 6887, 18 August 1835, Paddle Wheels. (Elijah Galloway)*

and an imaginary curved plate of this shape would enter the water cleanly at F. The portions of the float or bars are set up on this curve, radiating out from the common centre of the paddle wheel. This is the most efficient arrangement for a precise set of circumstances, but in some cases the true cycloidal curve will form too great an angle with the radial line DE, making the step or gap between bars excessive with the loss of propelling resistance, and therefore a compromise curve was chosen.

Cycloidal wheels fitted to the *Great Western* had four separate floats per arm, 4.5in, 12in, 10in and 8in, making a total depth of 34.5in, the narrowest float made of iron and fixed to the circumference. The external diameter of the wheels was 28ft 9in, and subtracting the floats the inner diameter corresponding to B, in Diagram 1, Figure 6:6 was therefore 23ft, with a circumference of 72.2857ft. Assuming the *Great Western* was floating on such a draught, that is, sufficient just to submerge the top edge of the floats in the vertical position, 900rph or 15rpm would give 10.7nm based on the circumference of 72.2857ft. Entering New York at the end of her maiden voyage her draught must have been close to this and in fact, by interpolating 900 revolutions against actual performance figures, ship's speed would have been 10.5 knots, so the inner paddle board rim was travelling faster by only 0.2 knot, very close to the theoretical optimum for a cycloidal wheel. At the time the water was smooth, the vessel having scarcely any motion, a light breeze of force 2–3 was blowing and no sail was set.

Problems with Paddle Wheels

However efficient the wheels were in terms of propulsion, they suffered from a problem common to all ocean going paddle steamers of the time, that is, the floats which were usually held to the framework by hook bolts and nuts frequently worked loose or dropped off altogether. An entry in the remarks column of the *Great Western*'s log of her first voyage on 14 April 1838 reads:

> At 10h. 33m. stopped the engines to examine the paddle wheels, having suspected a portion of them was not correct; found some of the bolts loose; set them up, and put aright the necessary jobs in engines, as per engineer's log. At 12h. 20m. P.M. finished the necessaries to the wheel, and set the engine to work again at full speed.

The constant concussion of the floats pounding the water each time they entered seemed to defy any amount of tightening of the nuts so that in 1844, when the original wheels were well worn and needed replacing, the new ones were not of the cycloidal pattern with multiple floats, having only a single one per arm.

Both the *British Queen* and the *President* had cycloidal paddle wheels fitted, but after some time in service a dispute arose over the patent rights; the subsequent threat of litigation forced

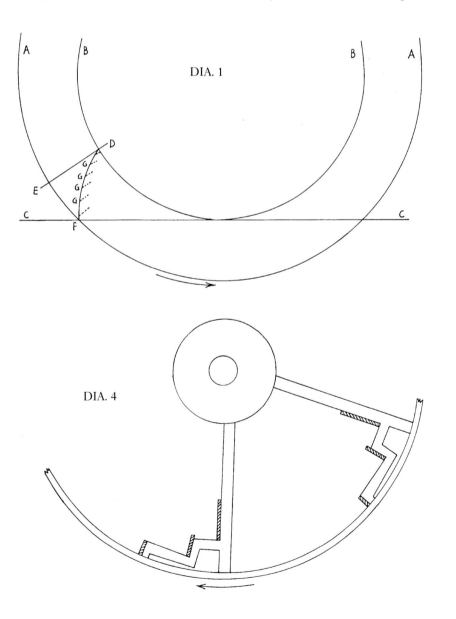

DIA. 1

DIA. 4

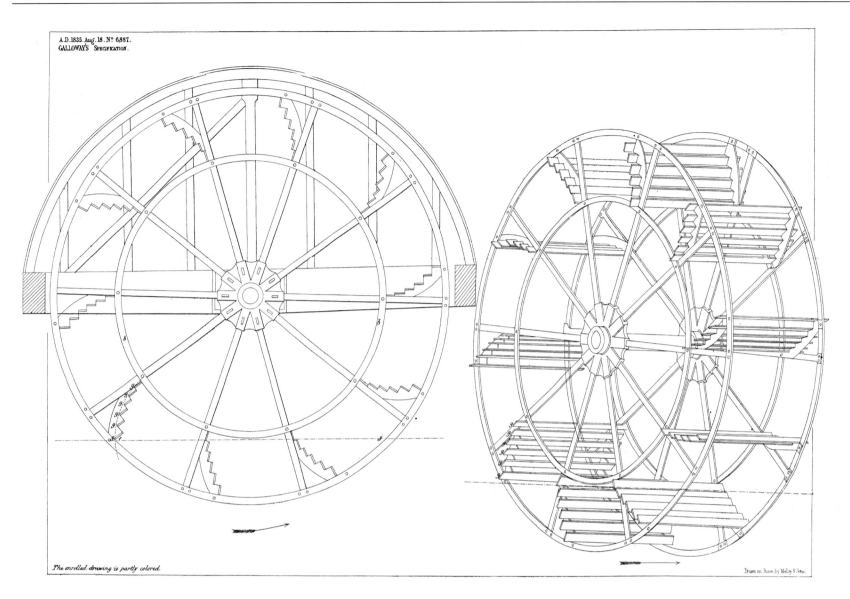

A.D.1835. Aug. 18. Nº 6,887.
GALLOWAY'S SPECIFICATION.

The enrolled drawing is partly colored.

Drawn on Stone by Malby & Sons.

the company to change over to single floats per arm and, as it transpired, the conversion was far from satisfactory. When bound for New York, the *British Queen* gradually lost all the floats from one wheel and was lucky to have a 6 hour break in the weather, enabling the crew to transfer half the floats from the undamaged wheel before the second and much worse storm blew up. This meant there were no spare ones on board or perhaps they had already been used up, for it made double the work to shift them over and would have reduced the efficiency of the good wheel considerably.

The same very stormy spell of weather caught out the *President* recently departed from New York. She was last seen by the sailing packet *Orpheus* 'labouring tremendously' in very heavy seas on the second day out and then disappeared without trace. As the weeks and months dragged on with no sign, speculation as to the reasons for her loss pointed to the vessel foundering, water getting below by some means, probably via

the deck openings. It is possible a contributory factor was the botched conversion to single floats, if the experience of the *British Queen* is anything to go by. This theory is discounted in Joshua Field's papers where he points out that on the outward crossing to the United States prior to the fateful return, the *President* did not have any problems with the paddle floats despite the heavy weather experienced. However, they may have been damaged by ice, which was reported in the area at the time, or from falling spars and rigging, making the vessel unmanageable for, even if her sails were not all blown out at the time, performance under canvas alone was considered inadequate for this class of vessel, and therefore probably useless in the dreadful conditions that prevailed. Joshua Field goes on to say she 'was thought by many to be ill adapted for fast sailing'. This opinion is further underlined by remarking on an earlier voyage, when she was returning from New York on 1 November 1840 that, 'after beating about in a heavy gale she put back to

Fig 6:7 *Part of Patent no 6887, 18 August 1835, Paddle Wheels. (Elijah Galloway)*

this place on the 6th having made only 300 miles in 6 days', which seems to justify remarks by her critics that she was underpowered as well as a poor sailer.

Commenting on this important aspect of steam propulsion, that is, the best type and form of paddle wheel, Robert Murray writes:[7]

Fig 6:8 From Patent no 5805, 2 July 1829, Steam Engines and Machines for propelling. (Elijah Galloway)

It is believed that the common wheel, if properly proportioned and allowed the proper degree of immersion is preferable, under ordinary circumstances, to any of the 'improved' varieties which have from time to time appeared. Of these, the only one which can be recommended, and that only under peculiar circumstances, is Morgan's Feathering wheel, by the use of which the boards may be made deeper, and therefore narrower than in the common wheel, and the diameter may be somewhat diminished; but it is objectionable from its weight (which is nearly twice that of the common wheel), from its complexity and consequent liability to derangement, and from its considerable additional expense. Mr. Field's 'Cycloidal' wheel, in which the paddle boards is divided into steps with an open space between, can hardly claim any superiority over the undivided board, but the simple modifications of this plan, formed by dividing the board into two breadths, and placing one on either side of the paddle arm, is probably the best form of wheel that can be adopted for large steamers.

He was mistaken in attributing the cycloidal wheel to Mr Field.

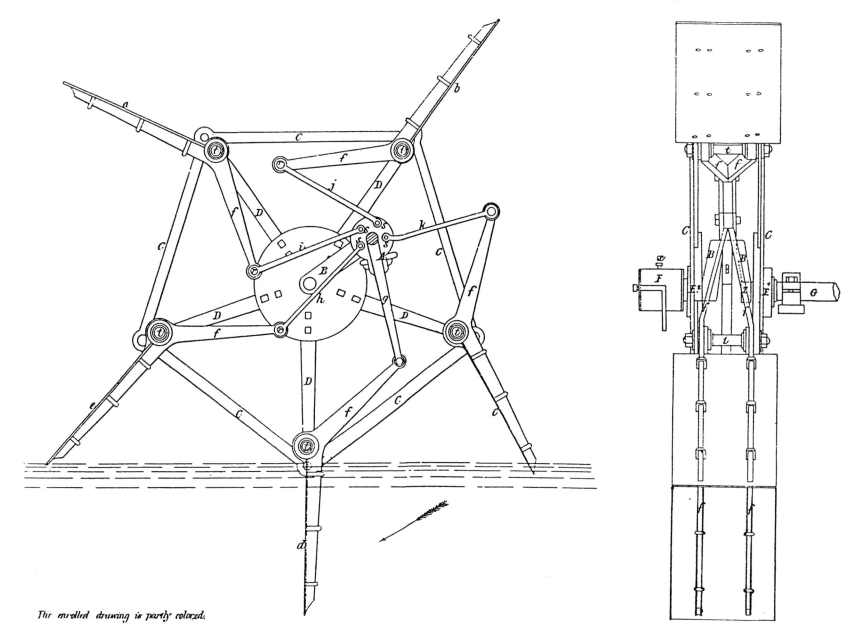

The enrolled drawing is partly colored.

The Feathering Wheel

Morgan's feathering wheel was in fact a modification of Elijah Galloway's original patent 5085, taken out in 1829; all rights were vested in 1838 to James L Lucena, barrister-at-law, who then licensed the patent to his partner, William Morgan, engineer, of New Cross, Surrey. Although none of the Atlantic steamers was fitted with the system because of the 'likelihood of derangement' due to its many moving parts, no appreciable advantage when deep loaded, and the extra expense, its greater efficiency could be used in vessels, such as harbour tugs that maintained for all practical purposes an optimum immersion of the floats and worked mostly in sheltered waters.[8]

As the wheel rotated, the better angle of the floats on entry, during immersion and when leaving the water, compared with the common wheel of the same diameter, is shown in Figure 6:8 taken from Elijah Galloway's patent of 1829. It can be seen that the boards A, B, C, D, and E, have bent stems F, linked by rods with the disc A, the axis of which remains in a fixed position in relation to the wheel, held by crank arm B. The king rod G, which in the drawing is connected to the lowest float D, is the only one rigidly fixed to the disc and thus imparts a rotary motion to it as the main frame C is turned by the engine.

Lucena and Morgan's alterations to Galloway's specification is shown in simplified form with only four paddle floats in Figure 6:9 (Fig 1). The main difference is that the stems are now bent at right angles to the boards with the consequence of longer rods connecting the ends to disc A, the improved geometry causing less stress in the system. The dotted lines indicate the float, stem and rod positions at entry and emersion, and if one imagines a common wheel constructed so as to have the same board angle by projecting them as if they were part of the radial lines, the centre of this circle will be above and outside the one drawn, and hence, at least twice the diameter.

Figure 6:9 (Fig 2) shows a further refinement, the floats virtually balanced on their supporting pivots, which are not in fact at half depth but slightly lower; the top section has a greater area to compensate as it will be working in more aerated water. Any residual difference in thrust above or below this axis, and hence a rotational effect, is further reduced by the pivot being arranged close up behind the float giving a relatively long lever action to the stem. The final loading on the rods as each float exerts maximum thrust is therefore minimal. This type of wheel could be seen on the paddle tug *Reliant* at the National Maritime Museum, Greenwich, London, and it was fascinating to watch the action of the mechanism as the wheel rotates.

Fig 6:9 *Improvements to the feathering paddle wheel. (Peter Allington)*

Fig 1

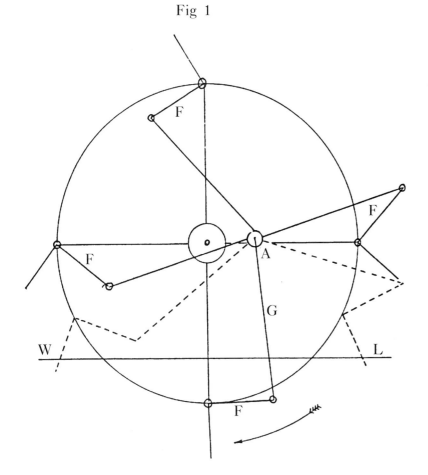

Fig 2

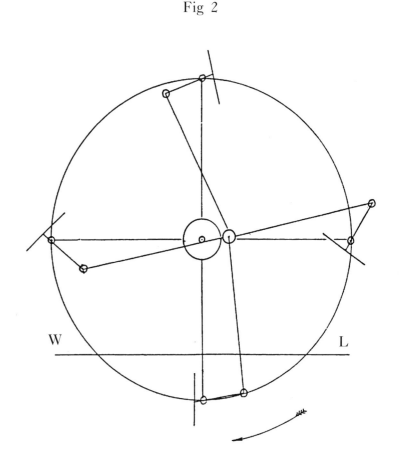

Other Paddle Wheel Designs

From the number of patents taken out at the time, there must have been a great incentive among inventors to improve the efficiency of the common paddle wheel. Most were complicated and involved many moving parts, with the attendant problems of lubrication under water and the liability of damage by floating debris. Among those inventions, which at the time were thought to overcome some of the disadvantages, several advocated angled paddle boards. The following is an extract from the *United Services Journal*, February 1841, under the title 'Notices of Steam Navigation', page 245:

> We come now to that class of paddle-wheels, the floats of which are placed in an oblique direction. The first wheel of this description, of which we have any account, is one patented by a Mr Robertson, of Liverpool, the action of which is thus described by Sir John Ross, in the advertisement to the second edition of his work on Steam Navigation, 1837: 'These paddle wheels,' says the author, 'were fitted to the *Victory* discovery ship, in 1828; and on her passage from Liverpool to London, notwithstanding the vessel was loaded, so as to bring the axle of the wheel within one foot of the water-line, she actually gained on her sister ship the *Harriett*, which used formerly to beat her; and she performed the voyage in less than four days, including her detention at several places. The floats of these wheels being diagonal, or fitted to the frame, at an angle of 45 degrees, enter the water without the splash which a vertical float makes; and both, on entering and rising, throw off the water instead of compressing and lifting it; and by immersing them to such a depth that they cannot be rolled out by any motion of the vessel, without any loss of power, makes the action of the engine more steady, while by meeting with more resistance at its deepest point of revolution, must have the effect of propelling the ship faster'.

Another unorthodox approach appears in 'Todd's specifications', patent no 8223, taken out in 1839, and appears, on paper at least, to have several advantages. He points out that:

> My improved paddles are self adjusting, and do not require the mechanical aid of any stops, cranks, levers, rods, grooves, eccentric wheels, pinions, chains, or any other kind of machinery, and that all extra friction is hereby avoided, also the tail or back-water. This is not the case with the common paddles at present in use, the said back-water being universally acknowledged to be a very great drawback on the effective power of the engine.

It can be seen from Figure 6:10, part of the patent, that the specially formed floats pivoted about a mid-axis and were weighted along the lower edge. He further states:

> My improved paddles, by entering the water vertically, or very nearly so, will not occasion the tremulous motion common to steam vessels, at present so injurious to them, and so much complained of by passengers; and by leaving the water in the same vertical position, the swell or back-water is avoided, and consequently the great danger to boats, in approaching the steam vessel under way.

It is doubtful whether the theoretical advantages put forward for this type of float were borne out in practice, for we can find no reference of any sea going steamer actually using them, although it would appear from the description that vessels working in calm water with the wheels always close to optimum immersion might benefit to some degree. On the practical side, damage to the floats was a constant hazard in harbour work and the expense of replacing a wooden board would certainly be less than trying to straighten out a bent iron one. Furthermore, there would be less chance of damage to the whole wheel, or indeed the engine, if the floats were simply of timber construction. It can also be seen that Todd's wheel would have to be more strongly built for the pivoting floats do not impart the same amount of rigidity to the structure compared with the common bolted-on boards.

Reefing Paddle Wheels

The difficulties experienced due to changing paddle wheel immersion has already been mentioned, particularly important in deep sea vessels where the length of voyage combined with a constant use of steam power could result in a change of draught amounting to several feet. This problem also affected smaller craft as the following contemporary press cutting makes clear (taken from the scrapbook of newspaper cuttings already referred to):

> Samuel Hall's patent reefing paddle wheels on Tuesday last propelled the Lee steam barge (to which they are applied) from Blackwall to Rochester bridge in seven hours and 18 minutes, being empty and drawing only two feet nine inches of water. On her return she was deeply laden, drawing five feet six inches of water, and performed the same distance in seven hours and 51 minutes, being by means of the reefing of the wheels only 33 minutes more in doing so when deeply laden than when empty. It is therefore evident how highly important it is to have reefing wheels for steam vessels making long voyages and of course greatly varying their immersion in the water.

While not detracting from the obvious advantages claimed, there is no mention of the wind or tidal conditions on each passage which would have a significant effect on the quoted times.

Hamond's specification for 'Improvements in the Mode of

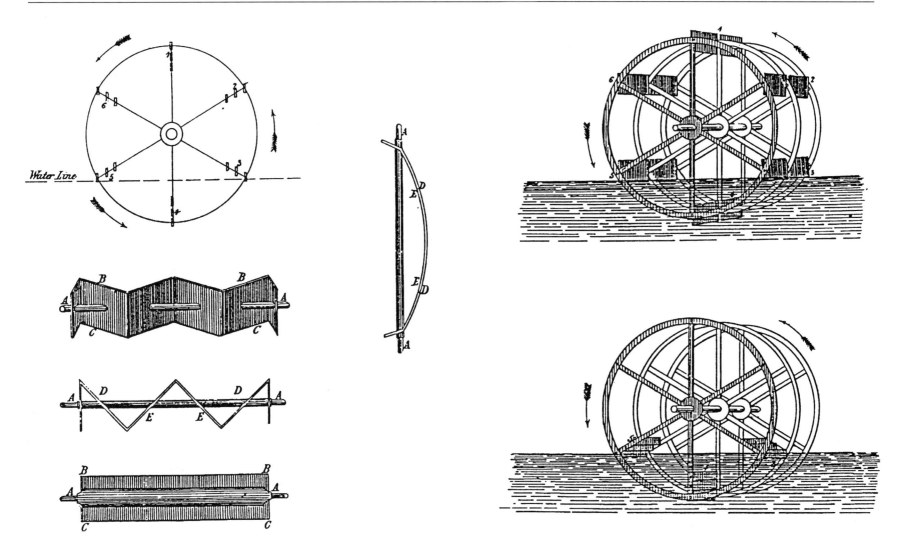

Fig 6:10 *Part of Patent no 8223, 19 September 1839, Paddles of Steam Vessels. (Todd)*

'Fastening on and Reefing Paddle-wheel Float Boards or Paddles' is an eminently practical solution, submitted by his father, Vice Admiral Sir Graham Eden Hamond, and granted a patent, entitled 'Paddle Wheels' no 10,349, in 1844, while Captain Hamond was at sea in command of Her Majesty's steam sloop *Salamander* stationed in the Pacific.

Because it contains so much practical advice and is the result of operational experience, it is worth including a large part of the patent, as well as a description of the actual drawings shown in Figure 6:11, for it serves to highlight the difficulties already mentioned with boards working loose and falling off:

Various modes have been adopted for fixing on paddle boards or paddles, and most of them very efficient, so far as the mere fixing them goes, being generally by iron hooks embracing the paddle arm, which, passing through the paddle boards, are secured by nuts and screws upon plates on the side of the boards furthest removed from the paddle arm. In process of time, however, coupled with the action of salt water upon the iron, the nuts and screws become so rusted together, that if occasion occurs for wishing them to be shifted, removed, or reefed, it is scarcely possible to be done without breaking off the end of the hook bolts, or, if not broken, the rust will be found to have so far corroded the screw part of it as to reduce it in size, and the inside of the nut will (subject to the same cause) become so enlarged as to render their further use impracticable, and recourse must be had to new bolts and nuts. Some very ingenious plans have been patented for quickly reefing and letting out paddle boards so as to keep them at a proper degree of immersion. They are, however, subject to strong objections in consequence of being composed of a complication of machinery constructed within the paddle wheel, which although beautiful in its original plan and construction in effecting the purpose intended (while new), yet, from the action of the salt water upon it (being constantly immersed therein), becomes oxidized, and soon altogether useless. From experience that

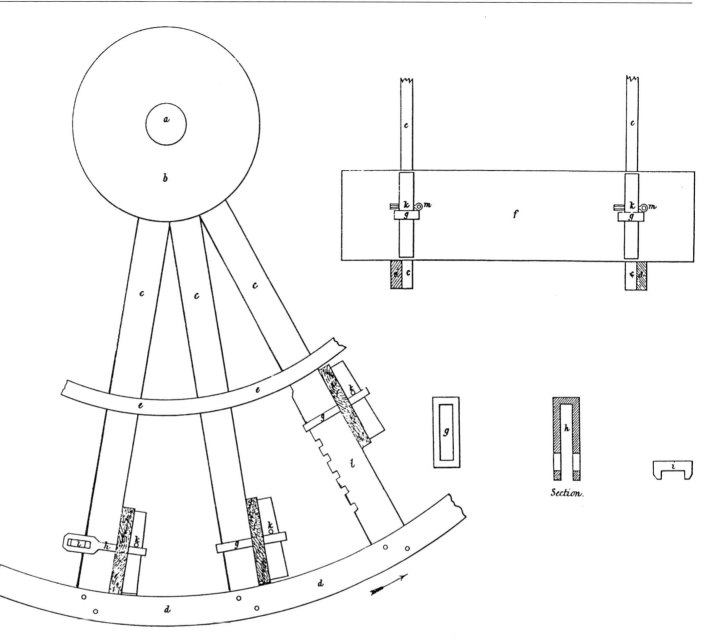

Fig 6:11 *Patent no 10349, 14 October 1844, Paddle Wheels. (Hamond) Using a scale of 1cm:1ft, the wheel as drawn in the patent has a radius of about 14ft and the floats 10ft in length. (These sizes closely approximate those of the Great Western.) At the same scale the floats measure close on 2ft 6in in depth with a thickness of 4in giving a volume of 16.5 cu ft. They would probably have been made of elm, a tough and durable wood, lighter than oak. However, if we allow 45lb per cu ft when wet then each float would weigh about 740lb. (20 floats per wheel – over 6.5 tons.*

It is likely that the wheel would be rotated so that the arm associated with the float to be 'reefed' or 'un-reefed' would be near horizontal with a slight gradient to assist the direction in which it was to slide once the wedges were knocked back.

Captain Hamond has obtained during his command of Her Majesty's steam sloop of war 'Salamander', in the Pacific, he turned his thoughts to endeavour to rectify the objections above raised against the present mode of fixing on and reefing of paddle boards or paddles, and he now ventures to offer an improved mode, which he considers of the greatest importance to steam navigation:

First, from its great economy in the first construction, it being fitted at half the cost of hook bolts, nuts, and plates.

Secondly, its great simplicity, and the easiness of its construction, as the whole of the iron work can be made by any common blacksmith, with no other tools than hammer and anvil.

He states also some of the advantages of his improved plan, more particularly for the information of those who are not practically acquainted with the difficulty and great loss of time in reefing, removing, or tightening up any one or all of the paddle boards when occasion requires, as they are at present applied, and when the nuts have become so corroded on the bolts that it renders it next to impossible to remove them without great labour.

First, the great facility with which the paddle boards can be reefed from there being no nuts to corrode upon the bolts, and the great desideratum which is thereby acquired of keeping, reefing, or letting out the paddle boards at the most advantageous immersion, according as the vessel varies in her draft of water at various periods of her voyage, and the consequent increased speed obtained by boards not being suffered to go deeper in the water than is necessary for that purpose, and which it is next to impossible to effect in the present mode of fitting them.

Secondly, the diminution in the loss of paddle boards from the nuts (when newly fixed) working off the bolts, a well known fact to those who have command of steam vessels, particularly when the vessel first comes from the dockyard, – the 'Salamander' having lost nine paddle boards between Plymouth and Madeira; the improved mode of fitting only requiring to be made fully effective by the blow of a hammer. It frequently happens in putting on float boards that the workman imagines the board to be fast from the nut merely working stiff upon the bolt, when, in fact, the board is quite loose upon the arm of the wheel, which also occasions great loss of boards, bolts, nuts, and plates, especially in severe weather at sea, when it is impossible to work a screw wrench or spanner in the paddle casing.

Thirdly, the great saving in expense in the improved mode of construction in comparison with that of the present, as well as of the saving of the annual loss of boards, bolts, nuts, and plates.

Fourthly, the ease and facility with which the improved mode of construction can be applied to the wheels of all steam vessels now in use, and also the facility of putting on or taking off or reefing the paddle boards at sea, or otherwise, and which, according to the improved plan as proposed by Captain Hamond, might be effected in the course of half an hour; whereas, in the old plan, and under favourable circumstances, it cannot be done under half a day.

DESCRIPTION OF THE DRAWING

An iron link or strap is first placed upon each paddle arm before the periphery or outer circle is fixed thereon. This link passes through a hole cut through the paddle board, and it projects through it so far as to admit a wedge of wood, and of nearly the breadth of the paddle board, to be inserted through such projection, and which, being tightened up by a few blows of a hammer, securely binds and fixes the paddle board to the paddle wheel arm. By way however, of additional security, a metal pin may be driven in above the iron strap to prevent the wedge slipping out, but which it will seldom or never do after it has become wet. When wishing to reef the boards or paddles, the wedge has only to be slackened, and the paddle board being placed at the required degree of immersion, the wedge is again driven up. In order to admit of this Invention being applicable to the paddle arms of steam vessels now in use, and without removing the periphery or outer ring from the wheel, an open iron link can be

substituted for the close one, as shown in the plan at h. This open link can also of course be used in cases where the close link has been broken or lost. A second link might also be added on each paddle arm in a very large steamer, if considered to be more advisable than a single one, and which would admit, of course, of shorter wedges, the paddle boards having additional holes cut through to admit of the second link; also, in constructing new paddle arms, notches or scores might be made in their outer extremities, as shown in the plan, so as to admit of the link taking firmer hold of the arm, and when wishing to reef the boards or paddles the exact distances of all the links might at once be given by naming the number of the notch from the periphery without using a rule to measure.

Another reference to this problem of variable immersion is contained in the prospectus for 'The India Steam-Ship Company' which appeared in the contemporary press and lists among the advantages of the proposed vessels:

The Company's ships will be so constructed and rigged as to possess both sailing and steaming powers. This grand desideratum is effected by an ingenious method of raising and lowering the paddle wheels.

This would seem a novel solution but we can find no details of this intriguing method having been put into practice; but if in fact it were, and the technical difficulties overcome, there is no doubt that a great saving in fuel could be made on the long passage out to India via the Cape of Good Hope which the prospectus estimates could be accomplished in 50 days.

Auxiliary Steam Power

Another scheme to reduce the passage time to India using 'paddle' propulsion that did not require 'raising and lowering the wheels' was put forward by the engineer Samuel Seaward.[9]

This involved fitting engines of only 30hp turning paddle wheels of 14ft diameter so arranged that they could be disconnected quickly. The drag could be further reduced if required by removing most of the wheel and bringing it on board, and with no paddle boxes or beams in the way efficiency was further improved when working as the floats could be reefed so that the proper immersion could be maintained. Unlike the Atlantic steamers, these vessels would not change much in respect of draught as only 90 tons of coal were carried. The object was to shorten the voyage under sail alone, as days or weeks could be added if long periods of calms were encountered, so a speed of about 5 knots in these circumstances was all that was required. The project was implemented by the East Indiaman *Vernon* in June 1839 and subsequently another vessel, the *Earl of Hardwicke*, had a small steam engine installed, but the experiment was abandoned in 1841. It was only a partial success as passage times were reduced but not by the significant margin that warranted the capital expenditure, fuel costs and wages for one engineer and one stoker. Furthermore, the space taken up by the engine and fuel which amounted to 115 tons could be better occupied for the carriage of freight and passengers.

Horizontal Paddle Wheels

Although not directly concerned with this problem of variable immersion it is worth mentioning that the US Navy built three vessels in the 1840s, the *Union*, *Waterwitch* and *Allegheny*, with Hunter's horizontal paddle wheels. These worked in special watertight compartments just above the turn of bilge, slightly aft of the mid-hull length, a sufficient section of the wheel working outside the hull in the slipstream. For the purposes of a man-of-war this arrangement allowed the machinery to be installed below the waterline and there was no interruption on the hull side, allowing a full broadside to be mounted. It is obvious that placed in this position they would be constantly immersed irrespective of the vessel's draught. However, the experiment was a failure in terms of high fuel consumption and low speed attained, and the peculiar inverted bell-shaped section of the hull was detrimental to sailing performance. Slip was estimated to be between fifty and seventy per cent.[10]

Conclusions

Despite all these attempts to improve the paddle wheel for sea going vessels, the screw was the real answer. Brunel in his 'Report' to the Directors of the Great Western Steamship Company in October 1840, advocated, subsequent to the trials with screw propulsion on the *Archimedes*, that paddle wheels should be abandoned for *The Great Britain*:[11]

> With paddles, the action is materially affected by the depth of immersion; when the vessel is deep, and consequently the paddles deep, the action is impeded, a greater part of the power of the engine is absorbed in driving the paddle, the speed of the engine is reduced and the effect diminished; when too light also the paddles do not take sufficient hold of the water, the amount of slip increased and power is wasted; in rolling the same effects are produced, and thus at those times when the greatest effect is required, namely, with deep immersion or in bad weather to overcome the increased resistance offered to the vessel, the propelling power is least effective, and Captain Hoskins actually estimates this loss as occasionally equal to two-thirds the whole power.

Despite the screw being shown in principle and by demonstration to be a more efficient means of propulsion, the design and manufacture of this expensive piece of machinery was far from being an exact science and a failure would only become obvious after trials had been made. The costs involved of dry docking the vessel and the making of a new screw should the first one not prove satisfactory was one of the reasons why merchant steamers in the 1840s, with few exceptions continued to use paddle wheel propulsion, a tried and tested system.

There was not much difference in the operational performance between the two, if both had a similar ratio of engine power to displacement, or so it would seem. This was 'proved' by comparing the average speed of screw-propelled vessels operating between Liverpool and Philadelphia and paddle-propelled steamers between Liverpool and New York, the respective distances 3,140 miles to the Capes off the Delaware River and 3,020 miles to New York.[12] These took place between November 1851 and February 1852, the screw vessels being *City of Manchester* and *City of Glasgow*, the paddlers being *Africa*, *America*, *Asia* and *Canada*. Average speed of the *City of Manchester* and *City of Glasgow* was 7.305 knots, and the paddle steamers were almost 2 knots faster at 9.132 knots. However, all the vessels were relatively close in size but the screw-propelled had engines of about half the nominal horsepower of the paddle steamers. It was calculated that if equal power had been given to the screw vessels then the average speed would have risen to 9.198 knots which is slightly more than the actual rate achieved by the paddle steamers at 9.132 knots. Conversely, had the paddle steamers' power been reduced by half, the average speed would have dropped to 7.27 knots. These calculations assume the screw propeller will transmit the same forward thrust as the paddle wheel for equal power, but at the time, this was not a foregone conclusion.

The navy carried out several trials between the screw-propelled *Rattler* and the paddle-propelled *Alecto* to determine which was the superior method. Both vessels were virtually identical in size and in the nominal horsepower of their engines. In the ninth trial, a straight tug-of-war between them, the *Rattler* came off best but it should be mentioned that her indicated horsepower was measured at 299.8ihp as against the *Alecto*'s engines which produced less than half at 140.7ihp.[13] These trials were essentially concerned with the efficiency of the vessels as tugs.

It took some time to demonstrate that the screw was practical and solved most of the problems which beset the ocean going paddle steamer. There were difficult technical problems to overcome: how to keep the thrust block cool, how best to raise the engine revolutions to that required for the propeller shaft, how to prevent wear and leakage in the stern gland, how to build the vessel strong enough to withstand the torque of the propeller shaft and, indeed, how to forge this massive piece of the machinery. Amongst other difficulties in the early days was the design of the screw itself in an age with little scientific knowledge of this subject, except that gained from working models and small vessels less than 50ft long, until the Ship Propeller Company built the *Archimedes* especially for testing the screw. All these questions had to be resolved before the screw could be considered definitely superior to the paddle wheel of merchant ships. As has already been explained, the navy had strong reasons for adopting screw propulsion more quickly as an auxiliary to sail.

1 Thomas Tredgold, *The Steam Engine,* vol 1 (London, 1838) p. 308

2 'Report on the Screw Propeller to the Directors of the Great Western Steam-Ship Company' by I K Brunel (October, 1840) Appendix II, p. 542

3 T Tredgold, op cit, p. 319

4 Part of the Field papers, Science Museum, London. Arch: Field 1/22–1/31

5 R Murray, *Marine Engines and Steam Vessels* (London, 1851) p. 72

6 Patent no 6887, Paddle Wheels 1835 Galloway's Specification, p. 4

7 R Murray, op cit, p. 109

8 B Greenhill and A Giffard, *Steam, Politics and Patronage* (London, 1994) p. 46

9 S Seaward, 'Memoir on the Practicability of Shortening the Duration of Voyages', *Transactions of the Institute of Civil Engineers* vol 3 (London, 1842) pp. 385, 400

10 Donald L Canney, *The Old Steam Navy,* vol 1 (Annapolis, Maryland, 1990) pp. 25–30

11 'Report to the Directors of the Great Western Steamship Company' 1840, Appendix II, p. 554

12 J Bourne, *The Screw Propeller* (London, 1867), Appendix 'Screw and Paddle Vessels on the Atlantic'

13 Bourne, op cit, p. 266

CHAPTER 7

Masting, Rigging and Sails

Figure 7:1 *HM Steam Frigate* Dragon, *a lithograph by Dutton after Lieut W G Masters, Royal Marines. The lithograph shows clearly the peculiar combination of a three-masted schooner with standing gaffs with their sails, 'spencers' as they were often called, brailing to the throat with a full-rigged ship's masting and rigging with which some paddle frigates and sloops were equipped. The spacing of the masts imposed by the presence of the engines and boilers did nothing to improve handiness and performance under sail. Note the linked rod funnel stays. (Private Collection)*

The Number and Placing of the Masts

As the position of the engines and the boilers, and hence the funnel, was of first priority, it was often the case in steamers with more than two masts that placing them in the optimum location for good sail balance could not be achieved, one at least having to be stepped at what was considered a safe distance from the smoke stack. This gave an odd appearance compared to the same type of rig on a pure sailing ship and was particularly noticeable on some naval paddlers where the original sail plan of a brig was changed to a barque with the addition of a fore and aft mizzen. This criticism cannot be levelled at the *Great Western* where the distribution of sail area seems about right, but even she suffered from the mainmast being too close aft of the funnel with a singed topsail, a real

problem when steaming into a light headwind with the canvas sheeted hard in for steadying purposes. There was a danger of not only the sail catching fire but the running and standing rigging as well.

With respect to the placing of the masts and other observations on the rigging of *The Great Britain*, Captain Claxton, in his description of the vessel, states the following:[1]

She has six masts, fitted with iron rigging, adopted in consequence of its offering two-thirds less resistance than hemp, a great point going head to wind. It was wished that five should have been the complement, but there was some difficulty in adjusting that number, and the alternative was either four or six. Economy of labour is a principle which has, in a great degree affected the mode

Figure 7:2 *The* Hope *steam screw auxiliary whaler, built by Alexander Hall at Aberdeen in 1873. In contrast with the frigate* Dragon, *(Figure 7:1) her screw machinery is placed aft and she can have the normal placing of the masts of a barque. (The late Captain J Gray)*

of rigging both the *Great Western* and *The Great Britain*. Nothing is so difficult to handle, under a variety of circumstances, as the sails of a steamer, unless the engine be stopped, which can never be allowed in Atlantic steaming, where onwards – and for ever onwards – is the rule. The greater the number of masts, the more handy the sails, and the smaller the number of seamen required to handle them.

Standing Rigging Development

It was the advent of the steamer that prompted an alternative to the universal use of hemp as standing rigging. The contemporary painting of the *Great Western* by J Walter showing her at the start of her maiden voyage off Portishead indicates that the funnel stays, mainmast shrouds and double forward leading mainstays were made from what appear to be short pieces of iron rod between 3ft and 4ft in length having an eye forged at each end and linked together, eye to eye, in the manner of chain. The method of tensioning is not clear but deadeyes could have been worked on the end of the lowest rod and set up with hemp lanyards as was the usual practice. Chain was also used on some vessels, either for the full length of the shroud or sometimes combined with hemp, the chain part being in the most vulnerable section near the hounds or where the rigging passed close over the top of the funnel.

One of the newspaper clippings found in the scrapbook already mentioned was an undated report of the French naval steamer *Veloce* in the *New York Weekly Herald* with the following description:

The three masts, top and topgallant masts, are stayed altogether with iron chains, and the upper masts and all the yards can, with little comparative labour, and in any weather, be lowered on deck. The main and foreyards,

Figure 7:3 *The* Great Western, *before the start of her maiden voyage, a contemporary lithograph from a painting by J Walter. (Private Collection)*

when sent down, fold up from the centre, parallel with the masts, to which they are secured.

It is also interesting to note later in the article that:

The wheels are of iron, similar to those of the *Great Western*, with this advantage, that when the wind is fair, in a short time, the paddles, which are of wood, may be unscrewed and taken on board, and nothing but the thin hoops of iron which constitutes the wheel be left to pass through the water. The *Veloce* makes as good headway, under sail alone, as most other vessels.'

She was a corvette, second class, launched in 1838 at Rochefort, and at the time one of the largest paddle steamers in the French navy, with a displacement of 1,259 tons and equipped with engines of 220hp by Fawcett of Liverpool.[2]

Chain was not the real answer, for not only was it very heavy but it lacked sufficient 'give', an important consideration with wooden hulls and being only as strong as the weakest link and liable to part without warning under a snatch load. Joseph Lidwell Heathorn's patent of 1832 (see Figure 7:4) tackles this problem with various spring devices, quoting from the specifications:[3]

. . . for the purpose of relieving the chain from sudden strain or pressure, by affording a certain degree of elasticity, and yet retaining the rigging with sufficient degree of tension.

Note the rigging is set up with deadeyes and lanyards which in themselves have a certain amount of 'give'. Furthermore some of the early mechanical methods for tensioning the standing rigging incorporated a lashing of some sort for it was considered essential to cut the rigging away in an emergency with no more than an axe or knife.

The real answer was iron wire rope and in 1835 Andrew Smith took out patent no 6743 entitled 'Standing Rigging for Ships'. As can be seen from Figure 7:5 the rope was formed from a single strand which consisted of a number of thin wire rods or wires laid parallel and made up into a circular section the whole being held together by a liberal coating of 'india rubber, oil and asphaltum', then covered in cloth soaked in waterproof composition and finally bound and served with tarred hemp (Fig 7 on the patent). It is also evident that no twist was applied to the wires or rods. The Atlantic steamer *Liverpool* most probably had this type of wire rigging as a press report prior to her maiden voyage on 20 October 1838, which was undated and part of the collection of newspaper cuttings already referred to, states:

The stays, shrouds and all the rigging that is fixed, or not intended to be movable, is of a new material. It is formed of wire rods bound together with thrums. It has the advantage of possessing great strength and of not offering any great resistance to the air.

The method of tensioning and connecting the ends of the shrouds is shown in the drawings that accompanied the patent (see Figure 7:5). While no bending of the wire rope or distortion by splicing was required in securing the end fittings, all the various parts including the device for setting up the rigging could only be made ashore by a specialist engineering firm, and any major fault in service would have to be repaired by a shipyard with the necessary equipment. The seaman could not in the ordinary way set up this type of rigging with his knife, fid, heaving and serving mallets, but would need specialised tools and even a small furnace to melt the zinc or lead fillings. It would appear that overall, except for the method of belling out the individual wires after passing the rope through the cone fitting and then securing it with molten metal, which is still used in the present day, the patent does not reflect practical sea going experience. For example, the cross-sectional view of the mast shows all the rigging at right angles when in fact, except for the forward one on each side, the shrouds will progressively look aft.

Perhaps to forestall any critisism of this new system of rigging by experienced seamen, a method of disconnecting the shrouds or stays under tension is illustrated in figures 11, 12, 13 and 14 on the patent drawing. According to the description, this involved removing two retaining links from either end of the two parallel pins located on each side of the cup-shaped fitting. This would allow them to be knocked out sideways from the recesses formed in the sides of the cup, allowing free exit of the collar and billed-out end of the wire. An ingenious but complicated device, which in practice, after years of corrosion, was likely to be difficult to let go in a hurry, and virtually an impossible task if a whole gang of shrouds had to be 'cut adrift' together.

[A further patent[4] by Andrew Smith was registered a year later and shows his single strand wire rope turned round a thimble, then divided in three or four 'groups' and spliced back into the standing part (see Figure 7:6). Having spliced cargo runners using both the 'Liverpool splice' with locking tuck and the 'over and under' method I would imagine great difficulty, even for an experienced shore side rigger, in doing this eye splice. (PA)]

Although not part of the patent application, it is interesting to note the illustration of a rigging screw, which in 1836 must have already been in existence for a year or two.

In 1839 Andrew Smith took out yet another patent,[5] an improvement on his first two. The wire rope now had a twist applied and instead of a single strand it could be formed of several strands, but there is no indication of the type of machinery to do this, other than a vague reference to using the same equipment and methods as for hemp or other fibre ropes.

It was not until a year later in 1840 that the real breakthrough occurred. Robert Stirling Newall of Dundee was granted a patent[6] for making wire ropes which contained comprehensive

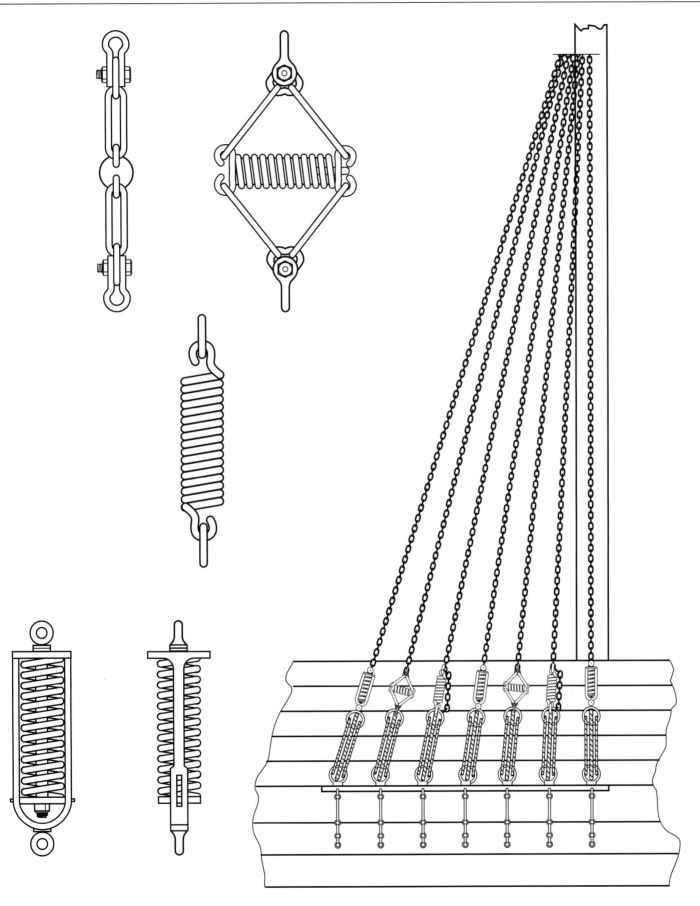

Figure 7:4 *There is evidence from contemporary paintings of early steamers that part hemp and part chain was used for standing rigging, the chain forming the upper section of the shrouds on the mast immediately abaft the funnel. Drawn from Joseph Lidwell Heathorn's patent of 1832.*

Figure 7:5 *From Patent no 6743, 12 January 1835, Standing Rigging for Ships. (Andrew Smith)*

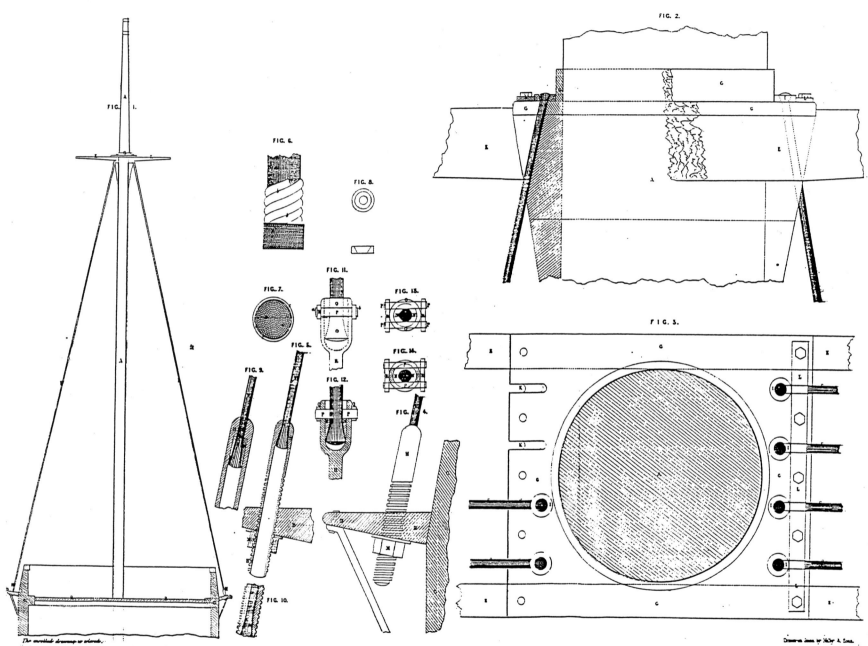

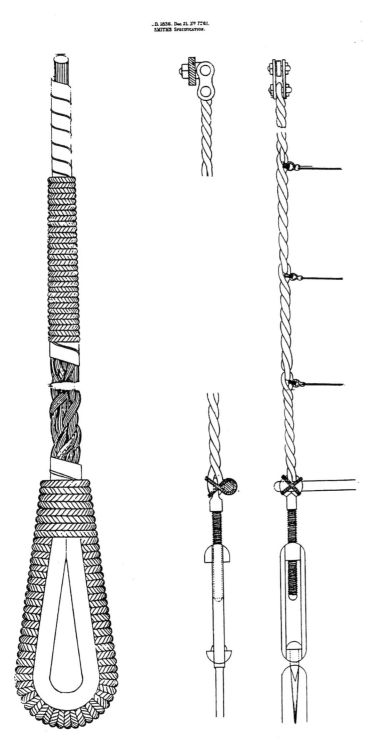

has a core of wire instead of hemp, or, 7×7 in which the heart is formed by one strand. This type of wire is used in standing rigging for it is not flexible enough to work around a sheave of small diameter, a common and versatile construction for this job being 6×19 or the even more flexible 6×37.

Figure 7:7 shows a section through Newall's wire rope and his method of securing fittings or joining, which he describes as:

The end of the rope is passed thro' a conical thimble, and the ends of the strands doubled in; the rope is then pulled back till the doubled in part fits the thimble, as represented. Melted brass is then poured amongst the ends of the strands, which will prevent their being drawn out of the thimble.

As already mentioned, modern practice has not improved on this method of fitting a lug on the end of a wire, although some terminals can now be fastened on mechanically or by the use of a special machine, which does away with the need for molten metal.

By 1843 when he applied for a further patent[7] detailing improvements to the machinery, Robert Stirling Newall gives his address as of Gateshead, in the county of Durham, wire rope manufacturer.

With the advent of iron wire, its initial use at sea was for the standing rigging and funnel stays on steamships, but it was not long before its advantage over hemp, in most respects, was recognised by the operators of sailing vessels, especially those with iron hulls. At about the same time as iron wire appeared on ships, new ways and means were devised for setting up this rigging. Over the centuries, deadeyes and lanyards had sufficed very well for tensioning the hemp shrouds and stays of the wooden sailing ship, and in fact continued to be used with wire right up to the end of commercial sail, and is still in evidence on survivors and older yachts.

Reference has already been made to a rigging screw having only one threaded part, which appeared incidentally on Smith's

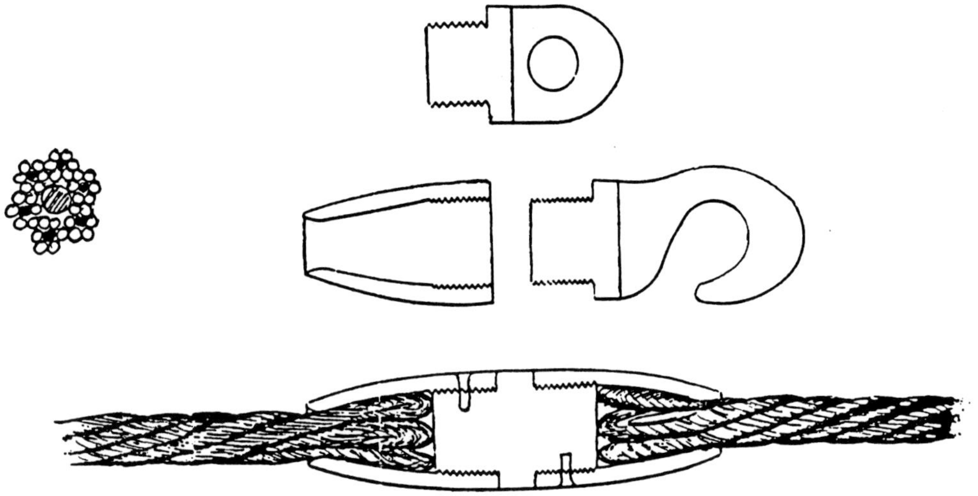

Figure 7:6 *Part of the drawings that illustrate Patent no 7261, 21 December 1836, Construction and Manufacture of Standing Rigging, Stays and Chains for Ships and Vessels by Andrew Smith. The section of shroud is formed from several long 'links' made from wire wound round a suitable mould, the separate 'links' joined like a chain and then twisted by some mechanical means and consolidated by solder, the finished lengths the same distance apart as the ratlines.*

Figure 7:7 *From Patent no 8594, 7 August 1840, Manufacture of Wire Ropes. The end fittings are shown with an internal thread to accommodate various securing devices. Using the same basic cone shape end method, the end fittings could be made much simpler and incorporate two lugs as an integral part with holes to take a securing bolt or pin, thus doing away with the more complex manufacturing process which involved the cutting of threads. (Robert Stirling Newall)*

details of the machinery and methods of manufacture. His iron wire rope is instantly recognisable today as 6×6 construction, that is, six wires are worked around a core of hemp or some other substance forming a strand, six of these strands being laid up around the rope's hemp heart. There are many variations in the construction of modern steel wire rope depending on its usage; 6×7 is more common now than 6×6, that is, each strand

Figure 7:8 *When the
Charlotte was built in 1840
at Plymouth she was smack-
rigged, her single mast stayed
athwartships with shrouds of
thick hemp rope set up with
deadeyes and lanyards. When
she was lengthened and
converted to ketch rig, as
shown here, her new mizzen
mast was supported by
shrouds of iron wire but still
set up with deadeyes and
lanyards. The difference in
thickness can be seen clearly
in this photograph. (Gillis
Collection)*

Patent no 7261 of 1836. The next development came in 1843 when James Greer invented his 'screw lanyard' having both left and right handed thread cut on the same bar (see Figure 7:9). He describes it as being:

Far more preferable to the present modes of securing the standing rigging, in as much as the rigging can be tightened or slacked at any time or in any weather without impeding the vessel's course. I consider it will be much

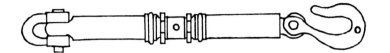

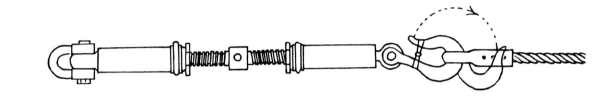

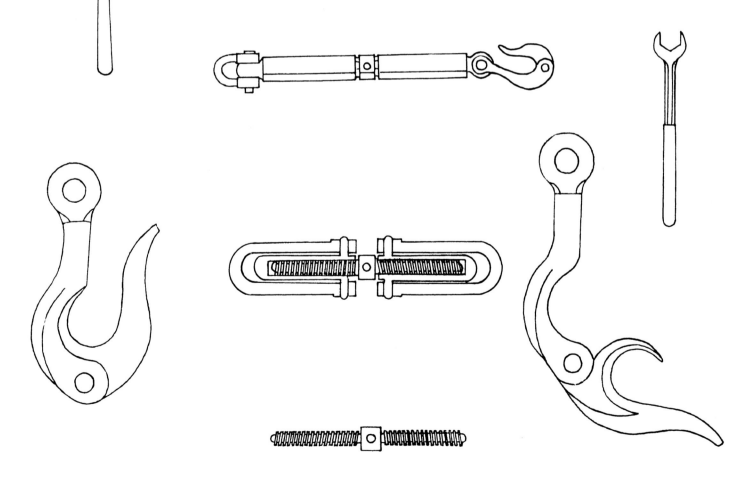

Figure 7:9 *From Patent no 9811, 1 July 1843, Securing Standing Rigging. Note the alternative method of securing an end fitting to wire rope which incorporates three pins through-riveted. (James Greer)*

more durable, and for ships of war save considerable space, and thus give greater range to those guns which may be in the proximity of the rigging or shrouds; and, from its cylindrical form, a shot striking it would be likely to glide off, thus preserving the shrouds; where as with the dead-eye and hempen or rope lanyard, the lanyard will be cut by the shot, and the shroud be set at liberty, to the great inconvenience of those working the guns, as well as a danger to the ship.

Of the specially designed quick-release hook which he recommends be used with the 'screw lanyard' he says:

. . . in case of a sudden storm, where it is necessary to cut away the masts or disengage the rigging as quickly as possible, simply place a man supplied with a knife to each shroud, and taking the precaution of cutting the lee rigging first, the mousing may be cut, and the masts with their appendages carried over the side and released from the vessel in a moment of time.

[Probably the first photographs of a vessel rigged with iron wire, and possibly the oldest photographs of a vessel of any kind, are the two in the Handels og Sjøfarts Museet at Helsingør in Denmark of the paddle steamer *Iris* (Figures 7:10 and 7:11). She was built by Halls of Aberdeen for service in the Baltic, and these photographs were taken in 1842, predating by a couple of years that of *The Great Britain* fitting out in Bristol and believed to be by Fox Talbot or a follower. Their importance as evidence for the development of rigging was first recognised by one of the authors in the 1970s. (BG)]

Looking at the photographs carefully and allowing for a slight distortion, an estimate can be made of the size of the running and standing rigging. According to tables in Harold Underhill's *Masting and Rigging* for this size of vessel, the jib and staysail halyards would be 2.5in circumference, (about 0.75in

Figure 7:10 *The* Iris *lying in Ålborg, Denmark, in 1842, starboard view. (Handels og Sjøfarts Museet, Helsingør)*

Figure 7:11 *The* Iris *lying in Ålborg, Denmark, in 1842, portside view. (Handels og Sjøfarts Museet, Helsingør)*

diameter). The forestay and shrouds are bigger in the photograph but not as large as the mooring ropes which would be about 4.5in circumference (about 1.5in diameter). As hemp shrouds for this class of vessel would be 5.5 to 6in circumference, only slightly smaller than the anchor stock, it can be seen that the standing rigging must be of iron wire of about 1in diameter or 3in circumference allowing for the serving. Underhill, in table No 15, gives 2.5in steel wire as the size of the fore and main shrouds required on a 300–400 ton barque.[8]

Furthermore, there are no deadeyes and lanyards in the *Iris*, the shrouds tensioned by some mechanical device in the form of a tube which is probably the outer protective sleeve of canvas or leather, having three white bands, at top, bottom and middle, possibly painted servings to seal the covering.

Figure 7:12 is a conjectural drawing by Peter Allington of this device, taking into account the following details from the photographs.

1) compared with other details, length approximately 30in,
2) proportion – diameter's length approximately 14:1 or 2–2⅜in diameter,
3) lower half slightly larger diameter,
4) shroud runs straight into the top – there is no swelling to indicate a shackle or thimble, except on the port forward shroud which is probably a coil of line.

Looking at the earlier rigging patents and the way in which the ends are treated it is possible the lower end of the shroud was passed through the upper tube, a shaped collar fitted, the wire splayed out and then molten metal poured over it to

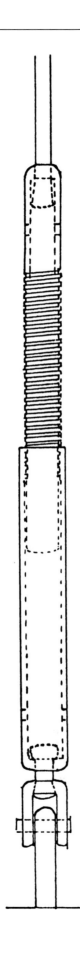

Figure 7:12 *Conjectural drawing of the tensioning device for setting up the shrouds on the P.S.* Iris *(see Figs 7:10 and 7:11). (Peter Allington)*

solidify the conical shape, thus preventing withdrawal. The tube could then be drawn back over it so that it seated at the top end as shown.

The lower portion may also have been a tube with a small section at the top threaded on the inside face or perhaps two metal straps joined the 'nut' at the top to the bottom part in which a swivel was incorporated. To tension the rigging a tommy bar would be inserted through holes provided in the lower section which was then rotated and worked up the thread of the upper tube, held stationary by another tommy bar. Greer's patent 'Screw Lanyard'[9] incorporating a left and right hand thread was issued a year or so after the *Iris* was built in 1842 (see Figure 7:9).

The topmast shrouds are more likely to be hemp as the slack has been coiled tightly and made up on the shrouds near the mast, but the centre section of the main topmast forestay where it passes over the funnel is wire, with fibre rope tails leading to either mast, the difference in diameter clearly visible.

Sail Handling

The rigging of the standing gaffs on the *Iris* and the way in which the boomless foresail is brailed into the mast has certain similarities to the fore and aft gaffsails on *The Great Britain*. Both have what appears to be single part peak halyards, but in the case of the *Iris* this could be a fixed length span, while those on *The Great Britain* led to a block on the mast, for the gaffs had to be adjustable, as will be seen later. The method of supporting the head of the sail by hoops and the use of an out-haul is the same on both vessels.

Unlike the Atlantic steamers that had to make a voyage of 3,000 miles non-stop, the *Iris* had none of the problems associated with a large fuel load or the consequences of variable immersion of the paddle wheels. Her trips were very short by comparison, only a day or so, evident from the livestock carried on deck, visible around the foremast in the photograph taken portside to; the falls of the running rigging made up in coils on the lower part of the shrouds clear from being chewed or trampled on. The photograph in figure 7:12 clearly shows the heavy gang plank used for the loading and offloading and as a further indication that her voyages were short, she carries her cargo gaffs rigged on the fore side of the mast probably at all times, as some of her destinations en route would be open roadsteads. The livestock would then have to be lifted in a purpose-made sling, swung out and lowered into a boat alongside, or loaded from boats in the same way; the most convenient place on board for this operation would be just ahead of the masts.

Both topmasts are housed and the jib boom run in, for, like the *Great Western* and *The Great Britain*, it is most likely these spars were only set up on those occasions when the extra canvas would be of use. All this indicates that due to the nature of the voyages, these sails were not much used, only the jib, forestay-sail and gaff foresail. In fact the mainsail is not bent on in either photograph, nor does it appear in a sketch of her entering Copenhagen a few years later. It is unlikely that it was ashore being repaired by the sailmaker, but permanently unbent as its use proved to be minimal and not worth the maintenance costs.

The foreyard has been lowered to reduce weight aloft and probably lashed in this position to the forward shrouds for both the lifts and braces which are still rigged are slightly slack. At this height it was easy to reach from the tops of the sponson houses but high enough to clear the alongside berths, for the predicted tidal range was minimal, only a few inches at most, although on occasions the wind direction and barometric pressure caused a surge in the Baltic which therefore increased or decreased these predictions. There is evidence that it was used at some time as the forestay has a baggy wrinkle or other anti chafe device, the spectacle block associated with a square topsail sheet can be seen hanging below the centre of the yard, and in fact what appears to be the topsail yard is lying fore and aft inside the port paddle box level with the top of the sponson houses (view starboard side too).

This would indicate that *Iris* when first built carried the rig of a topsail schooner with three headsails, fore topsail, boomless gaff foresail, gaff mainsail, probably with a boom although still brailing into the mast, and a main gaff topsail. Her much reduced working sail area, evident from both the photographs and sketch, must have resulted from operational experience: the inter-island trade mostly in sheltered waters with predominantly light breezes in the summer months. Her speed of 8 or 9 knots under steam would reduce the usable wind still further and therefore it would be logical to cut down windage as much as possible and dispense with the canvas that was of no practical use.

Objectively, the two topmasts could have been sent down altogether along with the main gaff, but the long tradition of seamen trained in wind-driven ships demanded they be retained for no other reason than they 'might come in handy one day', or more importantly, the vessel just would not look right without them; for one thing, if she had no main gaff, where would they fly the ensign?

This 'thinking' is reflected in the comments made by Jesse Gray, an engineer serving aboard the US warship *Mississippi* in the early 1840s. She was a paddle-propelled steamer, rigged nominally as a barque but distribution of sail and the position of the masts was closer to a brig, with a small fore and aft mizzen added and stepped well aft:

Figure 7:13 *This drawing of 1855 shows the* Iris *entering Copenhagen harbour. (Handels og Sjøfarts Museet, Helsingør)*

The sails are auxiliary to her steam; with her sails unaided by her engines, she is helpless; on the other hand, her engines are sufficient to handle her without the assistance of sail.

His views may well have been biased to some extent, not uncommon among engineers expressing an opinion on such matters, but his further remarks are of interest as he mentions the sails individually:

The mainsail cannot be carried – the main topsail is seldom used – steering sails have been useless – fore topsail useful – topgallant sails seldom used – fore topmast staysail and jib useful. The useful sails are fore and main trysails, fore topmast staysail and jib and occasionally the spanker with effect.

As with the *Iris* it was predominantly fore and aft canvas that provided any assistance to the engine, more particularly those in the fore part of the vessel. With the large crew on this type of steamer, topgallant masts would be sent down along with the upper yards in a moderate head breeze, and in stronger winds the topmasts would be housed and the lower yards braced up as

sharp as possible, reducing windage to the minimum, but in fine weather all was sent up again to 'improve the appearance of the ship'.[10]

The log book of the first voyage of the *Great Western* confirms that on average, sails in the forepart of a paddle steamer, making continuous use of her engines, were of more use than those in the after part. For some reason it was not until 18 April, 10 days out of Bristol, that the remarks column contains the entry 'Bending on the forestaysail' and despite confusion over the naming of the other sails it seems not to have been set before this date, the most likely reason being that it was under repair.

Due perhaps to the entirely novel four mast schooner rig, the terminology in the log book when referring to individual sails is not consistent. In the ordinary way, a vessel the size of the *Great Western* would have been rigged as a ship, that is, with square sails on each of the three masts. Some carried additional gaff-sails on the fore and main lowermast so the tendency was to refer to those in a similar position on the *Great Western* as if the masts were square-rigged. For instance, the gaffsail on the mainmast was named either the 'main trysail' or 'main spencer', not simply, as it would have been in later years, the 'mainsail'. The one on the foremast was called the 'foresail', 'fore trysail' or

Figure 7:14 *The United States Navy steam frigate* Mississippi, *built at the Philadelphia Navy Yard in 1841. (Illustrated London News)*

'forespencer', all referring to exactly the same sail. Some vessels, like the *British Queen*, did actually have two separate sails, the smaller one with a shorter gaff called the 'trysail' and used in strong winds. The lowest square sail on the foremast, which was not bent on permanently to the yard but set 'flying' from the deck, was named the 'square sail' to distinguish it from the gaff 'foresail'. As the maiden voyage progressed the word 'trysail' was dropped and the deck log book entries only used the word 'spencer', although the engine room log, which contained references to the sails in general, continued to use 'trysail'. For example, in the 19 April 1838 ship's deck log the column 'Sail' contains the entry 'Forestaysail and Fore spencer'; the engineer's log under 'occurrences and remarks' contains '4½ AM moderate breeze, SW; fore trysail and staysail set'.

An analysis of the sail set on the last 4 days when the winds were either on the beam or ahead indicates the forestaysail and fore spencer as used most often followed by the inner jib, fore topsail and mizzen spencer, then the square sail and main spencer. There is no mention at all of setting the fore topgallant, any gaff topsails and only once the sail on the fourth or 'after mast'. It must be said, however, that at no time was the wind abaft the beam during this short period.

Further evidence appears in a contemporary painting of the *British Queen* getting to windward in a fresh to strong wind, with only canvas set on or from the foremast. The main topgallant yard has been sent down, main topsail yard bare of any sail, and along with the main yard, braced round as sharp as possible to reduce windage.

Note also the linked iron rod forming the twin mainstays and the smaller sized but same construction used for the funnel stays (the same as on the *Great Western*). Some of the rigging detail seems incorrect, for example, the peak halyard blocks shown on the gaffs would prevent the head of the sail if supported by hoops, the usual method at that time, from travelling the required distance to the outhaul sheave. If, however, the gaffsails did brail up to the throat, then the position of the peak blocks would not get in the way, but as shown, the method of brailing is into the mast as used on the *Iris*. Furthermore, the lead of the main topmast stay, instead of terminating at the foremast cap, crosses the peak halyards preventing the gaff from

Figure 7:15 *The* British Queen *working to windward under sail and power. (NMPFT/Science and Society Picture Library)*

swinging over from one side to the other. Reef points are shown on the foresail, although the detailed specifications given by the sailmaker only mentions them fitted to the fore and main topsail.[11]

Despite some errors, one must assume the artist did not make a mistake with such fundamentals as the sails set, neither adding nor subtracting as he saw fit, for it represents perfectly the enigma of combining sail and paddle propulsion. In this situation, or at any time the vessel heels over due to wind pressure on the sails, the leeward wheel will be more deeply immersed. For paddle steamers that made continuous use of the engines, this unequal thrust was far more pronounced towards the end of a long passage. Stability being much reduced at that stage by the loss of weight from low down in the vessel, she heeled more easily, and even in a light breeze; her reduced draught allowed the weather wheel to rotate completely clear of the water for short periods. With propulsion therefore on one side only she had a strong tendency to turn towards the wind, which had to be countered by large rudder angles. This situation arose on the maiden voyage of the *Great Western*, when on 21 April, 2 days before her arrival at New York, the remarks column of the log book states, 'At 7, ship carrying weather helm, shifted the chain [anchor chain] over to windward'.

This was done to reduce heel, for even a few tons shifted over would make a difference, the vessel by then comparatively 'tender'. Wind at the time was given as force 3 on the beam and the sails set – inner jib, forestaysail, gaff foresail, fore topsail and unusually, right aft, the gaffsail on the fourth mast. It was probably set to act as a steering sail with the sheets eased off most of the time, but should the bows suddenly fall off to leeward, perhaps due to a temporary loss of propulsion as the lower or main driving wheel was alternately buried in a wave or came completely clear on the windward roll, or for whatever reason, the sheet could be hardened in smartly to help her regain the course. The whole purpose of the sail set on or from the foremast was to provide additional forward thrust, steady the motion, and assist with steering by counteracting the turning effect of the leeward paddle wheel independent of the rudder.

The Use of Square Sail

Steam propulsion required the weatherliness of the square sails to be improved, the yards having to be braced round closer to the fore and aft line than was customary in sailing ships of the period. This depended on several factors. The lower yard is limited by the foremost shroud on the leeward side, the angle and height of the forward leading stay above it, the futtock shrouds, and the manner in which it was slung ahead of the mast. The height of the lowermast related to the vessel's beam, which determined the athwartship spread of the rigging, also had an influence. On deep sea paddlers which used the engines continuously all the masts, irrespective of any square sails they might carry, were set up as on a fore and aft schooner, that is, a

pair of crosstrees extended the topmast shrouds instead of the larger and heavier tops associated with a fully square-rigged mast.

The lowest yard, more restricted in its arc of movement and the longer leech of the sail as a consequence of the tall 'schooner' lowermast, could not be carried with the wind so fine on the bow as the topsail, and therefore its use was limited to reaching and running. The practice was therefore to set this sail from the deck by hauling it up to the yard probably having been made up in 'stops', that is, first folded foot to head and then rolled up like a long sausage and held at intervals by rope yarns, which could then be broken by pulling down on the tack and sheet when required. There was no need for the gear usually associated with a course permanently bent on the yard, leech lines, clew lines and buntlines; therefore, the related blocks hung over the yard ahead of the mast on the underside of the top were no longer called for either. The expression used in the log book of the *Great Western*, 'Got the square sail up and set', leaves no doubt as to the manner in which it was handled. Getting this type of sail down was not so easy. The *Sirius* on her maiden voyage of 15 April 1838 reported that 'At 9pm stopped engine quarter of an hour owing to square sail flying to leeward' – it must either have ended up partly in the water or tangled with the paddle wheel.

The smaller spread of the topmast shrouds allowed the topsail yard, even when only partly hoisted, as with the sail reefed, to be braced just that bit sharper than the lower yard. However the twin crosstrees did not provide support to the topmast as effectively as the wider base of the 'tops'. This could have been a contributory factor in the *Great Western* losing her foretopmast on 15 April. According to the log book she was making 11 knots, wind on, or just abaft, the beam but squally, force 7 at times with a moderate sea. The sail was not reefed so its area must have been about 1,400sq ft.

How close to the wind could these Atlantic steam packets carry square topsails? The log book of the *Great Western* indicates that the true wind had to be 5 points (56 degrees) on the bow or more. For instance, approaching New York with a smooth sea under the lee of the land, her course west, speed 8.5 knots, wind northwest by north, force 5, apparent wind 40 degrees on the bow, her foretopsail was set. If this sail was to fill and provide any forward thrust, the topsail yard must have been braced round close to 30 degrees to the fore and aft line, and the sail made so that it could be set virtually 'flat as a board'. It is probable that in this instance the weather leech was regularly backwinded, but this would not have mattered a great deal as the main propulsion was from the paddle wheels, so any tendency to 'tack' the ship by coming completely aback could easily be corrected. In fact an hour later the wind had dropped to force 3 and backed northwest, her course was adjusted temporarily to west by south and the topsail furled. It follows that the lower yard to which the topsail was sheeted must also have been braced round very sharp, and to achieve this, it would have to be slung in the optimum position in relation to the forestay, shrouds and futtock shrouds, probably supported by a chain sling and held ahead of the mast by some form of metal truss, but no evidence has come to light confirming this on the *Great Western*. This type of gear was employed on sailing ships a few years later with the further development of the forward leading stay being placed higher up the masthead instead of at the same level as the shroud eyes.

Figures 7:16 and 7:17 compare the limitations of bracing the fore yard on HMS *Victory* and the SS *Great Western* drawn to scale. These are purely geometric illustrations and assume in both cases that the yard AB is slung at the same level as the intersection of the forward shroud and futtock shroud indicated by a and b. On the same horizontal plane but projected forward it will cross the forestay at c.

The angle of about 40 degrees achieved by the man-of-war can be considered about average for a merchant sailing ship of the 1840s with a fully square-rigged mast, while the *Great Western*, with her shorter schooner-type crosstrees and lower end of the futtocks on the mast, can manage 33 degrees with the yard touching both shroud and forestay. It can be seen that by raising the forestay the intersection c moves forward to c1, allowing an improvement of 5 degrees.

In practice these angles can be bettered by slacking up the weather truss which allows the yard to go farther ahead of the mast, heaving in any slack in the lee rigging in way of the yard, or in some circumstances by canting the weather yard arm down.

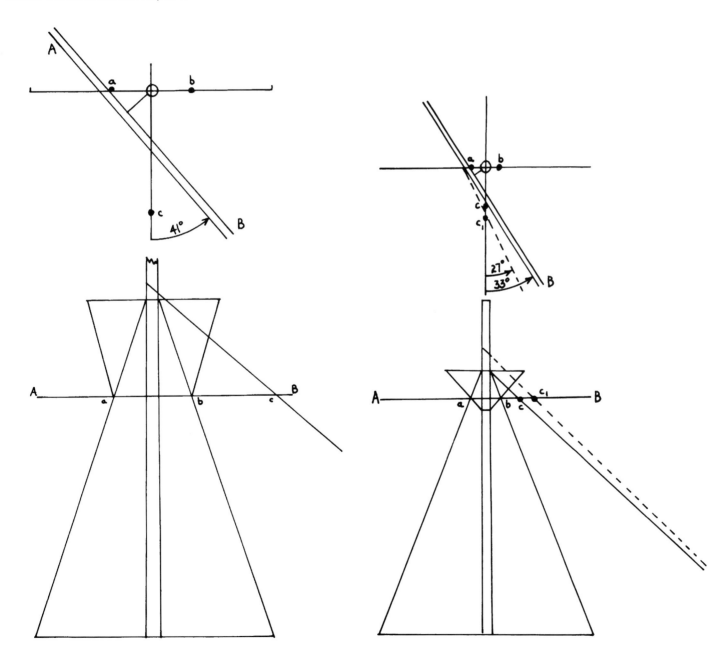

Figure 7:16 *Geometric limits imposed on bracing round the foreyard of HMS* Victory *by the standing rigging. However, various methods could be employed in practice to improve the situation. (Peter Allington)*

Figure 7:17 *Geometric limits imposed by the standing rigging on the foreyard of the* Great Western. *(Peter Allington)*

Gaffsail

The gaffsails on the *Great Western* (see Figure 7:18), although rigged with peak and throat halyards, remained aloft except in fresh headwinds or heavy weather when individual sails that were not required would be lowered, the peak kept topped up as in the illustration of her running before a storm (see Figure 7:19). It would not be strictly correct to call them 'standing gaffs' but as they were aloft more often than not, this term will suffice. The exception was the mainsail, which being close abaft the funnel and subject to heat and smoke, would, depending on the wind direction, be lowered regularly part way as shown in J Walter's painting of her passing Portishead (see Figure 7:20). It will be noticed that a span is used only on this gaff, all the others having the peak halyard blocks fixed directly onto the spar, and because of the heat, both span and halyard were therefore most likely made of chain.

As the forward leading stay of each mast, except the foremast, led down to the heel, or thereabouts, of the next ahead,

the gaffsails could not have a boom although this consideration did not apply to the fourth or 'after mast' where, being directly over the wheel, there would have been an advantage in having a boom. The aftermost gaffsail on the *British Queen*, *President* and *Liverpool* were all fitted with booms, so the reason why the *Great Western* was not is unclear. Her successor *The Great Britain* also appears in all the illustrations without a boom on her sixth mast but the log book entry for 30 July 1845 states '4.00 Carried away strops of fore peak halliards and boom outhauler of 3rd spencer'. This was the name given to the aftermost sail, the others being named fore, main, mizzen, 1st and 2nd spencers. The remark implies she did have a boom on this sail, although it might have been of a temporary nature. It is hardly conceivable that 'boom' and 'gaff' would be confused.

The sails on the *Great Western* are shown brailed up to the throat with the usual folds of canvas underneath the gaff. This method had the advantage of lifting the clew and sheet blocks clear of the deck, but in terms of windage and weight aloft, when the sails were furled, brailing into the mast or into the weather, as it was sometimes described, was a better option. This was the method used on *The Great Britain* and also shown in the photographs of the *Iris*; and, for it to work, the head of the sail, supported usually by hoops or rings, but sometimes a head lacing, must be able to slide virtually the whole way to the outhaul sheave. This means the peak halyard cannot be rigged in the usual way as the blocks or spans would obstruct the full travel. The modern solution of using a track and slides would overcome this problem.

It would appear from the photographs and the sketch of the *Iris* that the fore gaff did not have the usual throat halyard and it is also possible a gooseneck was fitted instead of jaws, or as is shown in Figure 7:21 support by a short length of chain rigged so close to the after face of the mast as not to be visible. The spar is probably held at the required angle by a fixed length span, and in common with the standing rigging, made up from iron wire. The head outhaul leads to a sheave worked through the gaff just inboard of the vangs then to a block on the lowermast cap. Without peak or throat halyards the sail was very easy to set – just cast off the brails and the head inhaul from the belayings pins, heave away on the outhaul and sheet and adjust the vangs as required. The shrouds have a considerable fore and aft spread so no backstays are fitted.

The manner in which the inboard end of the cargo gaff is supported is not clear, but rigged as it is at right angles to the mast, the jaws could rest on a saddle or chocks. These obstructions would not get in the way of the sail handling as the foresail did not have to be hoisted or lowered. The length is obviously sufficient for the cargo runner to plumb over the side and the whip and smaller stropped block, just inboard of the gin block, must have been used to control the lateral movement. So rigged, it would have a tendency always to swing outboard and aft, so the job of the whip would be to control this movement

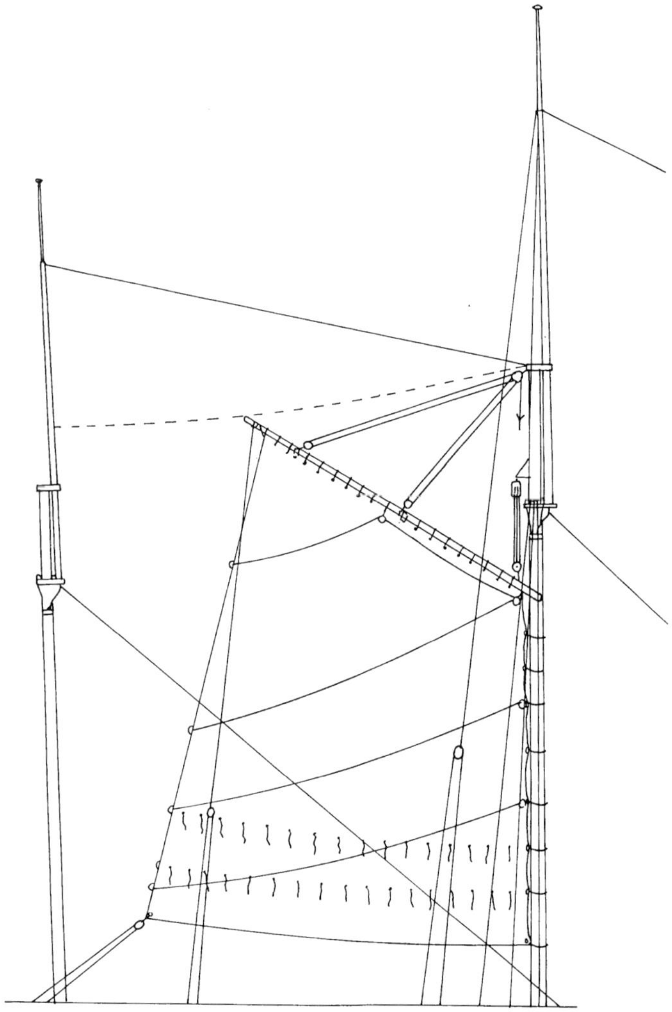

Figure 7:18 *Gaffsail as rigged on the* Great Western, *the detail based on contemporary paintings of the vessel. The dotted line shows the lead of the topmast forestay when the spar is housed. The shrouds on the mainmast being close to the funnel were made of linked iron rod. (A contemporary but unnamed model of an early steamship shows a single link joining the ends of the rods, rather than a direct connection.) Not shown on the drawing are the spreader and topmast shrouds. (Peter Allington)*

Figure 7:19 *The* Great Western *running before a storm. (Trustees of National Museum and Galleries on Merseyside)*

and to trim the gaff inboard. As no adjustment was required, the cargo gaff could remain at this angle with a fixed length peak span. The illustration of the much earlier Bristol Channel steamer *Severn* (1825) shows this type of gear rigged on the foremast (see Chapter 1, Figure 1:5).

The Great Britain

The gaffsail on the *Iris* demonstrates the advances made in steamship fore and aft canvas compared with the *Great Western*, while two years later in 1844 *The Great Britain* was completed

Figure 7:20 *The* Great Western *passing Portishead, Somerset, lithograph from a painting by J Walter. (Private Collection. Photograph by Bristol Museum and Art Gallery)*

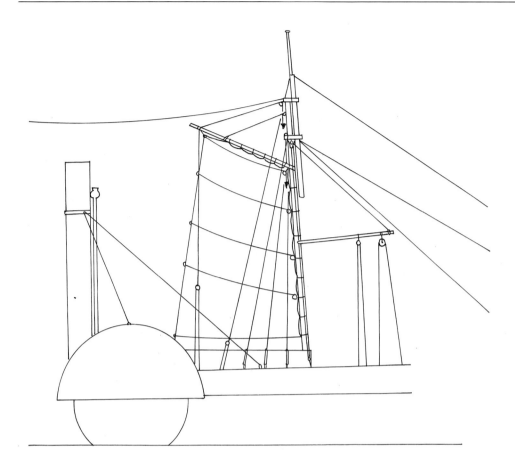

Figure 7:21 *Gaff foresail on the* Iris *drawn from details in the photographs (Figures 7:10 and 7:11). The considerable fore and aft spread given to the four shrouds per side provides good mast support for the cargo gaff. (Peter Allington)*

was probably a theoretical exercise, considered in the planning stage, which on further consideration was decided as impractical. The idea must have been shelved as the required gear on the stays were never fitted. However, the hinges or pivot at the heel would allow a limited fore and aft movement when pitching heavily without straining these tall masts as they worked alternately against the doubled stays and twin 'runner' backstays. The alternative of stepping them through the deck would require a much larger spar in terms of weight and diameter. For example, the second deck stepped mast was 68ft in length with a greatest diameter of 20in. Allowing an additional 20ft, which would still be above the shaft line, making 88ft in all, would need a mast between 24in and 26in in diameter. (The foremast of the American four-masted schooner *Bertha L Downs* was 88ft, maximum diameter 26in.)

This radical concept was not part of a slow evolutionary process in the development of sailing rigs but the work of an innovative and clever engineer looking anew at the functions of 'sail assist'. It is more likely than not that Brunel started, as it were, with a 'clean sheet of paper', and this must be borne in mind when interpreting the available evidence. As with some of his other ideas, the rig was far ahead of its time, too far perhaps for the conservative seamen of the day, and during her first refit changes were made, the masts stepped through the deck and the rigging set up in a more orthodox way. What appears a retrograde step and no more then stubborn prejudice may have been due to the failure of the iron wire on at least two occasions. *The Great Britain* lost her main topmast when returning from New York on her maiden voyage and the complete foremast over the side in a strong following squall in October of that year. Such accidents were almost certainly due to the standing rigging carrying away.

A close study of the Fox Talbot photograph (Figure 7:25) reveals what are most likely deadeyes and lanyards on the main and mizzen so it would be safe to assume the other masts were set up in the same manner. The fact that the *Iris* had some form of rigging screw 3 years earlier and Greer had issued his patent for a 'screw lanyard' suggests an engineer like Brunel might have considered some kind of mechanical tensioning device, but perhaps was not happy with its strength for use with such large masts. This is not to say deadeyes and lanyards are not compatible with wire rigging – far from it, as this method was used right up to the end of commercial sail.

Each succeeding mast working aft was given an increased rake; Figure 7:22 shows no 5 and no 6 and the sail as referred to in the log book, the 2nd spencer. Support on the forward side is provided by a doubled stay, the two parts leading down to the heel fitting of the mast ahead, or, in the case of the mizzen, part way up the mainmast. Athwartships, she has three shrouds per side with little fore and aft spread, designed primarily to support the mast laterally. Set up against the forestay, and providing the essential support from aft are two movable backstays. Due to the arc of travel required for the gaff and the interference with the sail, standing backstays with sufficient lead aft could not be

with an even more radical rig, combining recent developments with engineering principles and practice. Many of the features were unorthodox, such as stepping all the fore and aft rigged masts except the foremast on deck, dispensing with crosstrees (even on the mainmast) having the loose-footed gaffsails overlap the next most aft, and the use of moveable backstays.

Iron wire standing rigging was essential as the system required minimum stretch in the shrouds and stays. The *Great Western* and probably the *Iris* had the lower section of the mast within the hull, the mast heel stepped on the keelson and supported at deck level, the established practice on sea going vessels. The idea of stepping them with the heels on deck, with the consequent total reliance on the standing rigging, was a bold departure from tradition. Captain Claxton points out a reason for this in his description of the vessel:[12]

> Five masts of the six are hinged for lowering, when, in the Captain's judgement, contrary gales shall appear to have set in, as the westerlies do at certain seasons of the year, prevailing for months in the Atlantic. To a seaman's eye they have a look of insecurity; but if the strain which a fixed mast will stand is compensated by additional shrouding and stays, either in strength or quality, the same end is attained.

Claxton's proposal for lowering down the masts in a seaway

used. This point is borne out in the painting of *The Great Britain* saluting a man-of-war (see Figure 7:23). The wind is fine on the quarter, the sheets eased up with the sail blowing forward and the gaff squared off, virtually at right angles to the keel line.

A fair amount of detail with regard to the sails and manner of rigging is contained in the engraving of Walter's painting of *The Great Britain* being struck by a heavy sea (Figure 7:24). This shows two blocks on the aft face of the lowermast head, verified on sectional enlargements of the Fox Talbot photograph (Figure 7:25). All the fore and aft masts are similarly equipped. The upper one at the cap band is clearly used in conjunction with the head outhaul and what can best be described as the 'peak topping lift', for these gaffs stayed permanently aloft except on the rare occasions when lowered for repairs, but, as will be seen later, the angle needed to be adjusted.

The lower block slung on the after face of the mast level with the hounds is a heavy single sheave throat block (see Figure 7:26), the halyard bent on, probably with an eye spliced around the jaws, the fall leading down to the ship's side, and being considered virtually as 'standing' rigging, made up with deadeyes and lanyard, similar to the three shrouds ahead. (*The Great Britain* definitely had a throat halyard, the remarks column of the log book on 6 August 1845 stating 'Carried away throat halliard of No 2 gaff'.) A strong single part halyard would suffice as there was no need for the multiple sheave blocks to provide the mechanical advantage normally required for a hoisting gaff and sail of this size. Any stretch that developed in this hemp rope could be adjusted for with the deadeyes and lanyard. The single part fall is in fact the '4th shroud' on the port side (the usual convention is throat halyard to port, peak

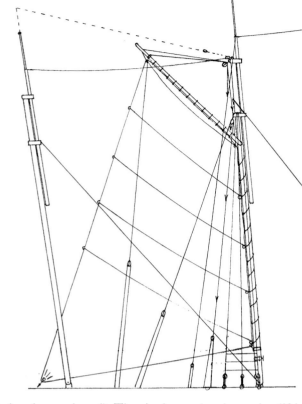

Figure 7:22 *Gaffsail on the fifth mast of* The Great Britain *referred to in the log book as the '2nd spencer'. All the contemporary paintings show the clew of these gaffsails overlapping the next mast aft and sheeted close to the deck. The luff is shown laced to the mast with the line forming a continuous spiral. This method will suffice if the sail is not raised or lowered as was the case. The peak halyard, or, more accurately, the gaff topping lift is shown leading down to a whip so that the angle of the gaff could be trimmed as required. (Peter Allington)*

Figure 7:23 The Great Britain *saluting a warship on 26 January 1845. This contemporary painting together with Figure 7:24 suggests that the vessel may normally have operated with topmasts housed. These topmasts may have been treated as studding sail booms and the gaff topsails set flying under conditions when studding sails would have been used on the main. (Private Collection. Photographs by Bristol Museum and Art Gallery)*

halyard to starboard). The single part 'peak topping lift' would be led down to the ship's side via a fairlead at the hounds. A direct lead from the peak block would place an unfair strain on the masthead which was virtually unsupported and would therefore be the '4th shroud' on the starboard side, probably

Figure 7:24 The Great Britain *off Lundy during trials. Lithograph from a painting by J Walter. This illustration is one of the sources used in researching the original method of staying the masts and rigging the sails. Some of the detail is not consistent and there are errors such as the wrong lead for the brail lines and inclusion of reef points, but one of the main features, the carrying of sails, close on 2,000sq ft in area in a force 9, is correct. The incident, as painted, occurred in the Bristol Channel prior to her entry into service on 24 January 1845 when she was struck by a heavy sea and suffered some damage forward. (SS Great Britain Project)*

with some form of whip or purchase at the lower end to provide the required adjustment. It was common practice to lead halyards away from the mast in such a way that some support was provided, not just a compression load.

The pendant section of the movable backstays were probably of iron wire, for they were, like the doubled stays and shrouds, an integral and essential part of the support system. Each pendant could have been made fast to the mast with an eye formed in the end, encircling it in the same way as the shrouds, and then, as shown, seized back on itself. The lower end may have been treated in a similar manner, taken around the whip block and seized back onto the pendant or eyespliced.

Mention has been made earlier in this chapter of *The Great Britain* losing her foremast over the side. The incident occurred on 2 October 1845 when bound for New York, when she was struck by a heavy squall, the wind direction northeast, probably on her starboard quarter. Running like this, she most likely had her gaff foresail, forestaysail and even the jib set, the weather shrouds providing some support, but by far the largest strain would have been on the weather backstay set up on the starboard side, the leeward one being all slack. In these circumstances, with the wind gusting to gale force or more, the foremast would have been subjected to maximum load from aft, much more than any of the other gaff-rigged masts which had no sail set ahead of them. Furthermore the foremast was right in the bows and suffered the most violent motion. It also appears from the illustrations to have had little if any rake aft and as the bow plunged downward, its tendency to pitch for-

ward and the kinetic energy generated, compared with the after four masts, which were smaller and had progressively more rake, placed a greater strain on the rigging supporting it from aft. When closehauled the vang and sheet would tend to pull the head of the mast aft, the foremast being particularly well supported with the headstays to resist strain from this direction. However in the circumstances, with wind on the quarter and both vang and sheet eased, they were in terms of providing additional support from aft, little if any help; all the sails worked against the weather backstay with some support from the main topmast-stay, if it had been set up taut. The most likely spot for the wire to fail would have been the neck of the eye around the mast where it would be subjected not only to the sharp changes in tension but a small regular working back and fore each time it was eased up and allowed to go forward or when the tension on the whip was set up again. As the sails on this mast, particularly the gaff foresail, were the most often used, the backstays would have had extra 'wear and tear'. There is no proof that the failure of the backstay caused the dismasting, but on the grounds of probability it was the most likely reason. Assuming this was the case and it was not the hemp whip that failed, or some other cause, the incident demonstrated that iron wire rope in its early form, lacking the flexibility of hemp, and likely to crystallise from repeated bending, was not applicable to all parts of a ship's rigging, and at the time justified the seaman's scepticism of it.

On the subject of the mast support the remarks of Captain F Liardet RN in his book on seamanship emphasise this point

Figure 7:25 The Great Britain *fitting out in Bristol in 1844. Photograph probably by Fox Talbot. (The SS Great Britain Project)*

and when applied to *The Great Britain*, with her deck stepped masts and small spread given to the shrouds, the importance of her movable backstays cannot be overstated:[13]

It has often occurred to me, that it would be a desirable thing if the after-pair of shrouds on each side of the fore and main-mast, were made of larger rope than the other shrouds; as in heavy pitching, the most of the weight and heavy jerking comes on these shrouds. The frequent carrying away of these shrouds, or their securing in the chains without previous chafe, or damage, led me to pay much attention to them; and the more I have watched the masts in blowing weather (more particularly in a head-sea), I have been convinced that it would add much to their security if the after-pair of shrouds on each side were made of larger rope, and the securings from them made stronger in the chains, and down the ship's side. If the loss of lower-masts were enquired into, most of them would be proved to have carried away by first losing the after-shroud. In reality these shrouds are the after-stays of the lower-masts, and more they are considered so, the better the masts will be secured.

The absence of crosstrees at the hounds meant the topmast could be housed closer to the lowermast with just sufficient gap between for the eyes of the shrouds, if indeed they were

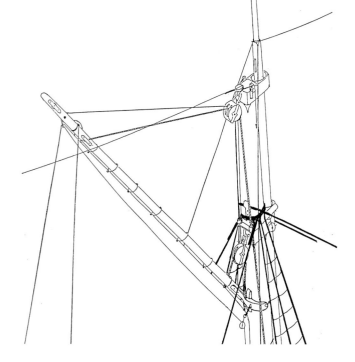

Figure 7:26 *Details of the mast head, standing and running rigging, gaff, and head of sail on the fourth mast (1st spencer) of* The Great Britain *(topmast housed). The wire rigging is shown with eyes around the mast in the conventional way but the evidence from a close inspection of the Fox Talbot photograph suggests the upper ends of the shrouds terminated otherwise. There were certainly not the usual wooden cheeks and trestle trees found on ships of this period. Note the absence of cross trees. (Peter Allington)*

Note. since this book has been prepared for publication, further research has revealed a far more sophisticated method of rigging the shrouds, underlining the fact that this was an engineer's rig.

formed around the mast, for it is possible some other method was used. With the topmasts sent up as shown in the Fox Talbot photograph, the stays lead down to the mast cap ahead, and, just discernible, is a block a few feet clear on the lower end of the stay. This is obviously used as the whip block to take in the slack when the topmasts are housed, the standing part made fast onto a lug on one side of the cap and the hauling part led to a sheave on the other, evident in the photograph as a 'bulge' protruding above the cap.

Walter's painting shows these topmast stays sagging slightly, and assuming the whip was tensioned as required, this would indicate they were made of wire rather than fibre rope being that much heavier. In view of the lengths required for the topmast backstays, it would be logical to make them of iron wire to minimise any stretch.

With the topmast housed, the peak of the gaff would have to be lowered to clear this stay or trimmed over to one side with the vangs. On the other hand, with the sail set and the vessel hard on the wind as shown in the painting, the gaffs are peaked up so that the ends are well above the height of the lowermast caps. This means a fixed length peak span was not used, the angle adjusted as required with a single part 'gaff topping lift', leading to the double sheaved upper block along with the head outhaul (see Figures 7:22 and 7:26). Like the *Iris* the head of the sail was supported by hoops rigged on the gaff and brailed into the mast.

Although the painting is vague as regards the details at the lower end of the gaff, jaws were fitted in the normal way, made of wood or possibly iron. The log book makes this clear, the entry in the remarks column for 0800hrs on 31 July 1845 reading, 'The jaws of the 2nd spencer gaff carried away, took in the sail'. The reason why a mast band and gooseneck fitting was not used was that the seaman still needed the facility of lowering the gaff for repairs, or indeed, had the original idea of lowering the mast been carried through, the gaff and sail would have had to be got down first. As the illustration shows the sail furled snug into the masts, the jaws would have been made in such a way as not to obstruct the hoops sliding down the full length of the spar.

Confronted with a fresh headwind it was common practice on these steamers to brace the yards as sharp as possible even when no square sail was set. The absence of crosstrees and hence the futtock shrouds beneath allowed the main yard on *The Great Britain* to be braced closer to the fore and aft line than usual. This angle could be reduced still more by lowering the weather yard arm which moved the point of contact with the mainstay downward, and, at the same time further ahead of the mast permitted the yard to come round a few more degrees. Walter's painting of her in heavy weather shows this technique very well; the topsail yard is similarly canted, but in this case it was to allow the lee yard arm to rise and contact the topmast backstays slightly further up, where the rigging was 'narrower'. Unlike the *Great Western*, where the square sail was hoisted up to the fore yard only when required, the main yard

of *The Great Britain* has the sail bent on permanently, probably because it is so much larger – double the size, at approximately 3,000sq ft.

Sail Handling

To set the spencers on *The Great Britain*, the first job would be to get the gaff over to leeward, then topped up and steadied in position with the vangs. If closehauled, as in the illustration just referred to, both movable backstays would be set up. This was possible as the beam on deck in proportion to the height of the mast would provide sufficient spread to clear both the gaff and sail, and this practice is quite clearly shown in the painting. Except in the case of the foresail, the single part sheet would be taken to the capstan just aft of the 5th mast, either directly, or via a messenger. When all was ready, any remaining sail ties would be removed, head inhaul and brails cast off and the head outhaul manned. Provided a change of heading did not cause any problems, it would assist this operation if the vessel was temporarily 'luffed'. After the outhaul had been sweated up and belayed the sheet would be hardened in with the capstan, final adjustments then given to the gaff, and if necessary the brails overhauled as any weight in them would curl the leech. Compared with a similar sized hoisting gaffsail and boom, there was much less work, as basically the sail was already aloft. Furthermore, there could be overlap of the next mast aft in the same way as the genoa on the modern yacht has the clew coming aft of the mast, the increased sail area giving greater efficiency when off the wind.

Taking the sail in, if short handed, would probably be a two-part operation. First wind would be spilled from the sail if possible, the outhaul let go and with little effort on the inhaul, the head, assisted by gravity, should come down the gaff to stow with the peak close in to the mast. At the same time the upper brails can be taken in as much as the part furled sail will allow. In just a few seconds the upper portion of the sail above the line from throat to clew is taken out of action. The second stage requires the sheet to be eased, or in light winds just let go and all the slack taken in on the brails, bringing the rest of the sail snug into the mast. The peak of the gaff can now be dropped if needed to clear the housed topmast stay and trimmed amidships or kept to one side with the vangs. [Throughout the operation the sail is under control and I can vouch for its efficiency, having a standing gaff and loose-footed brailing mainsail on my ketch *Crystal Stream*. (PA)]

There are disadvantages with this type of sail, as the gaff and sail cannot be easily lowered, nor can it be reefed in the usual way, but only as far as the crew could reach upwards from the deck to tie the points. It is evident in the painting of *The Great Britain* (see Figure 7:24) and from remarks in the log book that the wind was force 9 from the northwest and both foresail and 1st spencer are set full. Seamen of the day, well used to reefing sails and spars in such weather, must have viewed with suspicion such carrying on, for the system did not even allow a smaller sail to be set in place. The only mention of reefing in the log book refers to the square sails. However in light winds it does make reference to lacing a bonnet to the foot of the forestaysail.

Sail Assist – Then and Now

In terms of 'sail assist', the efficiency of the rig designed and built for *The Great Britain* has only recently been improved upon, and then only because modern technology has made the handling of large fabric sails on the specialised cruise liners, like the *Wind Star* (see Chapter 11, Figure 11:23), for example, so much easier. In her case no extra personnel need be carried above the normal complement. Not a line has to be hauled on or a gasket tied, the whole operation controlled by computer and the actual sail handling by hydraulically powered furling system. Judged by overall performance, or the forward thrust developed by a unit area of canvas, any improvements on Brunel's rig are probably only marginal. It can be argued that the original rig was designed only for the North Atlantic, as indeed it was, and for worldwide use, particularly the Australian run, more square sail was needed. However, apart from these qualifications the basic concept was outstanding in its simplicity, economy on manpower, and fitness for purpose, the only setbacks due to the materials available.

Ten years after *The Great Britain* was built, the reduction in sail area on certain classes of merchant steamship is evident from the Sail Drafts drawn up in 1854 by J Scott Russell (see Figure 7:27). As always, much depended on the operational requirements. The Clyde paddle steamer *Roven* (top) working in relatively sheltered waters or short routes has a minimal rig of two masts, setting only fore and aft canvas. Below is the North Sea trader *Baron-Osy*, a fairly large vessel, being 208ft on the waterline, virtually the same as the *Great Western*, but in comparison with her she has a much reduced rig: three masts with brailing gaffsails, no topsails and two headsails. All four vessels would have been operated under continuous steam, and service speeds of 12 knots were not uncommon at the time, so the three basic criteria for a sail assist rig in such cases would be – efficient with the apparent wind on or forward of the beam, of minimum windage, and the sail plan having a low centre of effort to reduce heel. As a sea going vessel the gaffsails on the *Baron-Osy* are rigged with vangs and booms for better control of the head and foot of the sail. The next illustration below is the *Malakhoff* designed for work in the Irish Sea, a significant portion of the total sail area made up from the square sails on the foremast, including a fore course, but she would still be classed as a schooner not having the 'tops' of a fully square-rigged mast. Except for the position of the mainmast, the rig of the *Pacific* (next below) is very similar, although, unusually, neither is shown with a headsail set from the end of the bowsprit, so the reason for having a spar of this length, or in the case of the

Pacific, having one at all, is not clear. Perhaps, if need be, the jib could be shifted further forward to obtain a better sail balance. It would also appear from the somewhat abbreviated rigging detail that the *Malakhoff* had peak halyards, suggesting the gaff and sail could be lowered, while the single part span in the same position on the *Pacific* would indicate that like *The Great Britain*, the gaffs were carried permanently aloft.

Alternative Rigs

Lug rig combines elements of both fore and aft and square sail and thus would appear ideal for the small to medium sized paddle steamers as it satisfies all the following requirements for 'sail assist':

1) providing sufficient sail area to get the vessel to its destination in the event of mechanical breakdown,
2) will perform efficiently when the apparent wind is forward of the beam,
3) the rig has minimum windage when the sails are not in use,
4) comparatively low weight aloft,
5) centre of effort of the sail plan can be kept low to reduce heel.

Despite these attributes it does not seem to have been popular, even on coastal steamers. The *Enterprize* which left Falmouth in 1825 bound for India carried a three-masted lug rig on departure but arrived at Cape Town with square sails on her fore and main having been converted on passage (see figures 7:29 and 7:30). Her fuel capacity and the length of voyage required more than 'sail assist', for whenever possible she stopped her engines to conserve fuel and continued as a pure sailing ship, the shortcomings of the lug rig in this respect evident soon after leaving the Channel.

At first glance a comparison of the two drawings of the *Enterprize*, irrespective of the difference in rig, gives the impression that they are not the same vessel. For example, the shape of the paddle box, position of the funnel and built up topsides forward complete with gun ports, all important details, are not consistent.

However, so many of the other features are identical that there can be no doubt that both illustrations are of the *Enterprize*. The mast positions are the same with the mizzen stepped well aft, the bumpkin used with the lugsail still retained; in both cases the main topmasts are rigged abaft the lowermast and neither vessel has external chain plates, which at this period was uncommon; and the shrouds have little fore and aft spread suggesting the same fittings were used for the standing rigging after conversion. Moreover, the hull retains the light coloured stripe extending the full length of the vessel, quarter windows, long poop with wooden rail, and the jib boom, bowsprit and head gear appear virtually identical; and overall, they look about the same size.

Figure 7:27 *Sail drafts of four paddle steamers designed by J Scott Russell dated 1854. Top to bottom: Roven 178ft LWL, day tripper and passenger paddle steamer on the Clyde;* Baron-Osy *208ft LWL, North Sea trader, passenger steamer;* Malakhoff *183ft LWL, Irish Sea trader, passenger steamer; and* Pacific *245ft LWL, foreign going steamer. (Basil Greenhill Collection)*

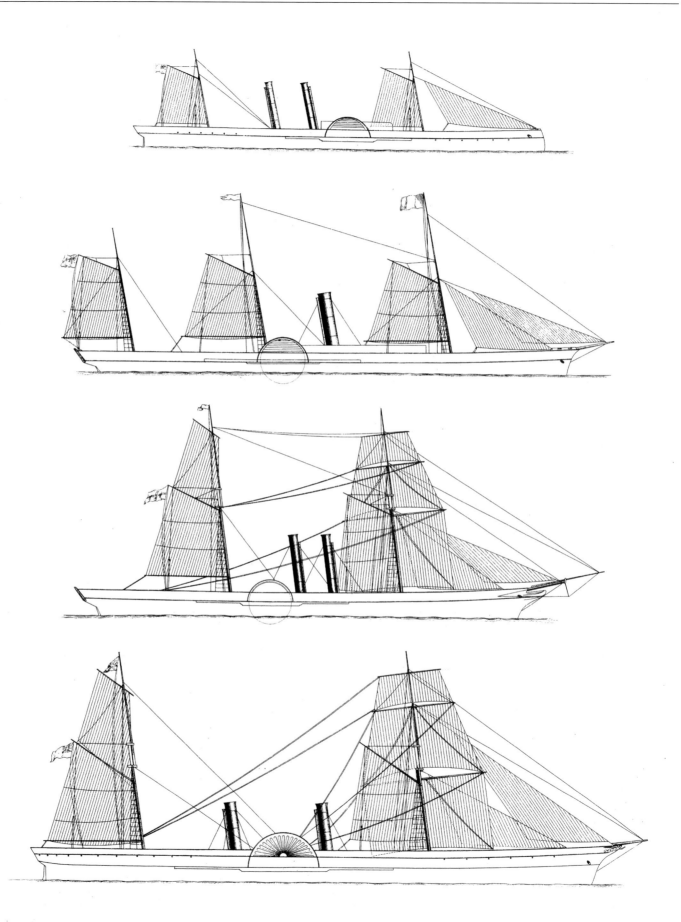

Figure 7:28 *Painting of the American coastal screw steamer* Hartford *of about 300 tons leaving New York on 20 February 1849 for the Californian gold rush, taking almost a year to reach San Francisco, a truly epic voyage. It shows a sail plan with three masts similar in many ways to the* Great Western. *The gaffsails are brailed into the luff, not up to the throat, the head supported by hoops; but as depicted, the peak halyard and associated blocks would prevent the required amount of travel. However, allowing for other mistakes by the artist, not only in rigging detail but in such fundamentals as the position of the mainmast (another illustration of the* Hartford *showed it stepped much closer to the foremast and the sail clear of the funnel), such evidence must be treated with caution. It is highly likely the gaffsails could be lowered being rigged with mast hoops and throat halyards.* (Museum of the City of New York)

Figure 7:29 *The* Enterprize *as she arrived at Calcutta. (From G A Prinsep,* An Account of Steam Vessels and Proceedings Connected with Steam Navigation in British India *(Calcutta, 1830))*

Figure 7:30 *The Enterprize of 1824 depicted in a painting in the Science Museum under lug rig. (Science Museum, London)*

It is interesting to note that ten years before the first Atlantic steamships, the standing gaff with a boomless sail brailing up to the throat was already common practice, and the linked rod standing rigging in way of the funnel, mentioned in connection with the *Great Western*, is clearly shown on the original lug-rigged main of the *Enterprize*, and subsequent to her conversion, used as funnel stays and the twin forward leading main stays. The *Enterprize* was certainly ahead of her time in many respects, and exhibits all the basic features of a rig designed for a power-driven vessel making continuous or frequent use of the engine as she would have done when employed on the Indian coast; that is, disregarding the square topsail on the mainmast which would have been of little practical use so close to the funnel, a fore and aft schooner with any square sails carried on the foremast only. It can also be seen that strictly she was not a 'barque' being fitted with twin crosstrees instead of tops on both the fore and main masts.

1 Capt Claxton RN, *A Description of the Great Britain Steamship* (Bristol, 1845) pp. 5, 6

2 J Fincham, *A History of Naval Architecture* (London, 1979 reprint of first edition 1851) p. 407

3 Patent no 6332, 'Rigging of Ships and other Vessels' by Joseph Lidwell Heathorn

4 Patent no 7261, 1836, 'Construction and Manufacture of Standing Rigging, Stays and Chains for Ships and Vessels' by Andrew Smith

5 Patent no 8009, 'Wire Ropes'

6 Patent no 8594, 'Manufacture of Wire Ropes'

7 Patent no 9656, 'Wire Ropes'

8 H A Underhill, *Masting and Rigging, the Clipper Ship and Ocean Carrier* (Glasgow, 1965) p. 265

9 Patent no 9811, 1843, 'Securing Standing Rigging, Chains and other Tackle'

10 Donald Canney, *The Old Steam Navy*, vol 1 (Annapolis, Maryland, 1990) p. 15

11 Daphne D C Pochin Mould, *Captain Roberts of the* Sirius (Cork, 1988) p. 126

12 Capt Claxton RN, *A Description of the Great Britain Steamship* (Bristol, 1845) p. 6

13 Captain F Liardet, *Professional Recollections on Seamanship, Discipline etc.* (London, 1849) p. 211

CHAPTER 8

Handling Sail and Steam – Passage Making and Navigation

How did the seaman combine sail and steam to best advantage? The answer lies in the fundamental requirements of these early transatlantic vessels, that is, to maintain speed and follow the course of shortest safe distance between ports. To achieve the objectives, continuous paddle or screw propulsion would be augmented whenever possible by the sails, but the heading was not changed to accommodate wind propulsion, except in particularly adverse weather or on the occasions when a small deviation, and hence extra miles, was more than compensated for by increased speed.

Most of the evidence has been obtained from the log books, those from the *Great Western* being particularly useful as the engineer's log, at least on the outward passage, is available. Additional and corroborative information has been obtained from journals, letters, reports, and contemporary publications.[1]

It should be borne in mind when referring to the following vector (Figures 8:2–8:6) showing ship's course and speed, true and apparent wind that they only represent an approximation. The campass heading given in the log book is to the nearest point (11.25 degrees), and both the wind's strength and direction were an estimation based on the sea state and a reference to the compass card, which, being far from steady in heavy weather, an error of one point was possible. (The compass heading and wind direction taken from the logbook are, for this exercise, assumed to be true.) When measuring wind strength, for example, force 5 is between 17 and 21 knots and force 6 between 22 and 27 knots. Therefore an error of judgement between these two could either be 17 knots at the least or 27 knots at the most. A mean windspeed has been used for each graduation on the Beaufort scale. Ship's speed and direction is indicated by the vector line with a single arrow, true wind speed by the double arrow symbol, and apparent wind by the triple.

Light Winds

Broadly speaking, if the wind was light and variable and the sea slight no sail was set, and the engines were, if the occasion demanded, at full power. However, as the economic use of coal was also a consideration, the expansion valve was sometimes set, not at 0, but at 2, 3 or 4 as the small loss of speed, when related to improved fuel consumption, would be acceptable in the circumstances. Another consideration was the number of boilers in operation, for in the same conditions of the wind and sea, the cam setting could be 0 when all four were producing steam, on the 3rd grade if three were working and on 7th when only two were fired up.

Experiments were carried out on the *Great Western* prior to her maiden voyage and it was established by calculations using data from the indicated card:[2]

> . . . that by means of the expansion valve, a great saving of fuel may be effected, with little loss of speed – that with half steam, two-thirds of the power may be obtained at all times.

Also contained in the Report (page 6) were the company's instructions to Captain Hoskins that:

> . . . he should endeavour to accomplish his voyage more with an eye to a discreet use of fuel, than to the constant attainment of maximum speed, through extreme consumption.

Headwinds

Should the breeze now freshen from ahead and the windage of the rig begin to slow the vessel, topmasts would be housed, the upper yards sent down, and those remaining braced sharp up: cam setting to 0.

In his book *The Economy of the Marine Steam Engine* Lieut Gordon RN made approximate calculations of the total retarding effect of the wind on a paddle steamer of 1,200 tons rigged as a brig. Steaming at 10 knots in a flat calm it would amount to 14.3hp. If the wind were as he put it 'passing the vessel at 20 knots per hour' (ship's speed not specified) it will have risen to 47.7hp. With the relative velocity further increased to 40 knots then the resistance in terms of horsepower was reckoned to be 114.4hp (ship's speed 6 knots). He goes on, 'it may be assumed, that striking the topmasts and yards would not reduce the above resistance by more then one-sixth'. Or 'that when the wind has a relative velocity of 40 knots per hour, it requires about one-third of the mean effective pressure on the piston to overcome its resistance to the hull and spars'.[3]

The above calculations assume there is no sea running and it was thought that the chief resistance to a steam vessel in adverse conditions was actually caused by the opposition of the waves.

As the *Great Western* started her voyage the next job after catting the anchors was, according to the log book, to 'strike the three after topmasts and gaffs, and fore top gallant mast; down top gallant yard', the wind being right ahead and fresh to gale force with a high short northwest swell. Despite these conditions she managed to maintain 9 knots as per common log, engine revolutions 690rph or 11.5rpm. Her 'effective' diameter of paddle wheel was 26ft 10in, or 84ft 4in circumference, so 690rph gives the distance by paddle revolution as 9.57nm (see Figure 8:1). Therefore 'slip' was only 6 per cent, which is remarkable for her deep-loaded state, so good in fact that some of the data would appear to be incorrect.

This brings into question her draught on departure, for it is both relevant to seaworthiness and paddle wheel immersion which in turn has a direct bearing on the performance and handling, yet the information for one reason or another is not contained in the log book, at least not in the published form by

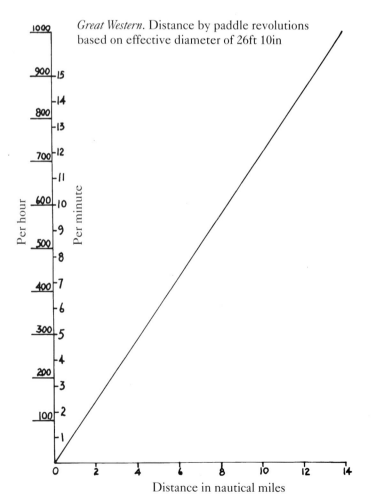

Great Western. Distance by paddle revolutions based on effective diameter of 26ft 10in

Per hour

Per minute

Distance in nautical miles

Figure 8:1 *(Peter Allington)*

Claxton. It was furthermore omitted on arrival at New York, and also, though not surprisingly, when she started her return crossing; the log book states on that occasion, 7 May 1838, 'vessel steering badly, in consequence of her being so much by the head'.

The painting of the *Great Western* off Portishead at the start of the voyage (Fig 7:20) shows her with a moderate draught but in fact she was probably drawing over 17ft aft with the extra fuel on board, which compared to a scale drawing of her hull lines would have submerged far more of the rudder, indicating a certain amount of artistic licence.

Looking at her actual performance, related to other information contained in the log book, reveals certain anomalies: at 1225hrs on the day of departure her position was one mile north of the island of Flat Holm at the top end of the Bristol Channel: the next definite location was at 2200hrs, when 'the lights of Lundy Island bore NNE 1½ miles'. Assuming these bearings were 'true', as the compass error is not given, the distance between them is about 62nm, which in the time interval of 9hs and 35mins would require an average speed over the ground of 6.5 knots. This is at odds with her hourly rate as per common log which gave her speed through the water as between 8 and 9 knots despite a strong headwind and nasty sea, which caused the following entry to be written up in the remarks column: 'Ship plunging heavy, and shipping water over the topgallant forecastle'. Any tidal effect, which is considerable in the Bristol Channel, would in 9hrs 35mins have largely cancelled out any gains and losses in terms of assistance, the maximum residual tidal effect plus or minus 6 miles, although the sea would be much worse on the ebb. This speed of 8 or 9 knots would, in the ircumstances, have been plausible if the fore and aft canvas had been set: the wind direction related to her course after rounding Flat Holm was broad enough on the bow to allow this, but the log book makes no mention of it; the crew were busily employed throughout getting the anchors and boats on board and stowing or lashing down loose gear on deck.

During her maiden voyage the *Great Western* once more experienced strong headwinds but this time she was in mid-Atlantic, the log book stating on 17 April 'vessel pitching and lurching deep, but very easy' into a short high sea. No sail was set, and hourly paddle revolutions were between 600rph and 800rph or an average of 11.7rpm, expansion valve set at 0. Speed by log was only 6.5 knots, slip now considerable at 34 per cent, and fuel consumption for the day was 32 tons.

It is probable that as the *Great Western* was steaming into a 'short high sea', the engines were much slowed at times or even forced temporarily to a standstill, as Robert Murray explains when referring to the fitting of flywheels on sea going paddlers. This effect would be more pronounced at the start of the voyage when the paddle floats were over 3ft deeper than optimum immersion:[4]

But in the case of a vessel at sea, the fly wheel is inadmissible for the following reason. Let us suppose a steamer to be leaving harbour with her wheels moderately immersed, and making perhaps 20 revolutions per minute. So as long as she is in smooth water the engines revolve with perfect regularity, but the first plunge she takes in the open roadstead immerses her wheels for some seconds nearly to the axis, and suddenly throws such additional load upon the engine that its speed is either greatly reduced or altogether brought up, until the vessel recovers herself and frees the wheels. Now, had a heavy fly wheel been attached, the consequences would have been that the engine must have revolved against this tenfold resistance and would have broken down.

Supposing the headwind were now severe gale to storm force, the early steamships would be almost stopped in the water, her wheels still rotating slowly, but not providing the propulsion required to maintain steerage way. At this point, or even before as the adverse conditions worsened, she was forced to change her heading so as to put the wind and sea on the bow sufficient to allow her storm canvas to be set.

This situation occurred on the maiden crossing of the *Sirius* when, after three days of steaming directly into a very heavy sea with no sail set, on 7 April her speed down to 3.4 knots and revolutions only 8 per minute, the log book states, 'the close reefed sails set'. The abstract does not give the actual heading but the following day her position indicated a more southerly course was taken, the wind being gale force from the westward.[5]

As the paddle wheels lost their forward thrust, the canvas provided a balanced sail area and combined with sufficient speed, rudder control was regained. She could heave to with her sails, or run before the storm under reefed fore topsail, if this was considered a safe option in the circumstances.

Wind on the Bow

If we take another situation in which the wind was broad enough on the bow to allow the fore and aft canvas to be set, in a light breeze all headsails and gaffsails would be in use providing significant forward thrust without too much heel, unless her stability was much reduced nearing the end of a long voyage. The expansion valve cam setting would now be on 1 to 5 with a small saving in fuel.

The vector Figure 8:2 illustrates this situation very well. Cam setting is 4 as the paddle wheels have a light load, slip working out at only 5 per cent.

Closehauled, with a freshening wind, heel would increase and with the leeward paddle wheel more deeply immersed, the rudder would probably be hard over at times, requiring sail taken in aft, thus compensating for the excessive weather helm caused by unequal paddle wheel thrust.

This situation is depicted in Figure 8:3. On 18 April the true wind was 5 points on the bow, force 5, paddle revolutions 840

Great Western: April 1838 Bristol to New York

Date: 9th   *Co:* W ∞ N½N   *Rate:* 11 knots   *Revs per hr:* 834
Distance by paddle wheel: 11.56   *Slip:* +5%   *Cam setting:* 4
No. of boilers in use: 4   *Fuel consumption this day:* 36 tons
Sea state: Slight
Sails set: 2 jibs, foresail, topsail, 3 spencers

	Direction	Force	Knots	Angle on bow
True wind:	SW	4	14	61°
Apparent wind:			21	35°

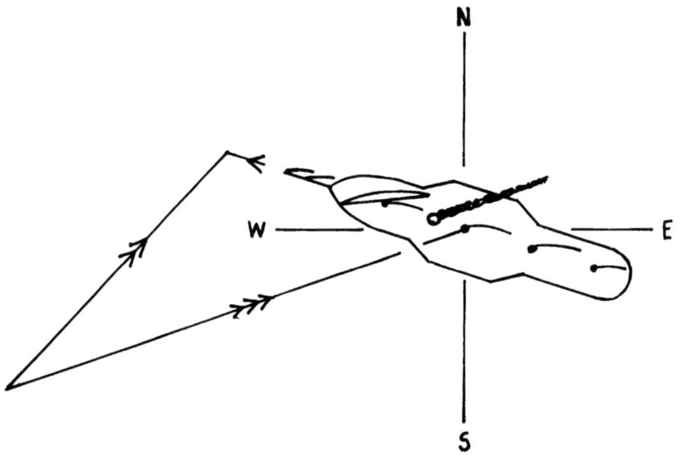

Figure 8:2 *After departure from Bristol, the* Great Western *making good speed despite being deep loaded and the paddle wheels therefore too much immersed. Good stability contributed to the considerable assistance from the sails which, even with a true wind nearly 6 points on the bow, would have been trimmed 'closehauled', the apparent wind only 35 degrees on the bow due to the ship's speed. (Peter Allington)*

per hour, cam setting 0, speed only 7.5 knots, slip 35 per cent. Due to a heavy head sea and swell only the reefed fore spencer (gaff foresail) has been set. A combination of the increased effect of windage and reduced forward drive of the sails required full steam, the cam setting at 0.

Later that day conditions moderated and the wind shifted another point broader on the bow, the reef in the fore spencer was shaken out and the forestaysail set, but no other canvas was used, due in all probability to the angle of heel and consequently unequal paddle thrust. Engine revolutions increased; at one stage the wheels were turning at 960 per hour, ship's speed had gone up to 11.5 knots with the full power cam setting of 0 maintained throughout. Fuel consumption rose to 39 tons from the previous day when 32 tons had been used, but difficulties in supplying all four boilers with sufficient coal meant that at midnight two fires, one in each of the fore boilers, were let out and cam setting shifted to the 5th grade.

Conditions at dawn on the 19th saw the *Great Western* pitching and lurching into a long high sea, still carrying only forestaysail and fore spencer, wind force 5 to 6 on the port bow. However she was making good speed at 10 knots and despite the cam setting still on the 5th grade, revolutions were relatively high at 840 per hour. Later in the day her rate dropped to 9 knots and the mizzen spencer was set. At 1730hrs the remaining fires in the two forward boilers were let out, and cam setting was shifted to the 7th grade, revolutions dropped

Figure 8:3 *Later in the voyage, the ship being lighter by about 300 tons, paddle wheel immersion would be close to the optimum but with little or no forward thrust from the reefed foresail and heading into a strong wind and heavy sea, progress is much reduced, slip of the wheels at thirty-six per cent. (Peter Allington)*

Great Western: April 1838 Bristol to New York

Date: 18th   *Co:* W ∞ N   *Rate:* 7.5 knots   *Revs per hr:* 840
Distance by paddle wheel: 11.65   *Slip:* +36%   *Cam setting:* 0
No. of boilers in use: 4   *Fuel consumption this day:* 39 tons
Sea state: Heavy head sea and swell
Sails set: Reefed foresail

	Direction	Force	Knots	Angle on bow
True wind:	NNW	5	19	56°
Apparent wind:			24	41°

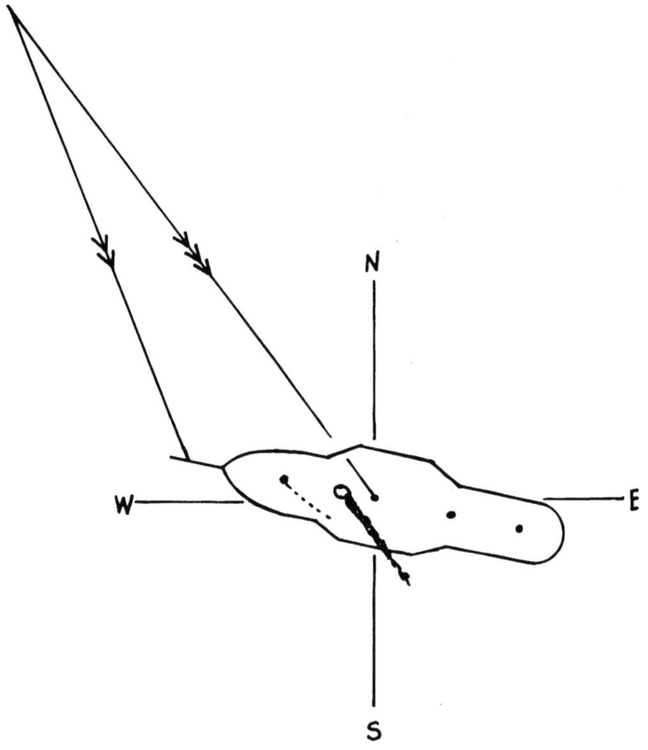

the fact, that the first lot of coal, which was the middle quality used, had greatly deteriorated in quality.

Not all the coal came from one source and it had often been left lying around outside in the wind and rain prior to being shipped on board. The report goes into much detail on the subject and ends, 'the rest of the coal came in as it arrived in the colliers, and no doubt a great deal of trash [steamingly speaking] was occasionally brought to the fires'.

It is also likely a great deal of steam was wasted as the wheels raced at one moment and came to a virtual halt as she rolled heavily to leeward, for by this stage of the voyage she was becoming 'tender'.

Next day, 20 April, with only two boilers still at work and cam setting maintained on the 7th grade, revolutions had reduced at one time to 600, ship's speed 7 knots, but consumption had also dropped considerably to 26 tons compared with the two previous days when, on each occasion, 39 tons were consumed. Some assistance was provided by two spencers, forestaysail and, for a short period, the fore topsail, but due to her reduced stability as she approached the coast of North America, almost at the end of the voyage, she must have heeled over considerably under this amount of canvas, wind force 6 at times fine on the bow.

As stated at the beginning of the chapter, there were occasions when it was advantageous to make a small alteration away from the optimum heading so as to keep the sails full, the true wind having shifted more ahead. For example, on *22 April 1838* the *Great Western* was only 24 hours from New York well under the lee of the land, and the sea was described as 'smooth, scarcely any motion'. The day opens with her course west by north, wind north-northwest force 6, 5 points on the starboard bow, ship's speed is given as 8.5 knots with the expansion valve set on the 9th grade, but steam production was well down. By 0800hrs 'kindled fires in after boilers, by reason that the coal in fore part of ship was becoming low'. In other words the sails were doing most of the work, and in the circumstances it would pay to keep them drawing. At 0300hrs the wind had backed a point to northwest by north, which if the course had been maintained would put the true wind 4 points on the bow. As the foretopsail was set at the time the heading was altered from west by north to west, keeping the wind 5 points on the bow. By 0600hrs it had backed another point to northwest so the ship's course was altered again by the same amount to west by south, the heading now 2 points or 22.5 degrees away from the desired course. Steam pressure, which had been low during the early hours, was increased with the after boilers in operation, so by 0900hrs the wind now further backed to west-northwest and reduced to force 4, all sail was taken in and the original heading of west by north resumed under power alone. By noon the wind had continued to shift and was now southwest, 5 points on the port bow, so once again sail was set, but the engines were turning over faster at 840rph compared with 780rph earlier in the day, cam setting 7 and ship's speed risen to 10 knots.

to 720 per hour and speed 8 knots. Despite the cam setting being only on 5 or 7 and not all the boilers working at full capacity, 39 tons of coal had been used.

These figures, which were the highest for the entire voyage when related to steam production, appear inconsistent with expected performance; for despite difficulties in getting coal to the furnaces the real cause was, as the log book states, 'during last night difficulty in maintaining steam; coal bad, viz, small and of little strength, making much clinker'.

This is the reason given in Claxton's report to the First Lord of the Admiralty where reference is made on page 3:

It will be seen that at times there is a vast disproportion in the consumption, on some days 39 tons, and on others even as little as 21 are in the return. The log gives fair reasons for the differences on most occasions, but not on all, as much of the larger expenditure may be attributed to

Wind on the Beam

A further change in direction of the wind to a more advantageous bearing, that is, on or just abaft the beam, provided it was not too strong, allowed all sail to be set including the square sails (see Figure 8:4). The angle of heel will be significant, but 'rig horsepower' being at its maximum, paddle wheel thrust can now be reduced with less tendency for the leeward one, although deeply immersed at times, to effect the steering. Cam settings now 7 to 9, with maximum advantage in fuel saving. In fact in these circumstances the paddle wheels were 'in the way', so to speak, and only enough steam was required to keep them

Great Western: April 1838 Bristol to New York

Date: 11th   *Co:* WNW   *Rate:* 10.5 knots   *Revs per hr:* 735
Distance by paddle wheel: 10.19   *Slip:* –3%   *Cam setting:* 7
No. of boilers in use: 4   *Fuel consumption this day:* 30 tons
Sea state: Long high swell from NW
Sails set: 2 jibs, topsail, topgallant, 3 spencers

	Direction	Force	Knots	Angle on bow
True wind:	NNE	4	14	90°
Apparent wind:			17.5	54°

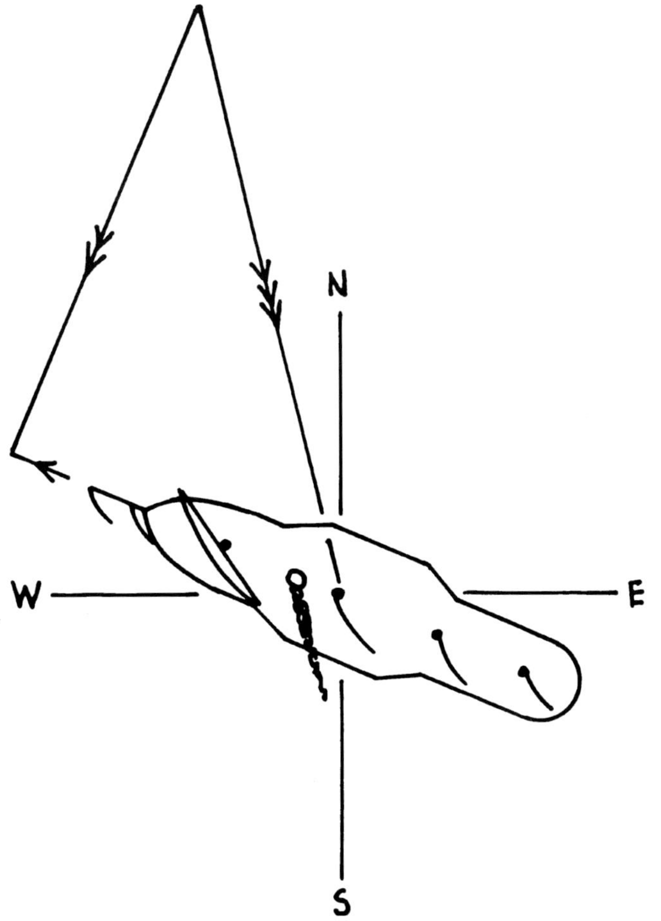

revolving fast enough relative to the ship's speed so as not to impede her progress. In this instance the speed by log was 10.5 knots and distance by paddle wheel only 10.19nm. Towards the end of the voyage, her much reduced draught and hence paddle wheel immersion as well as loss of stability would dictate the sails she could set.

Wind on the Quarter

Should the wind draw farther aft on the quarter, heel would be reduced, and providing the wind was not too light or too strong, every stitch of canvas would be set to advantage (see Figure 8:5). In these circumstances, if the breeze was fresh the vessel would attain near maximum rate under sail despite the true wind strength being reduced to some extent by her speed. A certain amount of rolling would be expected, but paddle thrust would be no more than required to keep pace and probable cam setting 7 to 9. Figure 8:6 shows the same situation but the wind is a lighter force 4 and from nearly right aft.

When homeward bound on 18 May 1838 the *Great Western* maintained a steady 10.5 knots for much of the day, her course was east with a strong breeze of force 6 from the northwest. Every available sail was set including the three square sails on the foremast. Engine revolutions are given as 13 per minute which gives a distance by paddle wheel of 10.82nm per hour (slip 3 per cent). Only two boilers out of four were working so cam setting was on 3. Fuel consumption for the day was only 20 tons and she covered 240 miles, or 1 ton for every 12 miles, despite stopping the engines one hour for repairs.

Wind from Aft

A wind from right aft will have little heeling effect although rolling will be heavier. The effective sail area will be reduced as those set in the fore part of the vessel tend to be blanketed by those aft. It would then be an advantage to carry all possible sail on the foremast and these would be her square sails and stunsails. The true wind strength will be reduced directly as the ship's speed and therefore must be 12 knots or more (force 4) to be of any use; and, to ensure a clean wind through to the sails on the foremast, some canvas would be taken in aft. The engines will be required to deliver more power unless the breeze is strong and cam settings vary from 0 to 5. If the sea becomes rough or the swell heavy the steering will become a problem, due principally to the alternate immersion of the wheels.

Thomas Tredgold calculated the sail area needed to produce 1hp, the vessel having the wind from right aft:[6]

> The average speed in still water, beyond which it does not seem desirable to go, is ten feet per second, that is, seven common miles or six nautical miles per hour; and at this velocity, when the wind is as powerful as is prudent to

Figure 8:4 *Wind direction and strength about ideal and if it were not for the long high swell fine on the bow, speed would probably have been even greater. (Peter Allington)*

Figure 8:5 *In this case the ship's speed has reduced the apparent wind slightly which is still fresh and on the beam. The sails would steady the motion and provide most of the forward thrust. (Peter Allington)*

Great Western: April 1838 Bristol to New York

Date: 15th   *Co:* WNW   *Rate:* 11 knots   *Revs per hr:* 870
Distance by paddle wheel: 12.06   *Slip:* +9%   *Cam setting:* 9
No. of boilers in use: 4   *Fuel consumption this day:* 27 tons
Sea state: Moderate
Sails set: Inner jib, foresail, foretopsail, 3 spencers

	Direction	Force	Knots	Angle on bow
True wind:	S	6	25	113°
Apparent wind:			23	87°

Great Western: April 1838 Bristol to New York

Date: 12th   *Co:* WNW   *Rate:* 10.5 knots   *Revs per hr:* 780
Distance by paddle wheel: 10.81   *Slip:* +3%   *Cam setting:* 5
No. of boilers in use: 4   *Fuel consumption this day:* 29 tons
Sea state: Swell long and high from NW
Sails set: 2 jibs, foresail, topsail, topgallant, 3 spencers

	Direction	Force	Knots	Angle on bow
True wind:	E × S	4	14	169°
Apparent wind:			4	142°

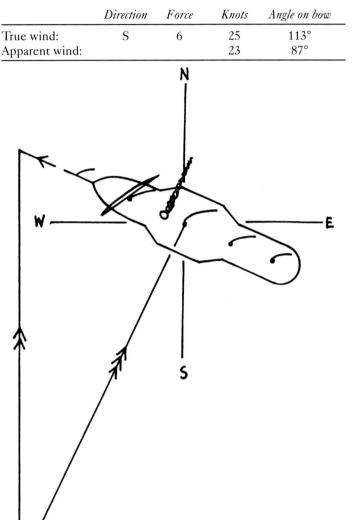

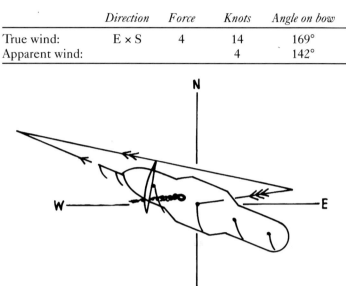

Figure 8:6 *Although all possible sail has been set with the ship's speed under power at 10.5 knots, apparent wind is only 4 knots from aft, hence, despite a great area of canvas, 'rig horsepower' is minimal. (Peter Allington)*

carry all the canvas, 'the direct effect will be only one horsepower for each thirty-two yards superficial.' [Using the conversion factor of one running yard, considered as 3ft by 2ft; 32yds would equal 192sq ft.]

From the formulae that accompanied the text a true wind speed of 18 knots would be considered 'as powerful as is prudent to carry all the canvas'. Therefore the apparent wind from right aft with the ship making 6 knots would only be 12 knots.

Assuming that close on 200sq ft of canvas would generate 1hp in these circumstances 24 knots of apparent wind would provide the equivalent of 4hp, or about 20hp per 1,000sq ft. (Tredgold used a definition of 1hp as 550lb raised 1ft per second.)

On her return to Bristol on 19 May, the *Great Western*'s course was east, the wind westerly force 3 to 5, that is, from right astern. Compared with the previous day, ship's speed was still 10.5 knots but engine revolutions had risen to 15 (12.48nm by revolution) so more power was being used. In fact daily consumption had risen to 24 tons but no stops had been needed so the miles covered increased to 252. Three boilers were working and cam setting was 7, a ton of coal being used for every 10.5 miles.

Comparisons can be made with 14 May when the winds were only light force 2 but out of the east, that is, right ahead, speed maintained at between 10 and 11 knots, no sail set, and consumption much higher at 33 tons per day.

Throughout the voyage difficulties were experienced at some time or other in getting the coal to the boilers and this task was given top priority, for the maintenance of steam pressure was considered in nearly all circumstances more important than setting or trimming the sails. Referring back to 19 April, all hands were involved: at 0430hrs the engineer's log states, 'engines almost stopped for want of coal being brought to

Figure 8:7 *This photograph, although taken probably in the early twentieth century, gives a good impression of the conditions in which the Great Western's firemen were obliged to work in a violently moving vessel. (Basil Greenhill Collection)*

furnaces to maintain steam; fore trysail and staysail set'. Engine revolutions had dropped to less than 4 per minute. Wind at the time was southwest force 5 to 6 with a heavy westerly swell right on the nose, ship's course west by north. The deck log remarks, 'All hands busily employed trimming coals from the peaks'. The vessel had just about come to a standstill and obviously lost steerage way for the entry of 0500hrs, 'ship not laying her course, kept her off one point northerly', thus putting the wind 6 points on the bow. However, no other sails were set to take advantage, or to balance up the two set in the forepart of the vessel, the forestaysail and fore spencer (fore trysail in the engineer's log). The most likely reason is simply that no hands could be spared. The remarks in the deck log that '. . . watch went below; much murmuring amongst the seamen respecting

coal trimming' must have been an understatement as they had already been hard at it for the previous 2 days. This entry is echoed in the engineer's log which ends the day with, 'During the night, much dissatisfaction prevailing amongst the stokers, declaring themselves all but incapable of work from fatigue; trouble to keep them at work'.

Coal consumption for the 18th and 19th, as already mentioned, was 39 tons per day which averages out 32.5cwt per hour or close on 1cwt (112lb) every 2 minutes. This would entail shovelling the coal into a basket or sack, working in semi-darkness, the only light at night a candle, all the while subject to violent motion described in the log book as 'vessel lurching and pitching deep'. As there was no direct access through the ship, the coal would have to be transferred along the deck.

Figure 8:8 *This late nineteenth-century photograph of the process of coaling the* Ophir, *built in 1891, at Port Said gives some impression of the labour involved in transferring the* Great Western's *coals along the deck from forepeak bunker to stokehold in bad weather. (Leicester Collection)*

Therefore every 2 minutes, night and day, some poor soul, covered in coal dust, was staggering along, tired out and trying to keep his balance on a heaving deck while using two hands to support the heavy sack on his shoulders. For the prime seaman who had joined the vessel to work the sails and maintain the rig, such menial tasks must have been extremely galling; for, if it was not humping coal, it was helping to haul up ashes.

This meant their proper duties were not attended to and with no one to keep an eye on chafe, freshen the nips, re-set up the rigging or do the hundred and one small jobs, damage both minor and serious was bound to occur. The more than usual amount of gear carrying away on the maiden voyage of the *Great Western*, a brand new ship, can be partly attributed to this cause.

The involvement of all hands shifting bunkers must have been commonplace. Lieut Johnston, commander of the paddle steamer *Enterprize*, writes in his journal on 4 September 1825:[7]

Calm and cloudy weather all the hands employed trimming Coals till 11 o'clock Since we have left England the duty to be performed has not admitted of any time being allowed the people for mending their clothes and only part of an afternoon for washing them. It has not been possible to keep the decks clean to point the ropes or do any of these little jobs which are necessary for the good order of the ship or for the preservation of her stores and Rigging for with the exception of one man at the wheel and one or two on the Sails the whole Crew must be employed in supplying Coals to the Engine This duty is fatiguing and very disagreeable The officers who we obliged to superintend are covered with Coal dust and exhausted by the close heat.

Passage Planning and Navigation

Steamers engaged on a voyage from the United Kingdom to New York would try to follow a great circle track across the Atlantic. This arc, passing through two positions on the earth's surface, is, because the earth is practically a sphere, the shortest distance between them, but in the case of a vessel proceeding from the Western Approaches or just north of Ireland such a great circle would pass over Newfoundland, Prince Edward Island, New Brunswick and Maine before it reached New York, as modern air travellers will be well aware.

Among Joshua Field's papers are several press cuttings, one[8] of which described the voyage of the *Sirius*, including extracts from the log book and comparisons with the *Great Western*:

The track of both the vessels across the Atlantic will be shown by the accompanying chart, on which we have also introduced the route which should be adopted to make the shortest passage. It is well known that the shortest distance between two points on the sphere, is the arc of a great circle, but this from the Lands End of England to New York, would pass over Newfoundland and Nova Scotia. As a convenient course, and one which may always be adopted by steam-vessels, we have taken a point about twenty miles South of Sable Island, and drawn the curve which therefore represents the shortest navigable distance between those places.

This distance is not more than 2490 miles and 645 miles further of navigable distance to New York, making 3135 miles for the passage: the distance on the arc from Lands End and New York, being 2976 miles, the excess will be only 159.

This figure of 3,135 miles from Land's End to New York is obviously in error as *Brown's Nautical Almanac* gives 3,049 miles as the total distance between Bristol and New York. Rechecking the calculations using, not Land's End as the starting point, but a position, latitude 50°30′N, 6°W, about 25 miles north-north-west, the distance to the point 20 miles south of Sable Island is 2,199 miles. If the 645 extra miles to New York are added and 150 allowed from Bristol to the position off Land's End, then the total is 2,994 miles. However, much depends on the exact point considered as the start of the passage and where exactly it ends. Furthermore, the gradual alteration in heading required to maintain the exact great circle course is impossible. A ship must necessarily hold a steady course (which means she follows a rhumb line while doing so) until a definite alteration is made.

A rhumb line is a line drawn on a sphere in such a manner that it cuts each meridian of longitude at the same angle and would thus appear as a curve but on a Mercator chart the rhumb line becomes a straight line, still cutting each meridian at the same angle. As such, it represents on the chart the track across the ocean of a vessel pursuing a steady course.

The track which a navigator works out when he wishes to steam along a great circle is therefore a series of rhumb lines joining successive points on the great circle. On a Mercator

Figure 8:9 *Sable Island from 6,000ft. A very dangerous navigational hazard on which many vessels have been lost over the years. (Public Archives of Canada)*

Figure 8:10 *Chart.*
(Hydrographic Office,
Taunton, Somerset)

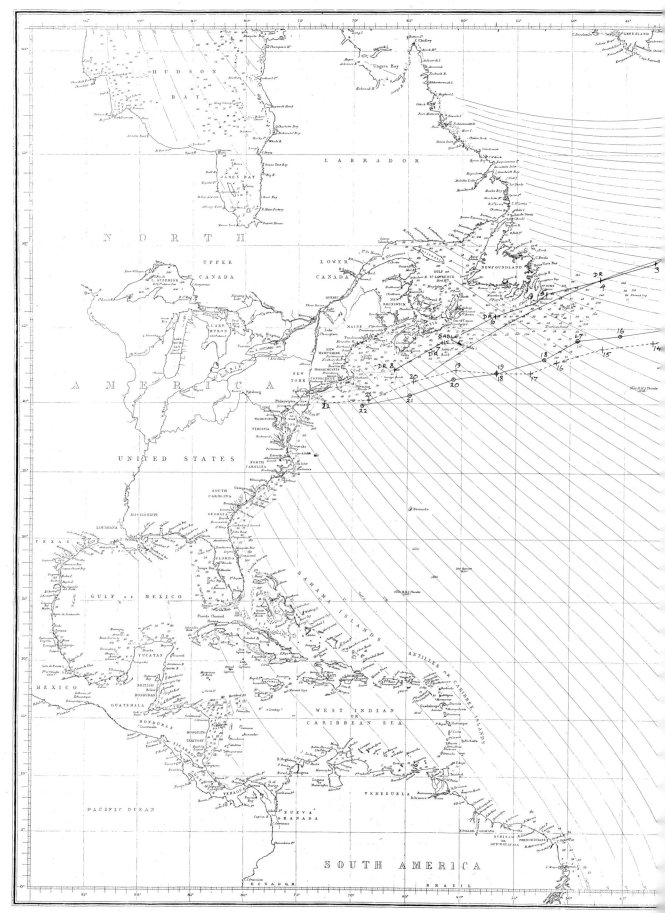

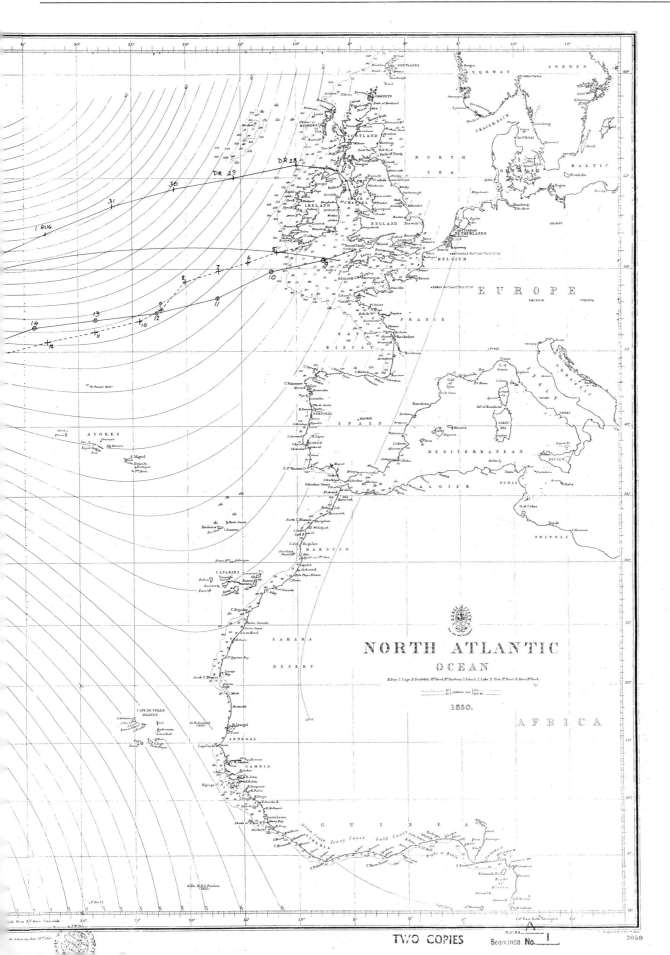

NORTH ATLANTIC
OCEAN

1850.

chart the great circle is a curve and the straight line course appears to be the shortest, but of course it is not in actual distance travelled because the earth is a sphere. Therefore this series of lines joining points on the great circle, if followed, will be of greater distance, and is known as approximate great circle sailing.

It will also be noted that the change of heading can be considerable if there is not a great difference in latitude, but a large one in longitude. (Position off Land's End 50°30′N, 6°W: Sable Island 43°30′N, 60°W.) In the example quoted, the initial true course off Land's End is, N80°W and the final heading south of Sable Island, S59.5°W. In practice a steam vessel proceeding from Bristol to New York would not come south to a point off Land's End but steer towards the Fastnet Rock off the southwest coast of Ireland.

The early transatlantic steamers, like all power-driven vessels, would try to maintain this optimum course of shortest safe navigable distance, but this was not always possible, or, as evident in the first crossings of the *Sirius* and *Great Western*, not even attempted. The route followed and daily positions are shown on the chart of the North Atlantic, Figure 8:10, and it is clear on this occasion that both followed a rhumb line course quite different from the great circle track, as indicated.

On passage, heavy weather, headwinds, poor steering and ocean currents may well force the vessel to the north or south. The practice was, once a new position had been established from observation and the vessel found to be off track, by say 30 or 40 miles, that a new initial great circle course would be calculated as there was no advantage in trying to regain the original. Despite, in this instance, not following a great circle track, it is evident from the abstracts taken from the log of the *Sirius* and printed in newspapers that, in addition to the noon position and true course and distance made good in the previous 24 hours, a bearing and distance was calculated, in this case to Sandy Hook, just south of New York. On good days, such as 13 and 14 April when wind and weather were favourable, there was little difference between the actual true course made good in the 24 hour period (S80°W), and the optimum great circle heading. The bearing on these successive days was Sandy Hook, S81°21′W, and S81°13′W. On a bad day of strong headwinds and heavy seas, such as 9 April, the optimum great circle heading using Sandy Hook as the destination was S79°5′W but the true course made good was S41°W and the distance covered in 24 hours only 94 miles.

The modern navigator has Polar Gnomic charts which makes plotting the great circle track much simpler as they are drawn as a straight line between the chosen positions. The latitude and longitude at various places along this line can then be taken off and plotted on a Mercator chart and a fair curve drawn through them.

In late spring and early summer the dangers from icebergs, particularly when associated with fog over the Grand Banks, off Newfoundland, required the prudent navigator to take this into account when plotting the great circle track. At this time of the year it would probably start or finish, as the case may be, further to the south and east (Sable Island the reference point) thereby increasing the distance between ports.

As the amount of steamer traffic increased after 1850, those bound to and from Europe, each following their shortest route all of which, irrespective of the port of departure converged, over the Grand Banks, were sooner or later bound to have a collision in fog, run into an iceberg or one of the many fishing vessels in the area. On 21 September 1854 the Collins Line steamer *Arctic* with 370 people on board struck, or was struck by the French steamer *Vesta*, at a position 50 miles southeast of Cape Race, each sustaining severe damage. Visibility at the time was poor and both vessels attempted to make St John's, Newfoundland. Tragically, the *Arctic*, foundered a few miles from shore, only forty-six survived, while the *Vesta* managed to struggle on and make port in a sinking condition. Not long after, the *Pacific*, sister ship of the ill-fated *Arctic*, disappeared in the same area, perhaps colliding with an iceberg or other vessel. These were serious and well publicised losses but there were many other incidents of a similar nature, causing concern to both travelling public and the Shipping Authorities. There is a very graphic description of a steamer ramming a fishing schooner in Kipling's *Captain Courageous* (London, 1897) pp. 142–7

A scheme was put forward in 1855 by Lieut Maury, an American naval officer who proposed two sets of routes across the Atlantic between New York, the English Channel and north of Scotland. The shorter one would be used in the winter months and the longer route well south of the Grand Banks in the summer when the danger of fog and icebergs was much greater. There would be two well-defined lanes on each route to separate these fast passenger steamers by a distance of about 60 miles, and it was suggested that other shipping, which included fishing vessels, sailing ships and low-powered steamers, if practical, keep clear. It was not until 1891 that these 'lanes' became formally recognised by all the shipping industry.[9]

The weather overall was also a factor but it is interesting to note the reduction in distance steamed by the *Great Western* between Bristol and New York in successive voyages starting with her first outward voyage in April 3,243 miles; June 3,176 miles; July 3,020 miles; September 3,030 miles; October 3,025 miles. Homeward bound, with a predominantly fair wind and reduced engine revolutions, she seems to have covered a greater distance: May 3,304 miles; July 3,094 miles; September 3,078 miles; October 3,088 miles; and November 3,172 miles. The shortest distance up to the end of 1839, which must have been very close to the optimum great circle track, was in August, when she covered only 3,005 miles, Bristol to New York.[10]

Until recent years with the introduction of the pocket calculator, the navigator used various tables and formulae to work out the initial course and total distances for a particular great circle sailing. Those known simply as ABC tables are used as a quick method to find the initial and final heading.[11] Parts A and B were first published in 1846 when an anonymous mathematician submitted them to the *Nautical Magazine*. Further refinement to improve accuracy has occurred and the revised edition of the tables by Rosser in 1882 is basically as they now appear in their present form. The early Atlantic steam navigators would have had to use the longer method of the haversine formulae to calculate the initial course and, in particular, the distance along the arc; which in fact cannot be done with the ABC tables. Therefore his knowledge of mathematics as applied to navigation must have been higher than most of his contemporaries, at least in the Merchant Shipping industry.

Also shown on the Atlantic chart (Figure 8:10) is the more northerly route taken by *The Great Britain* on her maiden voyage in 1845. Although Captain Hoskins reported it to have been without any incidents, the track after closing the land and the log book shows there was all the potential for a disaster. The log book, in the possession of the SS *The Great Britain* Project, is not the original, but a hand written copy, perhaps by one of the officers, the name of the person on watch being included but not their signature. Looking at the evidence from the chart, it is quite likely that certain omissions were made. The noon position on 4 August was by dead reckoning and the rest of the day up to midnight was foggy, speed maintained at an average 9 knots. It appears she may have stopped between 1400 and 1500hrs for soundings as the rate for that hour is only 4.5 knots. Some sails were set, but the wind was mostly light to moderate from the west. Early next day the fog lifted and at 11.45hrs land was seen to the northwest at about 30 miles but was not positively identified. It is quite possible the visibility deteriorated soon after, the land briefly seen was assumed to be Cape Spear and the noon position plotted accordingly. There were many small alterations of course during the early afternoon and she appears to have stopped at 1500hrs as the hourly rate is given as 4.5 knots, probably for soundings to be taken. Both these actions indicate the master was unsure of her position despite being quite close to land. Mist and fog are again a problem at 1800hrs but speed is maintained at 9.5 knots. She must have rounded Cape Race at about this time but there is no mention of it. The weather cleared at midnight, breeze was light and variable and sea smooth. Speed throughout the day was 9.5 knots, noon position was by dead reckoning which shows it was still relatively poor, perhaps a mile or so as colours were exchanged with several other vessels. At no time did the vessel stop to sound for the bottom. Conditions were about the same on the 7th until the afternoon. At 1500hrs the remarks column states 'thick fog', and at 1600hrs 'foggy', which continued to midnight, lifting occasionally. She must have passed north of Sable Island at some time. There is no evidence the vessel slowed at all during the fog or stopped for soundings. The day of 8 August started with mist and fog and the 1200hrs position was again by dead reckoning, 9.5 knots was maintained throughout despite the poor visibility, and by now the circle of uncertainty about the dead reckoning position was ever widening. The remarks column does however contain this entry for

0600hrs: 'Repeated continually striking the gong to warn vessels,' which were becoming increasingly numerous. At 1300hrs she stopped and found bottom at 70 fathoms, perhaps on the northeast corner of George Bank; with the dangerous Nantucket Shoal ahead, course was altered from west-south-west to southwest. In the early hours of the 9th bottom was found at 28 fathoms and the visibility must have picked up again after dawn as she exchanged colours with several vessels. No position is given at noon, but if some of these local ships were within hailing distance, *The Great Britain*'s whereabouts might have been established. In the early afternoon the course column states 'Various courses', and soundings taken with bottom at between 10 and 25 fathoms. There is a strong possibility that this was part of the Nantucket Shoal. Later the fog lifted and a sounding taken at midnight found no bottom. Early next morning she received on board the pilot for New York. Throughout the episode, despite being unsure of her position, much shipping in the area, and poor visibility for most of the time, the speed was not reduced in the slightest, except for those odd occasions when she stopped to take soundings. With strong tides in the area the recipe for disaster had more than enough ingredients.

On the next voyage she was not so lucky and found herself 'among the shoals of Nantucket on a thick dirty night' and it is likely she touched the bottom on this occasion as the screw was damaged, losing three blades. In such circumstances the paddle wheel (being less likely to contact the bottom) would have been an advantage.[12]

Log and Course

The term 'rate' has often been mentioned as it is the one used in the log books at the top of the column with sub headings of 'knots' and 'fms'. The patent or rotating log which recorded the distance run had only recently been introduced and was viewed with some suspicion.[13] The instrument could pick up weed or be eaten by fish, so the centuries-old reliance on heaving the common log every hour was still practiced even though the vessel might be streaming the new patent log. The log ship itself was a triangular board, the lower edge weighted and semicircular in shape, connected to the line by a three-legged bridle and so made as to float upright and thus offer maximum resistance. One leg of the bridle was fitted to the board with a wooden peg, thus if the line was checked suddenly it pulled out, allowing the board to float flat for easy retrieval (Figure 8:11).

The first part of the line, called stray line, had the end marked by a piece of bunting, thereafter the line was divided into equal sections of 47ft 3in marked by a piece of leather with 1 knot for the first, 2 knots for the second and so on. Two log sand glasses were used to measure the time interval, the long glass of 28 seconds and a short one of 14 seconds. The division of close on 48ft or 8 fathoms was subdivided into the corresponding quarter, half and three-quarter graduations, that is 2, 4

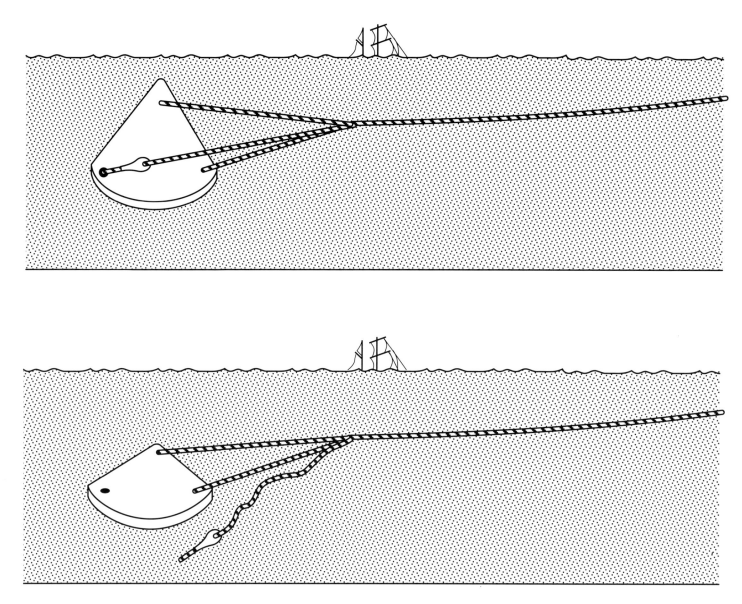

Figure 8:11 *Drawing based on The Common Log. (From John Todd and W B Whall,* Practical Seamanship *(1898))*

and 6 fathoms, hence the speed was expressed in the number of knots and fathoms that were pulled off the reel in 28 seconds. The performance of the vessel thus measured in the short space of 28 seconds at the end of the hour was taken as the rate for the whole hour, unless adjusted otherwise for soundings, engine breakdown, or some other cause (Figure 8:12). Therefore the term 'knots per hour' when used with the common log is quite correct. In fact the modern navigator should be working with the term 'nautical miles per hour', but by common usage the word 'knot' has come to mean just that.

The shorter glass was used when the vessel was making over 5 knots, the marks on the line would therefore indicate only half the actual speed and have to be doubled for a correct reading.

It is interesting to note that in *Practical Seamanship* by John Todd and W B Whall (1898), the distance between knots is given as 46ft 8in which is not correct mathematically, being 80ft short of the nautical mile. The ship would appear to be going faster than she actually was, perhaps a safety factor when closing the land in poor visibility, but the difference was minimal and for all practical purposes could be ignored.

There was also a considerable difference between the compass headings and the true course steered, for the variation as per the chart (1850) was as high as 39°W when *The Great Britain* was in mid-Atlantic, 30°W off the north coast of Ireland and at the northern edge of the Grand Banks, but only 5°W off New York. For example, her initial course when clear of Ireland as per log book, NW a quarter W–312 degrees, was, ignoring any deviation, 282 degrees true.

Figure 8:12 'Heaving the Log'. A posed photograph which illustrates the process described in the text. (The late Captain F C Poyser)

Compass Error

Every magnet possesses two poles, and regarding the world as a magnet these poles are named the north and south magnetic poles. However, they are not situated at the true north and south poles on the earth's surface, but some considerable distance from them, in recent years in Lat 70° N, Long 97° W and Lat 73° S, Long 155° E, respectively. The angle between true north and magnetic north is called magnetic variation, often referred to as just variation, and the isogonic lines drawn on the chart join places with the same variation. Due to the fact that the geographical positions of the magnetic poles are slowly altering, the variation at a particular point on the earth's surface will also change over the years. There would have been a small change in variation between 1845 and 1850 when the chart was produced, but for the purposes of this explanation, it is assumed to be the same.

Deviation is the compass error caused by the vessel's own magnetic field, usually associated with iron or steel ships, but any large amount of these metals placed close to the compass, even on a wooden vessel, will have an effect. The amount of error depends on the direction in which the ship is steering, and it will alter as the heading changes. In an effort to reduce this deviation to the minimum, the compass adjuster will place corrector magnets about the instrument so that the final error is of a workable proportion, at least, not greater than 5 degrees. The total compass error is therefore a combination of variation and deviation, but as there is no data for the iron ship *The Great Britain*, only the variation has been applied. Under sail, the deviation error can also be affected by the angle of heel; and if the vessel is navigating close to the magnetic poles, the earth's magnetic field will cause one end of the compass needle or card to be deflected downwards, or dip.

1 C Claxton, *The Logs of the First voyage, made with the Unceasing Aid of Steam, between England and America, by the* Great Western *of Bristol, Lieut. James Hoskins, RN Commander* (Bristol, 1838)

2 Report by Christopher Claxton to the First Lord of the Admiralty The Right Honourable The Earl of Minto GCB, 4 July 1838, on the first voyage of the *Great Western*, p. 3

3 Lieut W Gordon RN, *The Economy of the Marine Steam Engine; with suggestions for its improvement* (London, 1845) p. 141

4 R Murray, *Marine Engines* (London, 1851) p. 3

5 Undated and unattributed newspaper cutting from the Tregoning scrapbook entitled 'The Atlantic Steamers', which contained abstracts from the deck log book of the *Sirius* and 'A Table of the Observation made at Noon on each Day'

6 T Tredgold, *The Steam Engine*, vol 1 (London, 1838) p. 311, Art 647

7 Part of the Field Papers, presented to the Science Museum Library by Miss Gertrude Field, Arch: Field 1/22–1/31

8 Field Papers, 'Glances at Atlantic Steam Navigation', Science Museum, London

9 Frederick A Talbot, *Steamship Conquest of the World* (London, 1912) pp. 155–160

10 Field Papers, 'Glances at Atlantic Steam Navigation', pp. 8 and 9

11 Captain George P Burris, *Norie's Nautical Tables* (London, 1938) p. 52

12 E Corlett, *The Iron Ship* (Bradford-on-Avon, 1975) p. 117 (Captain Hoskins' report)

13 *The Great Britain* carried an entirely new device, an electric log, but it is not clear that it was used. E Corlett, *The Iron Ship* (London, 1990) p. 78

CHAPTER 9

Handling Under Power

The Importance of Steerage Way

The handling of the early paddle steamers which had a single crankshaft and both wheels fixed so they revolved together was, compared to a screw-propelled vessel, much more difficult to control at slow speed. If she were stopped in the water, sufficient way would have to be gained before the rudder had any effect on her heading; whereas, in the same situation the screw provided helm control as soon as the thrust race was established. This must have been a problem when berthing or getting clear of a dock, and paddle steamers of this period were liable to cause a certain amount of damage to themselves and shore installations.

Lieut W Gordon RN made the following observations and suggested improvements:[1]

> The proportions of the rudder should be increased, . . . a second rudder should be fitted at the stem, which would be a great convenience in turning in a narrow space. In practice, when backing a steam vessel, notwithstanding the action of the rudder, she will in most cases *come up* with her stern *towards the wind*.

The inability of gaining sufficient steerage way was partly to blame for the incident in May 1844 when HMS *Gorgon*, a first-class paddle sloop, went ashore in South America. The vessel was lying to a single anchor in the Bay of Montevideo on the River Plate when, in a rising gale, she started to drag towards the shore. Despite letting go a second anchor she continued, getting dangerously close to a group of rocks. Due to the direction of the tide, wind and sea were not from right ahead but 3 points on the bow, which ruled out the usual practice of steaming up to the anchors to relieve the strain, and attempts made to recover them by heaving on the cables proved futile. For the reasons just mentioned, the rudder would have had little or no effect in trying to bring her head to wind under the engines which were rated at only 320nhp, quite inadequate for the task, the *Gorgon* having a displacement of about 1,600 tons.

Brunel makes this point when referring to the screw in comparison with the paddle wheel:[2]

> . . . but even when the ship has no way, but the screw is at work, the rudder is acted upon by water moving perhaps two or three knots per hour, and the vessel is still under

command – this must materially diminish many of the greatest dangers arising from a strong headwind and sea, and at the same time and under the circumstances must increase the speed by improving the steerage.

It is open to speculation that the *Gorgon* would have recovered her anchor and got clear if she had been screw-propelled, for she would have had the added advantage of less windage without the wheels and paddle boxes. The illustration of the contemporary naval paddle steamer *Leopard* viewed nearly end on will give some idea of the enormous surfaces presented to the wind by a paddler (Figure 9:1), also shown in the photograph of the American passenger steamer *Fulton* (Figure 9:2).

The following quotations are taken from a book by Commander Astley Cooper Key RN, later Admiral Sir, which details the chain of events leading to the *Gorgon*'s stranding:[3]

> Our course was clear; a few minutes more and the ship would be on the rocks astern; two anchors had failed to hold her and there was no reason to anticipate that one could do better [the cable on the smaller anchor had just parted]. The best bower was therefore slipped, and full power given to the engines. The fury of the gale baffled all our attempts; truly mortifying was it to observe that, with full steam power, the helm hard a starboard, and the main trysail set, she would not come nearer than three points of the wind, and would then pay off.

After re-anchoring, and before additional ground tackle could be rigged, the single chain cable parted and her head payed off, the vessel now driving directly downwind towards the shore:

> Here was one of HM's finest steamers, with her engines, wheels, and gear in splendid order, perfectly unmanageable – able to steer but one course by the wind, which course would not carry her clear of danger: to wear was impractical, the attempt would have endangered the merchant ships in the harbour, and a glance of the eye showed that she could not weather the opposite point of the bay.

As the vessel was now in shoal water the engines were stopped and soon after she went ashore.

The cause of the disaster was attributed to the anchors and

Figure 9:1 *HM paddle frigate* Leopard *and HM steam sloop* Vesuvius *taking a salute from a merchant vessel in the Mediterranean, 1852. (Drawing by the Rev Calvert Jones in a private collection)*

Figure 9:2 *The American paddle liner* Fulton, *2,061 tons, built in New York in 1855 of wood and operating between New York, Falmouth (England) and Le Havre with a large US Government subsidy for carrying mail. She was obsolete at her launch. (John Bowen)*

cables being too small for the vessel, as the first point (every effort had been made to reduce the windage of the rig). Second, as the narrative continued:

> The next point to consider is, . . . what prevented the *Gorgon* from steaming out to the outer roads when the best bower was slipped? There are two reasons:- the want of power in the engines, and of sufficient after sail to bring the ship to the wind. The first of these were very apparent to all on board from the moment of slipping the cable: with power full on, the ship barely gained steerage-way; the rudder, therefore, could be but of little service towards bringing her to the wind. From the position of the mainmast, [the *Gorgon* was rigged as a brig] the effect of the main-trysail, for the same purpose, was but small,- it acted solely as a body sail, and its power was completely counteracted by the action of the wind on the paddle-boxes, which present an equal surface and are situated nearly as much before the centre of the ship as the close-reefed main trysail is abaft it. This would seem to point out the necessity of a mizzen-mast in large steamers.

The last point was acted upon and is the reason why, subsequent to this accident, a mizzen mast was fitted retrospectively on several naval paddle steamers, which, like the *Gorgon*, were rigged as brigs, making them barques of peculiar appearance as this third mast was stepped well aft.

Writing at the time, unaware of her recovery, Lieut Gordon RN made the following comment in his book published in 1845:[4]

> It is obvious that war steamers should have a very high proportion of power to enable them to chase, tow, or carry dispatches, in the teeth of gales; and it was owing to the very low proportion of power in the *Gorgon*, that she has been lately wrecked. A low proportion of power was recommended by Mr Seaward, who a few years since obtained nearly all the Admiralty contracts,and the result has been the loss of a fine steam vessel; but owing to the exertions of Captain Hoseason, the proportion of power has been nearly doubled, and vessels which have hitherto been fitted with engines of 320hp, will in future have engines of 560 horsepower.

After seven months of hard work and setbacks the captain and ship's company managed to free the *Gorgon*, which in fact had gone ashore, due to the storm surge, much higher up the beach than would be expected. She was finally hauled clear and anchored in deep water on 29 October 1844.

Figure 9:3 *HM steam sloop* Vesuvius *engaged in coastal bombardment during the war with Russia, 1854–6. The lithograph, from a drawing by Oswald Brierly, illustrates the unorthodox spacing of the masts very well. (Private Collection)*

Figure 9:4 *HM steam vessel* Virago *towing HMS* Queen *out of Malta, 16 June 1844. Lithograph by Dutton after Lieut G P Mends RN. (Parker Gallery)*

Figure 9:5 *The wooden clinker-built paddle tug* United Service *of Yarmouth, built at North Shields in 1872, demonstrates the manoeuvrability of vessels with paddle wheels which could be operated independently, by turning in her own length. (Basil Greenhill Collection)*

Early Paddle Tugs

Paddle tugs, once the strain was taken up on the tow line, but having no headway, could be turned independently of the rudder. The towing hook was usually positioned towards the centre of the vessel and provision made for it to be offset to one side or the other by lines or tackles. Depending on the amount of athwartship adjustment, the lever arm of the wheels would change accordingly and hence the tug would turn under the tow line, or, if a single post or bitts were fitted, the same effect was obtained with a 'gob' rope, that is, a bight of line set up to pull the tow rope off-centre. Later, when paddle tugs were built with wheels that could be controlled independently, they were very manoeuvrable indeed and used particularly on narrow twisting rivers and canals, where their advantage over screw propulsion saw them still working in the 1970s. The last

Figure 9:5 A. *Tug* United Service *towing a brigantine into Yarmouth in heavy weather, the line hanging slack over her port quarter: an anxious moment. (The late Captain Poyser)*

surviving example is the *Reliant*, with her side lever engines and feathering wheels, at present at the National Maritime Museum, Greenwich, a monument to the birth of steam at sea and of international importance.

Other Problems with Paddle Propulsion

Another important consideration with any power-driven vessel is its turning circle, and in this respect screw propulsion gives a much smaller one, size for size, than paddle wheels, unless of course they can be operated independently.

Paddle wheels were a problem in more ways than one. When coming alongside, should the lower edge of the paddle box fenders be above the level of the quay edge or small craft, the wheels would make contact first, and considerable damage would occur if they were still turning. They were also liable to pick up all manner of floating debris; and a situation such as getting set down on a navigation buoy or mark, which in a sailing vessel or one screw-propelled would cause no more than a slight bump, could end up with a smashed wheel and other damage leading to heavy expenses.

One of the most important functions of steam propulsion in the days when anchors were weighed by muscle power was to relieve the weight on the cable when heaving up, or to prevent the vessel dragging her anchor in extreme conditions by making use of the engine. However, it was not unknown to overrun and pick up the anchor buoy and line with one of the wheels. Of course, anything that can get tangled up, will, such as running gear washed overboard from forward, and that is the reason why cutting away the foremast on the *Gorgon* to reduce windage was not an option, as in her situation, with steam propulsion being her only hope, the paddle wheels could not be jeopardised, as they would have been, by falling spars and rigging.

If the paddle steamer were making way with the wheels turning and someone wished to board, it was not easy, for the small craft would be under oars or sail and have to avoid the obvious danger. The ideal place, just aft of amidships, could not be used because of the backwash, and ahead of the wheel was too dangerous, leaving the only place possible to scramble on board as right aft.

The steering difficulties were not confined to poor control at very low speed. In heavy weather the alternate immersion of the wheels caused the vessel to yaw badly either side of her course, so much so, that the compass heading was, judging by the *Great Western*, to the nearest point (11.25 degrees).

Commenting on this point, a seaman who had spent his early

Figure 9:6 *Paddle ferries alongside the congested landing stage at Liverpool. So as to bring the boarding position, which could be just ahead, or as shown, aft of the paddle box, close in to the landing stage, the shape of the rubbing band around the Seacombe required her to be made fast at an angle to it. In all probability, the vessel is facing the ebb tide and only two shore lines are required in this case; the after one, just visible beyond the gangway made up with a short nip, the forward one on the post having a greater length. It is interesting to note these well used shorelines are very pliable from the way the slack hangs down from the post, of 'left hand laid' construction, and from the evidence of the frayed section, probably made of cotton which size-for-size is stronger than manila and often used where elasticity is of great importance. (Before the use of manmade fibres and plaited construction most shipboard lines were three stranded 'right hand laid'.) (Postcard)*

working life as helmsman on a south coast excursion paddle steamer, working mostly out of Poole, said the main problem when steering directly into a rough sea was not so much the yawing caused by the alternate immersion of the paddle wheels due to the rolling, although this was a contributory factor, but a strong headwind catching the long bow on one side or the other and blowing the vessel off course. If not caught in time with the rudder she would sheer away badly to leeward with the helm hard over and then it was difficult to bring her back, at least with any dispatch.

The early Atlantic paddle steamers tried to follow the great circle track, in the same way as the modern commercial vessel where the optimum course alterations would be measured in a few degrees every 24 hours, but it is obvious from the foregoing comments that they could not steer to such close margins. The *Great Western* only managed a half point correction to headings if the sea was slight; at all other times it was a full point (11.25 degrees). A report to the commander-in-chief at Portsmouth by Captain Ramsay of the paddle frigate *Terrible* in April 1846 contains a reference to the steering of the vessel, which further underlines this problem:

> Their Lordships have also desired me to report particularly upon the steering of the *Terrible*. Going under 8 knots she steers easily, two men being sufficient at the wheel; above she requires three and sometimes four, with great attention.[5]

Comparison with Screw Propulsion

Compare this with the report of Commander Crispin RN of the Royal Yacht *Victoria and Albert*, who wrote to the Admiralty after his passage from Bristol to London on *The Great Britain*, dated 29 January 1845:[6]

> The screw far surpassed my most sanguine expectations on all points connected with it as a propeller, for, with all the disadvantages [heavy rolling] above related, against this heavy Sea and Gale, it propelled this large body of 3,500 tons at the rate of 4 knots. – At 10 we were enabled to set the Fore Staysail, the wind having come round to NNW steering West. – We then went 4 and 6 [4.75 knots] and what now struck me as most astonishing was that although this Sail – 320 feet from the Propelling power, with this heavy Sea on her bow, that the Rudder had perfect command of her, and that she did not fall off in the slightest degree from her course, and that one Man was sufficient to Steer her. – Shortly after this the Foresail was set, which increased speed to 5 and 2 [5.25 knots], from this time more Sail was gradually increased until the whole of her Trysails and Jib were set, at this period she had reached a speed of 8 and 2 [8.25 knots].

In fact, according to the log book, *The Great Britain* worked her courses to the nearest quarter point (approximately

3 degrees) even in heavy weather. Commander Crispin also mentions the working of the expansion valve and the comparison between a vessel with paddle propulsion and screw in respect of sail carrying. He reinforces some of the points already made:

. . . I again went into the Engine Room and found, still working with 9 tenths of the Throttle Valve shut and expansively cutting off the Steam at one sixth of the stroke, thereby proving the immense advantage of the screw as a Propeller over the Paddle Vessel as I am quite sure had a Paddle Vessel been similarly situated she could not have attempted to carry such a press of Sail: for had she done so, her lee wheel would have been so deeply immersed, and her weather one so much out of water, that her speed would have been greatly retarded. – Another vast advantage of the Screw was this, that although there was so much Sea, and the ship pitching considerably, yet the Machinery worked with almost the same regularity that a Paddle Vessel would have done had it been in the smoothest Water, and I am convinced with

the Screw as a Propeller, no Engineer will ever have the Slightest dread of his Engines overrunning themselves at one moment, and being as suddenly checked the next.

The Single Engine

The problem of slow speed handling and the lack of proper control of the engine movements combined to cause damage to both vessel and shore installations. The earliest steamers had only a single cylinder, which meant that if stopped with the piston at the top or bottom of its stroke the direction in which the paddle wheel revolved once restarted was far from certain. This, as can be imagined, created some confusion in close quarter situations.

Robert Murray makes the following comments in his book:[7]

River Steamers, however, are occasionally fitted with only one engine, the moving parts of which are 'balanced' (by means of a cast iron paddle board, or otherwise) in such a manner as may best assist the crank in passing the centres;

Figure 9:7 *This lithograph, made from drawings by Oswald Brierly, shows the steam screw battle fleet of 1854 with royal poles and topgallant masts and their yards sent down and topmasts housed, anchored and steaming to take the strain off the cables in a gale in the Baltic. There also appears to be a small steamer, with smoke from her funnel, alongside the port bow of the vessel in the foreground, perhaps assisting the operation. (Private Collection)*

but such an arrangement is always objectionable from the difficulty experienced in starting, and from the impossibility of preventing a disagreeable jumping motion in the vessel from the unequal speed at which the paddle wheels are driven.

This difficulty was overcome by fitting two engines to the paddle crank shaft so arranged that when one was at 'top or bottom dead centre' the other crank was in the optimum driving position. However there were times when one engine was disabled and both had to be stopped, and if need be the wheels locked while repairs were done, or the vessel could continue using just one engine while the job was in hand. To restart with one engine was as much of a problem as ever, and Murray suggests, 'If the single engine will not pass the centres on starting, it must be attempted to get way on the ship by the sails (towards any point on the compass), when the resistance of the water against the paddle floats will assist in enabling the engine to start and continue the rotary motion'. [This is no different in principle from bump starting a car or motorcycle down a slope. I have even heard of this method being used on a large yacht, the diesel engine having decompression gear and a manual clutch. A speed under sail of at least 5 knots was required and the clutch was then engaged to rotate the engine. (PA)]

Command and Control

The actual command and conning of these early steamers when entering or leaving port was not without complications. On the sailing vessel it was straightforward; even when under tow the master would be down aft close to the wheel or tiller, but on the steamer he was forced to come amidships over the engine room and therefore had to communicate two ways. To increase visibility a walkway was constructed between the tops of the paddle boxes, called the 'bridge', and it was from here that orders were issued for engine movements by shouting down and, similarly, to the helmsman aft. Such a system, especially at night when hand signals would be of no use, was not ideal.

A treatise on 'Navigation by Steam' by Ross (1828) shows a sketch of the various signals to be adopted by the master to convey the four basic commands, that is, Set on; Slow the engine; Reverse the engine; Stop the engine (See Figure 9:9).[8]

No definite evidence has so far come to light that steamers in the early 1840s, except for the vessels referred to in the next paragraph, were fitted with either a voice pipe or engine room telegraph, but it is likely that in a few instances at least, some form of mechanical communication had been developed and was already in use, as the safe handling under power depended much on the prompt and unambiguous transfer of orders.

Captain Basil Hall RN in the *Edinburgh Philosophical Journal* (July 1825) describes an invention by Messrs James and Charles Carmichael of Dundee, used on board the Tay Ferries.

Figure 9:8 *(facing page) The Swiss lake paddle steamer* Evian *demonstrated with her long bow the ease with which she could be blown off course in a strong headwind. (Basil Greenhill Collection)*

SET ON.
Or both hands raised as high as the head. The steam is then to be set on and the engine set in motion.

SLOW THE ENGINE.

REVERSE THE ENGINE.

STOP THE ENGINE.

Figure 9:9 *Sketch of signals for engine control. (From E G Smith,* A Short History of Marine Engineering*)*

It would appear to be the earliest recorded reference to not just a form of telegraph but actual 'bridge control' of the engines:[9]

By a simple motion of a small handle, or index, placed on a table, in view and in hearing of the man at the helm and the master of the vessel, every movement which the engine is capable of giving to the paddle-wheel may be at once commanded. The vessel may be moved forwards, or backwards – or may be retarded or entirely stopped, at any given moment, by merely turning the handle to the places denoted by the graduations of a dial plate. No skill is required for this purpose, so that the master himself, or a sailor under his direction, can perform the office as well as the ablest engineer. Thus the confusion which frequently arises at night in calling out to the engineer below, is avoided, and any ambiguity arising from the word of command being transmitted through several persons, entirely prevented. In point of fact, it places the engine as much under command as the rudder is – an undoubted improvement on the clumsy method of bawling out to the engineer below, who either may not hear, or may chance be out of the way – circumstances which may lead to the most serious accidents.

Improvements for the control of the engines by the officer on deck were put forward by Lieut W Gordon RN in his book on the marine steam engine published in 1845:[10]

It would be advantageous if the officer of the watch possessed the means of stopping the engines without reference to the engine room, in cases of emergency, or should the engineer be absent from his post. To effect the purpose, it is only necessary to have two levers, one connected with the throttle valves, and the other with the injection cocks, and to stop the engines it would only be necessary to *shut* both these cocks and valves.

The operation of reversing the engines could not be accomplished without more complicated machinery, which it would not be advisable to apply.

On each paddle box there should be a lever communicating with a pointer in the engine room, indicating distinct orders, such as –1. Ease; 2. Stop; 3. Back; 4. Go on; and each movement of the lever should ring a bell. The degree of power would be indicated by repeating the same movement.

1 Lieut W Gordon RN, *The Economy of the Marine Steam Engine* (London, 1845) p. 93

2 Report to the Directors of the Great Western Steam Company 1840, Appendix II, p. 556

3 Commander Astly Cooper Key RN, *A narrative of the Recovery of HMS* Gorgon (London, 1847) p. 4

4 Lieut W Gordon RN, op cit, p. 90

5 *South West Soundings* (magazine of South West Maritime History Society) No 29, p. 22

6 Crispin to Herbert, 29 January 1845, PRO ADM/87. Commander Crispin was, previous to his appointment to the Royal Yacht, commanding officer of the steam cruiser Vulcan and was on board the *The Great Britain* as an official observer for the Admiralty. B Greenhill and A Giffard, *Steam, Politics and Patronage* (London, 1994) p. 157

7 R Murray, *Marine Engines* (London, 1851) p. 3

8 Reference to Ross quoted from E C Smith, *A short History of Marine Engineering* (Cambridge, 1937) p. 156

9 An account of the ferry across the Tay at Dundee (Dundee, 1825) appendix 1, p. 2

10 Lieut W Gordon RN, op cit, p. 96

CHAPTER 10

Rules and Regulations

Accidents, as we have indicated in the last chapter, were common enough and a heavy financial burden for the owners, but more important was the injury and loss of life. It is hard to believe, but in the early 1840s there was no 'Rule of the Road' as we know it today other than a general code of practice established for sailing ships, which is recorded in a document by Trinity House, London, 30 October 1840:[1]

Whereas the recognised rule for sailing vessels is, that those having the wind fair shall give way to those on a wind.

That when both are going by the wind, the vessel on the starboard tack shall keep her wind and the one on the larboard tack bear up, thereby passing each other on the larboard hand.

That when both vessels have the wind large or a-beam, and meet, they shall pass each other in the same way on the larboard hand, to effect which two last mentioned objects the helm must be put to port.

And as steam vessels may be considered in the light of vessels navigating with a fair wind and should give way to sailing vessels on a wind on either tack it becomes only necessary to provide a rule for their observance when meeting other steamers or sailing vessels going large.

RULE

When steam vessels on different courses must unavoidably or necessarily cross so near that by continuing their respective courses there would be a risk of coming in collision, each vessel shall put her helm to port, so as always to pass on the larboard side of each other.

A steam vessel passing another in a narrow channel must always leave the vessel she is passing on the larboard side.

This rule for steamers was only a proposal. A letter from Messrs W and T Wilson, Mr Milcrest and Mr W W Russell, shipbuilders, Liverpool, in *The Times* newspaper of 4 October 1839 shows how serious was the lack of a universally adopted and mandatory set of steering and sailing rules. Part of this letter read:

. . . collisions are frequent, many lives lost, and immense damage done to property and vessels of all kinds, from

want of an universal code of night signals and the observance of a general rule of the road. The custom at Liverpool is, in meeting, for each vessel to starboard her helm, and in London to port it. Hence arose the violent collision between the *Royal William* and *Tagus* steamers. The first received the greatest shock, but from being divided into watertight compartments, though the forward one filled, she was saved.

The Introduction of Navigation Lights

The first point referring to navigation lights, is covered in the article in *The Mariner's Mirror*, quoted above, for there was no recognised way of identifying a vessel at night other than a long established tradition and general rule of the sea that a vessel at anchor, or a fishing boat, should exhibit a light so as to 'afford to the vessel whose duty it is to avoid her the means of doing so'. As regards vessels under way there was no rule about lights at night until near the middle of the nineteenth century. Regulations were finally brought in on 11 July 1848, and, 'required all steam vessels under way – within the limits mentioned in the Act – to exhibit a bright white light at the foremast head, a green light on the starboard side, and a red light on the port side, and provide for the side lights to be fitted with inboard screens'.

As far as sailing ships were concerned they could virtually do what they liked as regards lights for another 10 years. Even after another Act of Parliament in 1851, which included regulations for sailing vessels, they were only required 'when under sail or being towed, approaching or being approached by another vessel, to show a bright light in such a position as could be best seen by the other vessel and in sufficient time to prevent collision'. Sailing vessels at anchor were to show 'a constant bright light at the masthead': the under way light was only shown when the occasion required. These rules were revoked as from 30 September 1858, after which date the red and green sidelights were ordained for sailing ships as well as steamers.

Safe Navigation

It was the rapid increase in the numbers of steamships and the collisions they were involved in that forced the authorities to

Figure 10:1 *This photograph, believed to be of the polacca brigantine* Peter and Sarah, *built at Cleave Houses, Northam, North Devon, in 1809, must have been taken between October 1858, when sidelights with screens, clearly visible in her mainshrouds on the port side were made compulsory for sailing vessels, and her loss on 1 November 1859. It is probably the earliest photograph of sidelights on a sailing vessel. Note also the very thick hemp shrouds on the fore. (Gillis Collection)*

standardise the lights carried at night and subsequently those required for sailing vessels.

When only wind-driven ships were under way in thick fog and calm weather, not much harm was done if there was a 'coming together'; but this situation, due to the advent of the steamship, changed to one of great danger, for the sailing ship was literally a 'sitting duck'. She might drift down on another anchored vessel and sustain damage, but by comparison, being hit by a steamer at 10 knots would be far worse, for what was considered a 'safe speed' was left to the discretion of the master or mate in charge. Both the log books of the *Great Western* and *The Great Britain* do not show any reduction of speed in fog, at least when clear of the land.

For example, the *Great Western* was making between 10.5 and 11 knots between midnight and noon when returning to Bristol on 14 May 1838, the remarks column stating, 'light airs intermixed with calm and fog throughout; took in and made sail as required'. She was in mid-Atlantic at the time and any sailing vessel she came up with would have been virtually stationary. Similarly, *The Great Britain* on her maiden voyage made no reduction of speed from 9 knots, despite the entry in the remarks column of 'thick fog' although on a previous occasion it does mention 'Proper lookouts stationed'.

For a large sailing vessel working around the coast, a 'safe offing' from headlands and other dangers was considered normal practice and unless circumstances dictated otherwise, she would not close the land until approaching her destination. Steamships, not subject to the risks of a lee shore or other hazards peculiar to wind propulsion, would take the course of shortest navigable distance around the land, and therefore passage planning was fundamentally different. Fierce competition demanded a fast passage and therefore the temptation to cut corners was ever present (as it is today).

While not ignoring the fact that many sailing vessels ran aground in poor visibility it should not have occurred in steamers on the scale it did, for they were far more manoeuvrable, and as passenger vessels should have been handled with greater caution.

The following extract is taken from a report of the Committee of Nautical Inspection of the Board at P&O in 1849, and recommended to the notice of the Main Board:

As likely to lead to the improvement of the mode of navigating the ships of P&O Steam Navigation Company by again pointing to the commanders the imperative necessity of running no risk that can possibly be avoided and thus insure the safer navigation of the company's ships.

Much of the danger to which steamships are subject consists in the facilities with which they are gifted to avoid those dangers that so often prove fatal to them. Almost all the losses of steamers have been occasioned by hugging the coast and shaving headlands, while a sailing ship not knowing but the wind however favourable might suddenly fail her and even blow in an adverse direction, cautiously abstains from any act involving risk; but the commanders of steamers, presuming on the artificial power conferred by their engines, shave the headlands too close and creep into the sinuses of the coast with the view perhaps of saving an hour in the performance of the voyage, upon which to ground a claim for extraordinary zeal and exertions on the part of the commander thus for reducing the direction of it.[2]

Subsequent to enquiries into the various losses, circulars were forwarded on to all commanders of the company's ships, of which the following is a typical example:

Figure 10:2 *The* Albion, *built at Clydebank in 1893, was bound from Newport to Bristol on 1 April 1907 with 400 passengers when she was run ashore in dense fog close to the Black Nore Lighthouse on the Somerset coast, near Portishead. In this case there were no casualties and the passengers walked ashore over gangways.* Albion *was refloated and broken up in 1919. (The late B J Greenhill)*

With reference to the recent cases of two of the company's vessels on the Peninsular Line being placed in critical positions;

The Court of Directors desire to draw the attention of the Commanders of all the ships to the state of their compasses, any doubt, as to the trust of which, or as to the local alterations existing on board their respective vessels is to be immediately communicated to the Company's Superintendent at Southampton, and that officer is to satisfy himself from the Column in the Report of State and Condition, headed state and condition of compasses signed by the Commander that they are true and efficient before the ship proceeds on a voyage. The Directors further feel themselves called upon to enjoin the utmost vigilance and caution in approaching the land on all occasions, particularly during the night or in thick or foggy weather, and that the use of the lead in such circumstances be never neglected.[3]

Certificates of Competency

Nearly all the accidents were as a result of human error and the competence of many of the masters and officers to conduct a steamship safely was open to doubt. The expansion of steam navigation attracted a new type of shipowner, who, not having had any sea service himself was not in a position to judge the competence of the person he placed in command. Those with a naval background and experience in steamships or from the ranks of first-class merchant shipping, particularly the East India Company, provided the recruits to the better-run companies, but these qualifications did not always establish the competence of the individual. The Royal Mail Steam Packet Company started with fourteen large steamers in 1840, nearly all of which were commanded by naval officers, usually lieutenants on half pay, but within eight years of the start, the company had lost six vessels.[4]

A system of voluntary examination for deck officers was set up by the Board of Trade, the actual tests carried out by various branches of Trinity House. The scheme was not very successful as by the end of 1846 less than 200 had passed. The Admiralty, however, made it compulsory in 1847 that no vessel taken up by them in government work would be considered, unless the master and mates were properly qualified. This order was extended to include passenger ships and mail packets over which they had control. By 1850 some 3,000 had passed the tests.

The Mercantile Marine Act, CAP 93 of 14 August 1850 which became law on 1 January 1851 applied to all 'Foreign Going' ships, both steam and sail, covering not only the

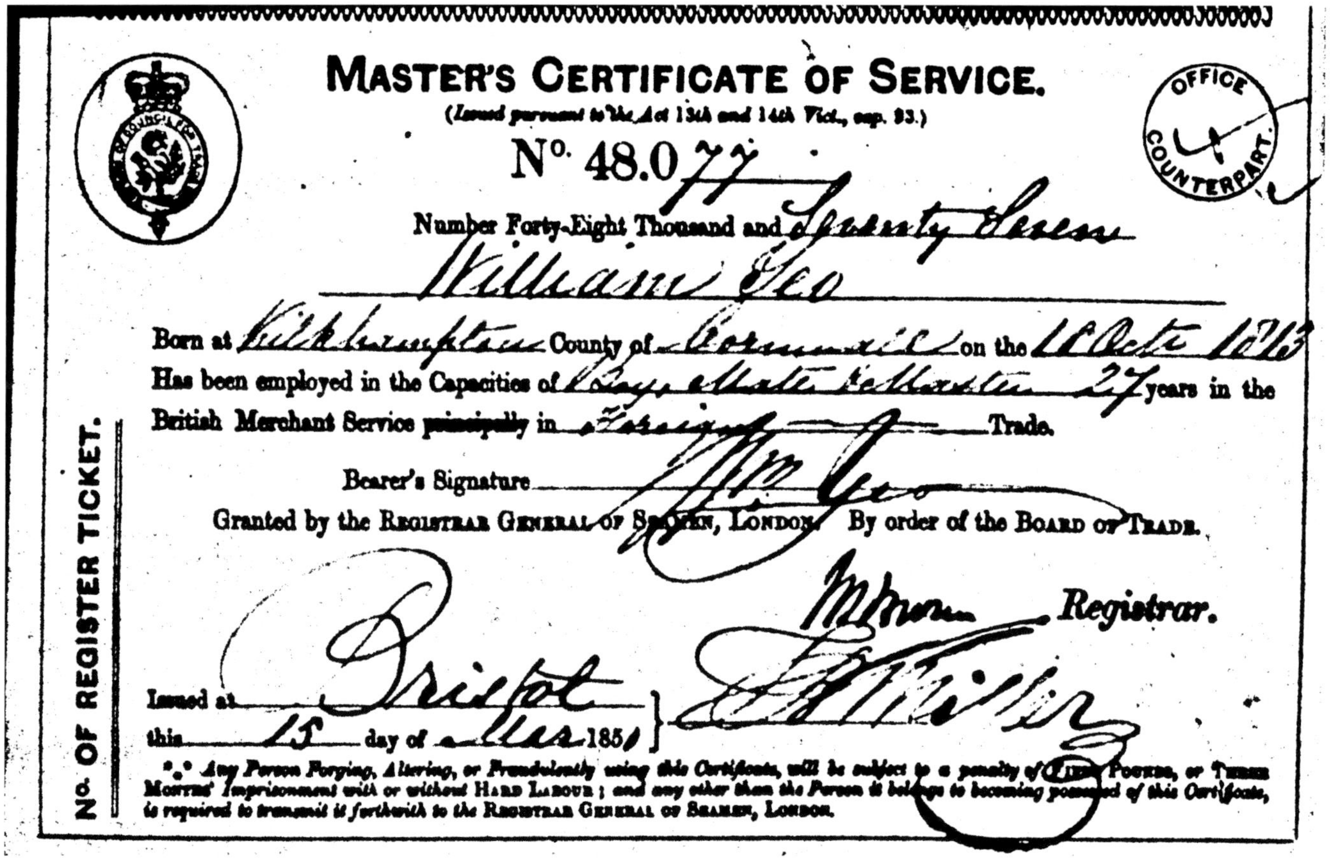

MASTER'S CERTIFICATE OF SERVICE.

(Issued pursuant to the Act 13th and 14th Vict., cap. 93.)

No. 48.077

Number Forty-Eight Thousand and Seventy Seven

William Yeo

Born at Kilkhampton County of Cornwall on the 16 Octr 1813

Has been employed in the Capacities of Boy, Mate & Master 27 years in the British Merchant Service principally in Foreign Trade.

Bearer's Signature Wm Yeo

Granted by the Registrar General of Seamen, London. By order of the Board of Trade.

Registrar.

Issued at Bristol this 15 day of Mar 1851

** Any Person Forging, Altering, or Fraudulently using this Certificate, will be subject to a penalty of Fifty Pounds, or Three Months' Imprisonment with or without Hard Labour; and any other than the Person it belongs to becoming possessed of this Certificate, is required to transmit it forthwith to the Registrar General of Seamen, London.

No. OF REGISTER TICKET.

OFFICE COUNTERPART.

Figure 10:3 *A Masters' Certificate of Service issued under the Mercantile Marine Act of 14 August 1850 on 15 March 1851 at Bristol, to William Yeo who claimed 27 years of experience as boy, mate and master in foreign trade. William Yeo subsequently became a very prominent shipowner and merchant. (Basil Greenhill Collection)* certificates of competency or equivalent Certificates of Service for Master and Mates, but, 'Agreements with "seamen", Advances and Allotments of Wages, Health on board Ship, Desertion, Discipline, Log Books, Payment of Wages, and discharge of "Seamen"' (page 1063 of the Act, section 5).

The passage of the Bill through Parliament was not without strong opposition from a section of the shipowners who attempted to 'water down' the requirements, and in particular objected strongly to such examinations being made compulsory.

The existing powers held by the Admiralty were transferred to a new body under the control of the Board of Trade:

Those who had obtained certificates under the old scheme could exchange these for the new B of T certificates and those already in command but without certificates were granted a Certificate of Service.[5]

These improvements to safety at sea, which benefited all seafarers irrespective of being employed on a steamer or sailing vessel, were introduced as a direct result of the increasing numbers of steamships and the heavy financial losses occasioned by them.

1 W Senior, 'The Beginning of Sidelights', *The Mariner's Mirror,* vol 3, no 9 (September, 1913) p. 261

2 From a paper by H Campbell McMurray, Royal Naval Museum, P&O SN, Notes and Proceedings of the Nautical Committee, 1847–74, p. 37, National Maritime Museum P&O/3.3

3 P&O SN, Notes and Proceedings, p. 17

4 Paper by H Campbell McMurray, quoted from reference 79

5 Paper by H Campbell McMurray, reference 41

CHAPTER 11

Further Development of Sail Assist: Modern Applications and the Future

Figure 11:1 *The wooden barque* Sigyn *of Wårdö, Åland Islands, Finland, built at Göteborg, Sweden, in 1887, now preserved in her own floating dock at Turku, Finland, is the last wooden three-masted square-rigged merchant sailing ship in the world. (Basil Greenhill)*

Further Rig Developments

Robert Murray writes in 1851 that:

The success of auxiliary screw merchantmen has already been such, that it appears probable that the whole commerce of the country will be carried on by them at so reduced a cost as to beat out of the field all sailing vessels, not only of this but of other countries: the value of speed and regularity being now so greatly and so truly appreciated by merchants.[1]

These remarks were premature, as until the 1870s at least, sailing vessels, most of them wooden barques – of which the last in

Figure 11:2 *The steel four-masted barque* Pommern *built at Glasgow in 1903, now preserved at Marieham in the Åland Islands. She is the only big steel sailing vessel in the world which is intact, unchanged as a merchant vessel. (Basil Greenhill Collection)*

Figure 11:3 *The four-masted wooden schooner* Helen Barnet Gring *built at Camden Maine in 1919. (Captain Francis E Bowker)*

the world is the *Sigyn* of Wårdö, preserved in her floating dock at Turku in Finland – were to continue to carry the bulk of the world's cargoes. The large steel four-masted barques were still to prove profitable in some bulk cargo trades until the late 1890s, even in competition with the triple expansion engine steam vessel. One of these, the British built *Pommern*, is preserved unchanged, just as she came in from the sea in 1939, at Mariehamn in the Åland Islands of Finland. Their American contemporaries, the multi-masted schooners of Maine and of the Pacific coast, remained commercially viable until the early 1920s.

It can be argued that the progress of the sailing ship after 1870 was made only by adapting steamship industrial techniques into the sailing culture – iron, later steel, construction, iron lower masts and yards, iron wire rigging, screw tensioning devices for standing rigging, labour-saving machinery on deck, donkey engines, braces winches, halliard winches. All these products of the heavy industry culture enabled the sailing

vessel, steadily increasing in size, to compete with steamers in an ever decreasing number of bulk trades for one more generation. The sailing vessel then was no longer a self-supporting entity, as she had been in the days of wood and hemp, but one dependent on shore support. Thus the *Pommern*, built 1903, is nearer to a contemporary steamer than she is to the *Sigyn*.

Great changes took place in the 30 years after the *Great Western* was built and the transitional ships continued to develop, taking advantage of the industrial expansion ashore. The problems associated with brass bearings and lubricants were largely overcome; new alloys were introduced and mineral oils became available to replace tallow, various animal fats and vegetable oils. Iron, as a shipbuilding material, essentially a product of steamship development, was increasingly used not only for hull construction, but for the standing rigging, lower masts, and even yards on larger vessels.[2] The compound engine, once its reliability was established with the greater economy – virtually half the consumption per horsepower per

Figure 11:4 *The Cunard liner* Etruria, *built of steel at Glasgow in 1884, single screw, triple expansion engine with vestigial sail assist, photographed off the New England coast in 1896. She ran in the Liverpool–New York service and was broken up in 1909. (Society for the Preservation of New England Antiquities, N L Stebbins Collection, plate 1031)*

hour of the single expansion condensing engine – allowed the steamship to compete on long haul routes with sailing ships carrying general cargo. Sails were still of use on steamers but were less important in terms of the vessel's propulsion, at least on fully-powered merchant ships, and the screw had virtually replaced the paddle wheel.

Such canvas that was still carried, particularly on the ocean liners in the last decade of the century, was insufficient in respect of total area related to the size and speed of these vessels to be of use as sail assist; and in the event of a total breakdown its 'fail safe' function, once proved vital on *The Great Britain*, was, to say the least, inadequate. This was proved on several occasions; for example, the Inman liner *City of Paris*, built in 1889, having both square and fore and aft canvas, drifted for days after suffering a complete loss of engine power, despite being twin screw, and had to wait until another steamer came along and took her in tow.

With the ever increasing windage of the superstructure, the only practical use was to damp down the rolling and steady the vessel in heavy weather. Masts and sails probably impressed passengers, 'improved' the appearance of the ship, and, although not openly admitted, satisfied the deep seated traditions of masters, mates and owners who had spent their early years in sailing vessels.

The Last Fully-Rigged Steamers

As we have explained in this book the fully square-rigged vessel with power propulsion was, commercially, a non-starter. She had of course to carry the full crew of a barque or full-rigged ship – depending on her size up to forty skilled men, to work her, in addition to the engineers and firemen. Potential cargo space was occupied by engine, boilers, stokehold and bunkers. But more important than all this, without power the ordinary bulk-carrying fully-square-rigged vessel is lucky when sailing to windward to point better than 70 degrees off the wind. When she moves under power the apparent wind immediately shifts

Figure 11:5 The USS Vandalia (1870–89) at the New York Navy Yard. She is rigged as a ship setting 14,000sq ft of canvas, the standing rigging being of wire rope set up by deadeyes and lanyards. (US Navy Photograph – released)

Figure 11:6 *The barque-rigged iron screw steamship* Durham. (Basil Greenhill Collection)

ahead and in no time at all she is pushing her masts, yards and complex rigging against the wind and getting no help at all from it unless allowed to fall off to leeward of her course. A powered fully-square-rigged vessel can, depending on her speed under engine, use her sail assist only with the wind on or abaft the beam.

It was for these reasons that 'steam auxiliary' square-rigged vessels were never operated in any numbers in ordinary ocean trade. As we have also explained, the navy, with its totally different operating situation, used them in large numbers right up to the end of the nineteenth century.

The barque-rigged screw steamer *Durham* (Figure 11:6), built in 1874, and similar vessels – *The Great Britain* re-rigged as a ship was in the same business – could operate profitably until the 1880s in the Australian trade with passengers and high value light cargo by sailing under square sails without power when conditions were favourable (as when running the easting down)

and steaming, with or without the use of her fore and aft canvas as conditions dictated, when the wind was forward of the beam.[3]

It has been recorded by John Malster in *North Star to Southern Cross* that many first-class passengers in fact preferred to travel by the *Durham* and her sisters rather than by the full-powered steamships of the Peninsular & Oriental Line, which did not provide a service direct to Australia for another ten years.

The *Durham* was built of iron at Blackwall for Money Wigram and Company, a very old established firm of London shipowners in the Indian and Australian trades. She was of 2,284 tons with a small compound engine. By the early 1880s the passenger business had finally moved away from vessels of her type and she was therefore chartered for voyages to New Zealand and Australia with cargo, the latter passage being made via the Suez Canal. After only eight years operation as a steamship the obsolete *Durham* was sold and and her new owners converted her into a purely sailing vessel.

Proposed Improvements

Even in the 1860s strategic considerations still demanded that some classes of naval vessel should continue to carry what was virtually a full sailing ship rig. Although steam propulsion was adopted in the British navy as fast as advancing technology allowed, and by the 1850s the battle fleet comprised vessels equipped with auxiliary steam engines driving screws, the old problem of combining sail and steam still existed. Being able to retract the screw up into the hull when not required was a big advantage but the existing rig needed to be modified, or indeed completely rethought. H D P Cunningham, a naval officer famous for his design of reefing square topsails, explained his ideas in a paper 'On the Rig and Sails of Steam Ships of War' which was presented at the third session of the Institute of Naval Architects in March 1862:

When we contemplate the maze of rigging and spars which constitute the rig of a first-class steam-ship, when we consider the huge yards extending their arms on either side as if on purpose to resist the progress of the ship, and which cannot be effectually got rid of even when braced forward as far as they will go; when in a calm we see the ensign of a fast screw-ship blowing out as if acted upon by a strong wind, and consider what inconceivable resistance must be opposed to the ship's progress when steaming against a strong breeze; when we consider, too, the immense weight aloft, the flywheel-like momentum which must be given to the ship in rolling by all this weight, I believe that the impression cannot fail to be received that the service of the sail-power are defective, and not consistent with the progressive improvements that have been made in the steam-ship otherwise.

It was Cunningham's belief that one of the problems (that of the hulls being strained) was caused by the excessive weight and leverage aloft and he lists measures to reduce this defect and improve overall performance by:

1st. That the required area of canvas shall be spread by the most simple means, and with as little rope as possible in the shape both of running and standing rigging, not only to reduce the weight aloft, and the resistance to the wind, and, at the same time, to render the arrangement of the rigging more simple, but also to lessen the danger of the screw steam-ship of war fouling her screw in the event of her losing masts or spars in action.

2nd. That the arrangement of the spars should also be very simple, and so adjusted as to admit of the yards being

Figure 11:7 *The two-bladed screw which could be retracted into the hull of the polar exploration ship* Fram, *now preserved under cover near Oslo. (Basil Greenhill)*

braced up as sharp as possible, not only to enable the square sails being used close to the wind, but also to diminish the resistance of the yards when steaming head to wind; or, if attainable, that means should be adopted for dispensing with the yards, yet still possessing the power of using square sails. This simplicity is also desirable, not only to reduce the number of joints in the masts, by which much standing or supporting rigging can be dispensed with, but also to diminish the number of spare spars, all of which add weight, and encumber the decks of the modern fighting-ship.

3rd. That a copious system of fore and aft sails should be provided, the effect of such sails, being considered of the greatest possible value to a screw steam-ship.

4th. That the power should exist of setting, and taking in the square sails from the deck without sending men aloft, such an ability being considered of the greatest importance with reference to the casualty of the screw power being disabled in action, and the necessity arising of resorting to the sails, when the men required to go aloft would be exposed to much danger from missiles employed in modern warfare. That otherwise, too, the power of working the sails from the deck must be considered a desirable accomplishment.

5th. That the protection from fire of the masts, spars, and even of the sails and gear, should be a subject for much consideration.

6th. That attention should be given to provide the means for easing the ship aloft as much as possible, not only by the actual reduction of weight, but by keeping it as low down as can be; such being considered, with reference to former remarks, most important.

At the time it was still considered necessary to have men-of-war with full sailing capabilities, at least those on the more distant stations, as the cost of fuel, the amount that could be carried, and the difficulty of procurement in some parts of the world demanded the vessel be operated if need be as a pure sailing ship. Therefore the rig was, unlike her contemporaries in the mercantile marine, still of utmost importance.

Specifically, he advocated:

1) standing rigging of ships to be of iron wire,
2) lower masts, as in the recently built *Warrior*, to be of iron,
3) iron lower yards and topsail yards to be fitted with his patent reefing gear,
4) the reduction in running rigging associated with his reefing systems,
5) a different method of staying the masts which allowed the yards to be braced up more sharply,
6) greater importance given to fore and aft sails which are to be as large as possible.

He concludes this section with the following remarks:

You will thus see that my arrangement of rigging admits of a large amount of fore and aft sailpower, the value of which, I must also point out, is greatly enhanced by the ability to brace the yards up sharper than upon the old plan; and this, together with the reduction of rigging, and consequent resistance to the progress of the ship when head to wind, which now almost neutralises the energy of the small amount of fore and aft sail power provided, must greatly add to the efficiency of the steam ship.

He advocated more masts on long vessels – four instead of three if the length exceeded 280ft – and also considered a proper balanced sail plan could be achieved if the concept of the vessel was to build the engines to suit the ship, and not the ship for the engine, thus allowing greater flexibility in the placing of the masts.

Even more radical proposals were put forward in the paper: the placing of the square sails on the after face of the mast supported by a yard hinged at the centre, combining the advantages of both fore and aft and square rig and a complete reversal of the established practice of supporting the mast, the shrouds being led forward and the backstays secured on the centre line.

Several illustrations were included at the end of Cunningham's paper, two of which are reproduced in Figure 11:8. Further clarification of this idea is shown in the drawing, Figure 11:9, which shows a foremast with only two sails, the upper brailed into the mast, the two half yards lying fore and aft; the lower having the starboard or weather section taken in, assuming the vessel is closehauled. A rope or reinforced canvas strip was probably worked down the centre of the sail with cringles either side at intervals to take the brailing or leech lines, and set up taut by means of a tackle as shown. However, if the full sail was required this tackle would have to be slacked up to allow the sail to assume the correct shape, for in this instance the two halves of the 'yard' are not in a line when set up but form an obtuse angle of about 160 degrees.

The foregoing remarks are based on Cunningham's practical but small scale experiments and therefore are to a degree speculative as to the operation in a full-sized rig. Furthermore, as the efficiency of a sail depends much on a clean airflow over its leading edge, the brailed in section when closehauled would generate considerable turbulence in this area causing a loss in performance, particularly limiting how close the vessel could lay to the wind.

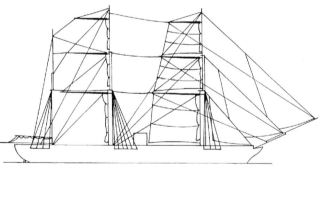

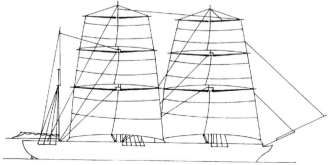

Figure 11:8 The forward leading braces were needed to steady the half yards, those on the foremast leading down to the bowsprit. The corresponding ones on the main mast yards have been omitted in the drawing but in both cases would have to run outside the standing rigging, and unless temporary stops were used, considerable chafe would result from those on the leeward side with the sails set as in the lower illustration. (From H P D Cunningham, On the Rig and Sails of Steam Ships of War*)*

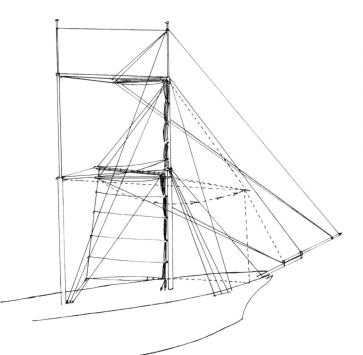

The Staysail Schooner Rig

The last quarter of the nineteenth century and early years of the twentieth century saw the development of the huge multi-masted American schooners, which in terms of manpower to tons carried were the most efficient pure sailing vessels ever built. By way of comparison the *Edward H Cole*, a big four-master of 1,791 tons gross, had a crew of eight whereas the full-rigged ship *A J Fuller*, 1,848 tons gross, needed twenty-one men.[4]

With such a small crew, a steam donkey boiler was essential to drive the deck winches and windlass for the sails were huge, 70–75ft on the hoist, some with an area of almost 6,000sq ft, such as the aftermost gaffsail on the six-masted *Wyoming* of 1909. Despite the availability of power on deck, reefing was a problem and the constant pumping action of the gaffs in a seaway strained both rig and hull. Furthermore in the larger vessels there were difficulties with the standing rigging, the common weakness due to every mast being supported in the fore and aft line by a triatic or springstay between the mast heads which ultimately relied on the headstays and bobstays. The whole system was subjected to tremendous strain in heavy

Figure 11:9 *Simplified drawing of Cunningham's revolutionary rig. How the topmast and topgallant mast were supported athwartships is not clear from his drawings – see Figure 11:8. (Peter Allington)*

Figure 11:10 *The American wooden six-masted schooner* Wyoming, *built at Bath, Maine, in 1909. On leaving the Kennebec her aftermost gaffsail, sometimes called the driver, is being set with the aid of the steam hoister, the exhaust of which can be clearly seen. (Maine Maritime Museum)*

weather and on occasions some part would fail, particularly the bobstay, leading to a partial or complete dismasting as occurred to the nearly-new five-master, the *Gov Ames* (shortened from *Governor Ames* so as to reduce the cost of telegraphic communication). During a hard gale her standing rigging began to stretch badly so the vessel was brought to anchor and the sails furled. However she was still in an exposed position and the violent pitching that ensued caused a splice to fail in one of her headstays, the result being that almost immediately both fore and main masts fell over the side. As all the masts were held together by the springstay, it was inevitable that the after three masts, now with the principal fore and aft support destroyed, would likewise come down.

As shown in the photograph of the *Gov Ames* the springstay was in the way of the gaff topsail when the vessel tacked, and to avoid damaging them the halyards have been slacked up. A hand would have to go aloft and bring the topsail into the mast so that he could reach and unbend the chain sheet, pass it over the springstay and than refasten it to the clew. Furthermore the tack line would also have to be shifted to the other side by heaving it aloft and likewise passing it over the stay, then dropping it down the other side to leeward of the peak halyard but on the weather side of the gaff jaws. What has all this to do with sail assist, for these were pure wind-driven ships? The answer

is, only indirectly, for the solutions to these problems put forward by R B Forbes, a distinguished American shipowner and merchant of the 1880s, have many of the attributes required for a sail assist rig and are in fact reflected in the barquentines *Star Flyer* and *Star Clipper* of the 1990s. Despite the readiness of the American shipowners and masters to accept innovations, this totally new concept was perhaps a step too far, and was never adopted. His plan for a staysail rig is reproduced in the book 'The Schooner *Bertha L Downs*', page 37, the original in the W J Lewis Parker Collection, and contrasted with his drawing of the *Gov Ames* as she actually was: a typical multi-masted gaff-rigged schooner of the late 1880s. For the purpose of the comparison, and sufficient to illustrate the differences, only the fore and main masts are shown in Figure 11:13, the shrouds having been omitted as there would have been little difference between the two in this respect, except, however, that he recommends more spread fore and aft for his staysail rig.

It can be seen that the large gaffsail normally carried has been virtually divided in half. The lower nock staysail with a boom, the topping lift led to the crosstrees of the next mast aft, has above it what can be described as a 'fisherman staysail', although strictly speaking the head is not hanked to a stay, at least, not on the one shown between the main and fore mast. However, the head of the corresponding sail between main and

Figure 11:11 *The American wooden five-masted schooner* Gov Ames, *built at Waldoboro, Maine, in 1888. (W J Lewis Parker Collection)*

Figure 11:12 *The late twentieth century cruise barquentine* Star Clipper. *(Star Clippers, Miami, Florida)*

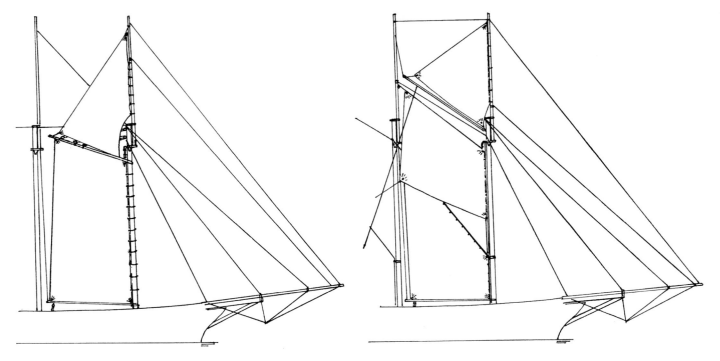

Figure 11:13 *Comparison between orthodox gaff foresail and topsail (left) and Forbe's idea for improvement (right). The head of the middle sail should be hanked to the stay immediately above for efficiency and ease of handling although this is not evident in his drawing of the rig and sail plan. (Peter Allington)*

mizzen is shown with hanks, but the weather or luff, unlike that on the sail between fore and main, does not appear to have any. The sail is controlled with two lines, the upper leading to a block part way up the main topmast and the lower one, or sheet, leading from the clew down to the deck. This type of sail would be difficult to set in a fresh breeze even if it was stopped off with rope yarns and broken out when required, and until it was in the lee of the lower staysail, would shake about a lot when taking it in: unless the plan was to stow it aloft, in which case the head would normally be hanked to a stay. If this sail could not be made to work closehauled as efficiently as the lower nock staysail then the loss of area and 'leading edge', compared to the gaffsail it was designed to replace, more particularly in a light breeze, would put the whole concept in doubt. It did however overcome a problem that is synonymous with gaff rig; that is, if no vangs are rigged to steady the gaff in light winds and a heavy swell, it will jerk and swing wildly from side to side on those occasions when the puffs die away. In the case of the American schooners, such circumstances could periodically roll the whole lot, sail, gaff and topsail to weather, most likely brought up sharply by the topsail hitting the springstay (see the photograph of the *Gov Ames*).

Shown in the photograph of the *Gov Ames* as she was actually rigged (Figure 11:11) is the large size of her aftermost gaffsail; a typical feature of this type of schooner. Forbes wrote:

> The aftermast is invariably the longest and is generally so far from the stern that the mizzen or spanker is the largest and most unwieldy sail when it should be the smallest [referring to three and four-masted vessels]. In squally weather this sail when lowered in gybing sweeps the whole after deck where the steering gear is placed, and greatly encumbers the wheel unless that is protected by a strongly built house; this is a fact so well recognised that the mizzen or after sail is generally the first of the large ones taken in.
>
> If we must have gaff rig the after mast should be nearer the taffrail than usual, and the sail should be fitted to brail in on the gaff and to the mast, but it should be so fitted as to be lowered entirely to the deck at times; this arrangement leaves the much smaller gaff and boom to be cared for.

His 'improved' staysail rig as drawn for the *Gov Ames* has a gaffsail on the after mast not only much smaller than the one she actually carried but considerably less than the other four gaffsails, which were about equal in size.

Sail Assist in the Twentieth Century

The use of sail assist on fully-powered screw steamers persisted into the twentieth century. Some steam drifters carried a gaff mainsail and a mizzen into the 1930s (Figure 11:14). In the 1860s and '70s wooden barques and barquentines, built to very high standards for work in pack ice, were launched in Dundee for Arctic whaling. As this business waned some of these vessels were sold to Newfoundland merchants and were still employed in the 1930s in an annual voyage into pack ice after seals. They were always under steam, but as Figure 11:15 shows very clearly, they used their staysails, and even on occasion their remaining square canvas, as sail assist.

The development of the marine diesel engine resulted in a great resurrection of sail in the early twentieth century and hundreds of German, Dutch, Danish and Swedish vessels were designed and built to use both sail and power. They were mostly small, though there were some four-masted schooners built of steel, polemasted and rigged with gaffsails. Perhaps most of them did not operate continuously under power and were therefore auxiliary sailing vessels, rather then sail assisted motorships. Many vessels were built, however, which were designed to operate continuously under power with sail assist, such as the British steel ketch *The Motoketch* (Figure 11:16). Some fine small Swedish motorships were launched in the 1930s rigged with gaff or jib headed sails (Figure 11:17) largely because the cost of fitting and maintaining them was less than that of carrying the certificated marine engineer then legally required in a vessel without sail.

In order to avoid restrictions placed on the building of fully-powered tonnage in Germany immediately after the First World War, five five-masted steel schooners fitted with 350hp diesels, originally intended for submarines, were launched in 1921–2 by Krupps for F A Vinnen of Bremen. Although built to the same dimensions their gross tonnage varied slightly, from 1,827 tons for the *Carl Vinnen* to 1,860 tons for the *Adolf Vinnen*. They were equipped with very square double topsails and a topgallant on fore and mizzen, and despite the unorthodox rig, were very handsome vessels. The sail plan – not falling into any established category, the term 'five-masted two topsail schooners' given to them by Harold Underhill – was as good as any. In continuous employment all over the world, they were probably the most commercially successful big sail-using vessels of the twentieth century. A breakdown of passage information contained in the German publication *Bark, Schoner und Galeass* for the *Susanne Vinnen*[5] (at the time named *Patria* and operating as a cargo-carrying vessel under the Italian flag) from June 1932 to December 1933, when she completed six deep sea voyages, shows that 75 per cent of the time she was under sail alone and 25 per cent under power and sail. Her average speed both under sail or sail and motor was about the same at 5.5 knots, although during this period her mean hourly rate dropped from 6.04 knots under canvas to 4.83 and under sail and motor from 6.96 to 5.22 knots, probably due to an increasingly foul bottom.

Data for the *Carl Vinnen* under the German flag show a greater use of the engine combined with sail when engaged in a similar trade to South America, the destination being ports in Northern Europe rather than those in the Mediterranean. Between September 1926 and September 1927 she crossed the

North and South Atlantic eight times, making four voyages that averaged out at 45 days, about 23 of which were under power and sail. Much would have depended on the destination, but wherever it was, the route chosen was that of a pure sailing ship, evident from the miles covered and the track as plotted on a worldwide chart. For example, an eastbound run from Hamburg to Melbourne (she was also in the Australian trade)

would be expected to have a higher percentage of days under canvas alone.

A comparison of total sail area shows that these schooners, despite having an engine, were indeed first and foremost wind driven, setting 2,321sq m or 24,983sq ft in twenty sails. The three-masted full-rigged ship *Acamas* of virtually the same length and gross tonnage, built in 1897, had 22,945sq ft in

Figure 11:14 *This ketch-rigged steam drifter, the* Kipper, *was built by Robert Cock and Sons, Appledore, North Devon, in 1908 for Yarmouth owners. (The late Sir Barnet Cocks)*

Figure 11:15 *Steam sealers with sail assist in the ice off Newfoundland in the 1920s. (Public Archives of Canada)*

twenty-eight sails as per measurement of a sail plan drawn up by Harold Underhill (see Figures 11:18 and 11:19).[6]

However, the *Acamas* could carry 3,200 tons of cargo when down to her marks at 21ft, while the Vinnen schooners loaded about 2,400 tons on a draught of 19.1ft. Not all this discrepancy can be attributed to draught alone as the engine occupied space, as did the double bottom water ballast tanks. In many ways this was a revolutionary rig, the sail plan resulting from a tremendous amount of practical experience combining to best advantage a high proportion of fore and aft canvas for wind-ward work (often under power as well), and a more balanced distribution of square sails on two masts for those times when wind was on or abaft the beam.

However, Herbert Karting, in correspondence with one of the authors (BG), makes some interesting points on their sailing characteristics which he describes as being good going to wind-ward although they had a notorious tendency from the amount of sail aft to head up into the wind (for this reason the aftermost gaffsail was sometimes cut down to a 'leg of mutton', or dispensed with altogether); and that the company standing orders stated the engine should be started only when absolutely necessary.

The long schooner lowermast raises the height at which the fore and mizzen square sail yards are slung, virtually at a level of the lower topsail yard on the *Acamas*, and in terms of length these yards were the same at 80ft, while the fore and main yards on the *Acamas* were 90ft.

The photograph of the *Carl Vinnen* (see Figure 11:20) was taken from the deck of the Finnish (Åland) four-masted barque *Viking* on 18 July 1937 when the *Carl Vinnen* was bound from Tyneside to Riga for a load of timber destined for Ghent. The breeze was moderate and from almost dead aft and in these

Figure 11:16 The Motoketch, *a sail assisted motor vessel with a 70bhp engine built on the Thames in 1910. One of the authors (BG) was familiar in the 1930s with her very similar sister vessel, the* Traly, *which was certainly operated with the continuous use of power. (Basil Greenhill Collection)*

Figure 11:17 *A Swedish motor schooner of the 1930s or early '40s, photographed in the English Channel in 1948 when bound from Teignmouth to the Baltic with china clay. (Basil Greenhill)*

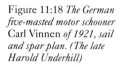

Figure 11:18 *The German five-masted motor schooner* Carl Vinnen *of 1921, sail and spar plan. (The late Harold Underhill)*

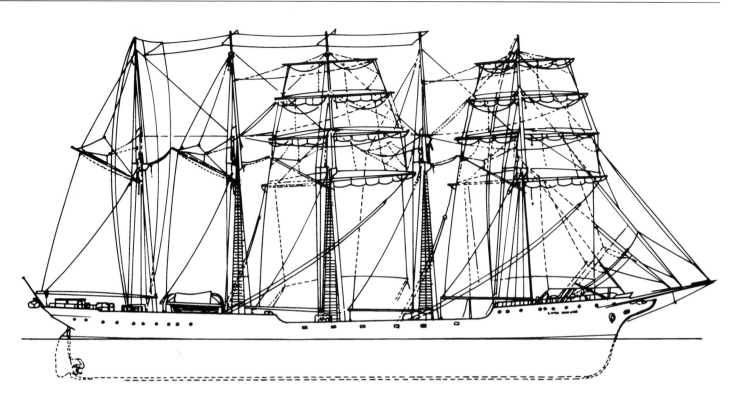

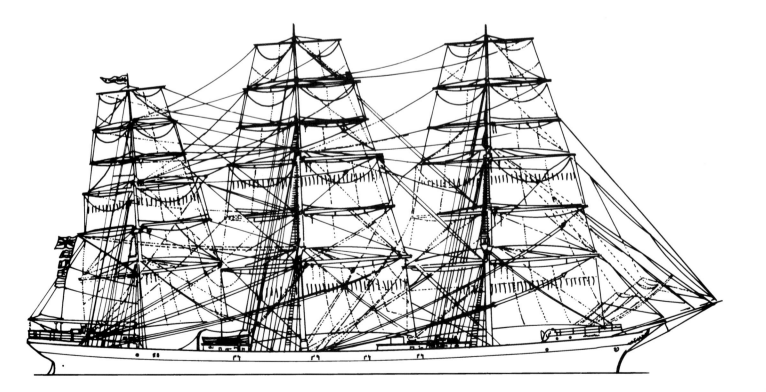

Figure 11:19 *The British steel ship* Acamas *of 1897, sail and spar plan. (The late Harold Underhill)*

circumstances only such sails as would have been of practical use were set, the engine running at the time. It is also evident that the fore and mizzen gaffsails have been set with a reef in to assist the wind flow to the square sails. (In this photograph the fore and mizzen 'courses' have not been set for some reason.)

The Canadian Motorised Fishing Schooners

A good example of the commercial use of sail assist as an essential part of the operation of vessels in the mid-twentieth century is provided by the two-masted fishing schooners working the North Atlantic cod fishery from Lunenburg, Nova Scotia, at this period. They were rigged with gaff foresail and forestaysail but used a jib-headed main of peculiar shape (Figure 11:21).

These vessels were designed and built to have full power, and the purpose of the sails was to provide extra drive, steady the vessel in a seaway, and allow her to maintain station or heave to in the fishing grounds without having to use the motor. The total sail area was about the same as the earlier sailing schooners would have set when well reefed down, and was a snug all in board rig, ideal in heavy weather. [One of the authors of this book sailed in the Lunenburg schooner *Bluenose II*, a reconstruction of the classic sailing schooner of that name. In force 6 the sail area was reduced to the level of a Lunenburg-type motor schooner. Without the help of the engine she sailed very fast and handled well. (BG)]

The following quotation is taken from *History of the Lunenburg Fishing Industry*:[7]

Before the 1920s were far advanced, motorised craft had begun to end the reign of the classical semi-knockabout-type in the Lunenburg fleet (without bowsprit or with a vestigial bowsprit). The first gasoline engine used in the fleet was installed in 1919 on the deck of the schooner *Vivian Smith* and was used for hoisting sail and weighing anchor. In 1919 the schooner *Edith Newhall* had a 200hp gasoline engine installed on her quarter, while the schooner *George M Cook*, the first schooner built in Lunenburg with an engine on the centre line, was launched in 1919 . . .

During the early 1930s the knockabout design evolved into the 'Lunenburg Type'. These schooners featured the round bow of the old semi-knockabout but without bowsprit. The sail plan had been reduced to the amount 'sufficient to enable the schooner to be hove-to when at sea, or to keep her moving without using the engine'. The Lunenburg-type schooner also featured a wheelhouse aft. The *Marjorie and Dorothy*, built 1934, typified this design. She was equipped with a 300hp full diesel engine, the largest yet installed in a Lunenburg fishing vessel, and with a speed of 10 knots, she was capable of employment in either the fresh or salt fishery.

These sail assist schooners were used in the Lunenburg

Figure 11:21 *The Canadian dory fishing motor schooner* Lilla B Boutilier, *built at Lunenburg in 1938 and lost at Carbonear, Newfoundland, in 1971. (Knickles Studio, Lunenburg)*

Figure 11:22 *The 'Lunenburg-type' motor schooner* Theresa E Connor *is preserved at Lunenburg at the end of the twentieth century. This photograph shows the master's berth, electronic equipment of the 1950s and the after end of her 300hp Atlas Imperial diesel. (Basil Greenhill)*

fishing industry into the 1960s. They ceased to be employed only when it proved impossible, with the rising standard of living and enhanced relief payments, any longer to recruit men ready to accept the hardships, dangers and low returns of fishing from small dories, launched from the schooner each morning.

Recent Developments

As ships were fitted with ever more powerful engines and fuel economy continued to improve, the reliance on sail diminished and so did the impetus to develop even more efficient rigs, for it was apparent that except for a few specialised categories there was no practical use for auxiliary sail, or sail assist, on the fast ocean going steel ships being built by the end of the nineteenth century. However, in recent years there has been a renewal of interest in wind propulsion of one kind or another and mention has been made of the cargo ship *Minilace* and the cruise liner *Wind Star* both making use of fabric sails, and proving each in its own way a success. In the mid-1990s there are a number of vessels of similar type making a living in various ways in different parts of the world.

The *Wind Star*, built in 1986, is 440ft long and sets four large boomed staysails, mizzen and jib with a total area of 21,500sq ft. She suffered many teething troubles with structural failure in the aluminium luff extrusions and difficulties with the computer-controlled, hydraulically-operated roller furling sails, but once these problems were sorted out her performance was better than expected. On her first real trial using sail and engine with the breeze forward of the beam, the speed increased from 10 knots to 13.8 knots when the canvas was set and allowed a throttling back on the screw propulsion. However, it was estimated that her speed under sail alone in the same conditions would be down to 6 knots with a good deal of leeway. In ideal conditions with a fresh breeze on the quarter she could manage 8 knots under sail alone.[8]

Another recent development has been the building in Ghent, Belgium, of two sailing cruise liners, the 360ft *Star Flyer* and *Star Clipper*. Both have 36,000sq ft of dacron sails and are rigged as four-masted barquentines with a potential speed of 17 knots under canvas alone, which compares with only 8 knots on the *Wind Star*. Therefore these two vessels can be considered as auxiliary sailing ships and in fact passages are done mostly under sail, the 1,370hp Caterpillar diesel used on occasions to maintain a schedule and for manoeuvring in port.

Modern technology has facilitated the furling and stowing of the five square sails on the foremast within the hollow yards and there is no need to go aloft other than for repairs and maintenance, hence the absence of ratlines on any of the masts. Unlike the *Wind Star*, which used computer-controlled and hydraulically-operated furling gear on all her headsails and staysails, both the *Star Clipper* and *Star Flyer* hoist these sails in the 'old fashioned' way and they are either stowed on the bowsprit or booms, as the case may be, with the exception of the main masthead staysail which appears from the photographs to be roller furled. This would allow 'passenger' involvement to some degree and therefore is a different concept from the *Wind Star*.

Except for the facility for 'housing topmasts' (the masts are all in one piece) many of the ideas and recommendations of both Forbes and Cunningham have been incorporated in this barquentine rig with its high percentage of fore and aft canvas complemented by the easily handled square sails on the foremast, a most efficient combination and ideal for this type of vessel.[9]

The Future

Despite a narrowing in recent years between what has become technically feasible, not just in the field of sail assist but in other forms of wind propulsion, and economic viability, the gap is still too great for the vast majority of the shipping industry. While fuel prices remain relative to their present levels, the financial incentive is not sufficient to warrant the necessary risk capital for design, development and installation of sail assist on a large scale. However, in some specialised instances such as the cruise ships, sail assist was part of the overall concept and built in from new, while other experimental rigs such as that on the *Minilace* have been fitted retrospectively after careful research. Japan launched its first successful wind-assisted vessel, the *Shin Aitoku Maru*, in 1980 which demonstrated that significant savings in fuel and overall running costs could be achieved.

In recent years the countries of South East Asia have shown interest, and financial backing has been made available by government agencies for several schemes. Using fabric sails and relatively cheap 'low technology' systems of control and handling, small vessels on short haul routes have shown that at least one quarter of the fuel costs could be saved. A typical example is the Fijian inter island cargo passenger vessel *Na Mata-I-Sau* of 350 deadweight tons which was fitted in 1984 with a ketch rig, the staysail, main, and mizzen all roller furling and rigged with booms, the one on the main doubled as a cargo derrick of 1.5 tons capacity.

To predict the future in a rapidly changing world is impossible but in terms of transportation one thing is certain: the world's fossil fuels are finite, and unless a totally new system of propulsion is invented it is inevitable that in the next century prices will rise as diminishing reserves are set against increased demand. There will be a greater incentive to develop other means of propulsion, which at the moment means wind, solar power, and possibly, gas-powered engines. This being the case, there are several ways in which they could be combined, for it is unlikely that only one system would prove viable on its own, once even the natural gas reserves have become depleted. If, for example, the main propulsion unit was gas/electric, wind powered alternators and solar panels could assist indirectly, or either fabric or wing sails provide the auxiliary backup allowing reduced engine revolutions to the extent of shutting down

Figure 11:23 Polaris *of Stockholm with a 1,000kw diesel has three jib-headed sails and a staysail totalling 650sq m. She is used in the cruise and charter business and was photographed in the harbour at Visby, Gotland, in August 1995. She was originally the Swedish torpedo boat T103 Polaris, built in 1956 by Fr. Lürssen Werft, Bremen-Vegesack. In 1977 she was withdrawn and sold to a private owner at Stockholm. (Basil Greenhill)*

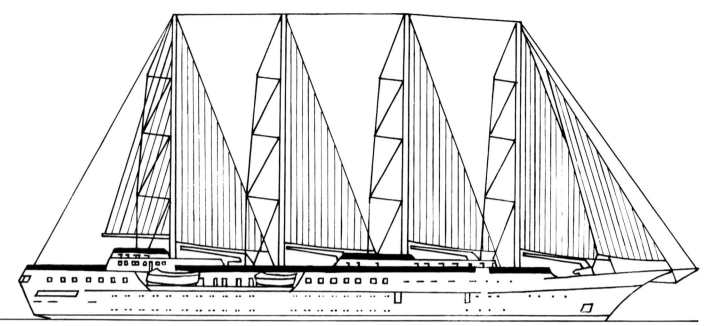

Figure 11:24 *The four-masted schooner-rigged motor cruise vessel* Wind Star *built in 1986. (Wind Star Sail Cruises Ltd)*

completely in a fair wind, while the solar power could virtually replace the generator used for ancillary services via a bank of storage batteries. The rising cost of fuel oil will undoubtedly, in the first instance, result in even more fuel efficient engines, and the development of gas-powered machinery, but that alone will not be enough: economies will also have to be made in the size of the propulsion unit leading to a slower service speed, which of course will affect the apparent wind. Nuclear-powered merchant ships are a possibility, as the experiment with the American-built *Savannah* in 1962 demonstrated, at least technically, but not as a commercially viable alternative at the time. In an increasingly 'green planet', which harbours in the world would admit such vessels? But who knows what will transpire in the future; attitudes can change when 'needs must' prevails.

Predicted climate changes brought about by a rise in global air temperature will lead to melting polar ice which in turn will probably modify existing ocean currents and hence the weather patterns they influence. How this will affect the established 'trade wind' and 'monsoon' cycle is unclear but it may be considerable.

If wind power, in whatever form, is reintroduced on a large scale, it will be a gradual process, a reversal of the slow decline of the importance of sail on the transitional steamships of the nineteenth and early part of the twentieth centuries.

1 R Murray, *Rudimentary Treatise on Marine Engines and Steam Vessels* (London, 1851) p. 134

2 By 1865 British yards were already building more steamers than sailing vessels. In 1860 iron construction had represented rather more than one third of new tonnage built. By 1870 no less than five-sixths of new tonnage was iron. Dr Thornton, *British Shipping* (Cambridge, 1959) p. 59

3 Rear Admiral P W Brock and B Greenhill, *Steam and Sail in Britain and North America* (Newton Abbot, 1973) p. 86

4 B Greenhill and S Manning, *The Schooner* Bertha L Downs (London, 1995) p. 11

5 Herbert Karting, *Die Motorsglar der Krupp-Germaniawerft* (Rendsburg, 1987) pp. 102–3

6 H A Underhill, *Sailing Ship Rigs and Rigging* (Glasgow, 1938) p. 27

7 R A Balcom, *History of the Lunenburg Fishing Industry* (Lunenburg, NS, 1977) p. 46

8 Joseph Novitski, *Wind Star* (New York, 1987)

9 Details of *Star Flyer* and *Star Clipper* from *Ships Monthly* magazine (October, 1992) p. 13

Epilogue

This history of the trans-oceanic steamship begins on the North Atlantic with gropings towards a regular service between Britain and North America. This book has been about the pioneers and principally deals with the one vessel which proved in the late 1830s that a regular service could be maintained, the *Great Western*. Her success was a technical achievement in developing new seamanship skills in which steam power and sail were used in conjunction with one another.

Whether this vessel, or any other packer, could ever have been made to pay adequate dividends on capital invested as a carrier of passengers and limited high-value cargo is very unlikely. Professor Francis Hyde in his excellent account of the history of the Cunard line[1], wrote, '. . . It soon became obvious that the paddle steamship, with it's limited cabin capacity, was un-economic as a means of ocean transport, unless supported by large mail subsidies'. We have suggested in this book that there was rather more to the commercial disadvantages of the wooden paddler than simply the matter of passenger accommodation. But the statement is, of course, correct. The paddler was a dead-end in commercial terms, as, indeed, she was also as a vessel of war.

In awarding mail contracts the British Government was concerned, as it was at the same period with the development of screw propulsion at sea, with the security provided by the financial backing of the promoters and with their political and social connections in a world in which these were all important[2]. As Francis Hyde has made very clear[3]. Samuel Cunard worked with great success in this world of 'Steam, Politics and Patronage'. Straight competitive commercial success on the North Atlantic had to wait to be demonstrated with the Inman Lines' iron-screw steamships in the 1850s.

There remains a matter to be cleared up. What motivated the original backers of these schemes, who invariably were called upon for extra funds and continued to accept no return on their capital? Who were these entrepreneurs and where did they obtain the capital for these ventures? These questions are for economic and social historians to answer, as are others relating to the financing and management of early steamships. The answers will, of course, involve contemporary attitudes to the investment of risk capital, with their social, political and psychological undertones.

One thing is certain, this must have been an even more challenging time in which to be alive than is the late twentieth century. For the first time in history it was becoming apparent that the hand of man, through the engineer, could rival, to use contemporary terms, the hand of God, in re-ordering the world.

1 Hyde, *Cunard and the North Atlantic* (London, 1975) p.29

2 Andrew Lambert, *Battleships in Transition* (London 1984); and 'The Ship Propeller Company and the Promotion of Screw Propulsion 1836-52', in Basil Greenhill, Ed., *The Advent of Steam* (London, 1993); and Basil Greenhill and Ann Giffard, *Steam, Politics and Patronage* (London, 1994)

3 Hyde, op cit, pp. 5–8

Bibliography

ARMSTRONG, Warren, *The Collins Story* (London, 1957)

ATHERTON, Charles, *The Capability of Steamships* (London, 1853)

BOURNE, John, *A Treatise on the Screw Propeller* (London, 1867)

BROCK, Rear Admiral P W, and GREENHILL, Basil, *Steam and Sail* (Newton Abbot, 1973)

BROWN, D K, *Paddle Warships. The Earliest Steam Powered Fighting Ships 1815–1850* (London, 1993)

BURNEY, Staff-Commander C RN, *The Boy's Manual of Seamanship and Gunnery* (London, 1871)

CANNEY, Donald L, *The Old Steam Navy. Volume 1* (United States Naval Institute, 1990)

COOPER KEY, Sir Astley, *A Narrative of the Recovery of HMS Gorgon* (London, 1847)

CORLETT, Ewan, *The Iron Ship* (London, revised edition, 1990)

CRADOCK, Lieut C RN, *Wrinkles in Seamanship* (Portsmouth, 1894)

CUTLER, Carl C, *Queens of the Western Ocean* (Annapolis, USA, 1961)

EMMERSON, George S, *John Scott Russell* (London, 1977)

The Greatest Iron Ship, SS Great Eastern (London, 1953)

FARR, Grahame, *The Steamship Great Western, The First Atlantic Liner* (Bristol, 1973)

FINCHAM, John, *A History of Naval Architecture* (London, 1851, reprint 1979)

GORDON, Lieut W RN, *The Economy of the Marine Steam Engine* (London, 1845)

GREENHILL, Basil Ed, *Sail's Last Century* (London, 1993)

GREENHILL, Basil Ed, *The Advent of Steam* (London, 1993)

GREENHILL, Basil, and GIFFARD, Ann, *Steam, Politics and Patronage* (London, 1994)

GREENHILL, Basil, and MANNING, Sam, *The Schooner Bertha L Downs* (London, 1995)

GRIFFITHS, Denis, *Brunel's 'Great Western'* (Wellingborough, 1985)

HARLAND, John, *Seamanship in the Age of Sail* (London, 1984)

KARTING, Herbert, *Bark, Schoner und Galeass* (Rendsburg, 1987)

KENNEDY, John, *The History of Steam Navigation* (Liverpool, 1903)

KENNEDY, Capt Nigel W, *Records of the Early British Steamships* (Liverpool, 1933)

LARDNER, Dionysius, *Steam and its Uses* (London, 1850s)

LEATHER, John, *Gaff Rig* (London, 1970)

MacGREGOR, David, *Fast Sailing Ships* (London, revised edition 1988)

Merchant Sailing Ships 1815–1850 (London, 1984)

McMURRAY, Campbell, *Old Order, New Thing* (London, 1972)

MURRAY, Robert, *Marine Engines and Steam Vessels* (London, 1851)

NICHOLLS, A E, *Nicholls's Seamanship* (Glasgow, 1905)

NORTH, Terence, *Yacht Sails* (London, 1938)

NOVITSKI, Joseph, *Wind Star. The Building of a Sailship* (New York, 1987)

POCHIN MOULD, Daphne D C, *Captain Roberts of the Sirius* (Cork, 1988)

POND, E LEROY, *Junius Smith. A Biography of the Father of the Atlantic Liner* (New York, reprint 1971)

RIDGELY-NEVITT, Cedric, *American Steamships on the Atlantic* (East Brunswick, New Jersey, 1981)

ROBINSON, Commander R S RN, *The Nautical Steam Engine* (London, 1839)

ROWLAND, K T, *Steam at Sea. A History of Steam Navigation* (Newton Abbot, 1970)

SMITH, Capt Edgar, *A Short History of Naval and Marine Engineering* (Cambridge, 1937)

SPRATT, H Philip, *The Birth of the Steamboat* (London, 1958)

Outline History of Atlantic Steam Navigation (London, 1950)

Transatlantic Paddle Steamers (Glasgow, 2nd edition, 1967)

TAIT, Capt James, *Tait's New Seamanship* (Glasgow, 4th edition, 1940)

TALBOT, F A, *Steamship Conquest of the World* (London, 1912)

TAYLOR, Capt L G, *Cargo Work* (Glasgow, 5th edition, 1959)

TREDGOLD, Thomas, *The Steam Engine. Volume 1* (London, 1838)

TYLER, David Budlong, *Steam Conquers the Atlantic* (New York and London, 1939)

UNDERHILL, Harold A, *Sailing Ship Rigs and Rigging* (Glasgow, 2nd edition, 1955)

Masting and Rigging, The Clipper Ship and Ocean Carrier (Glasgow, reprint, 1965)

Deep Water Sail (Glasgow, 2nd edition, 1963)

VILLIERS, Alan, *The Cutty Sark* (London, 1953)

Primary Sources

I K Brunel, 'Report on the Screw Propeller to the Directors of the Great Western Steam-Ship Company' (October 1840).

The Mariner's Mirror, vol III, no 9 (September 1913).

Capt Claxton RN, *A Description of The Great Britain Steam Ship* (1845).

United Services Journal, extracts from vol I, II and III, 'Notices of Steam Navigation', April 1840 – November 1841.

Hand written fair copy of Deck Log of *The Great Britain*'s maiden Voyage: 26 July 1845 to 11 August 1845.

Christopher Claxton, published version of 'The Logs of the First Voyage between England and America by the Great Western'.

Goodrich Collection 1875, Science Museum, London.

Journal of the *Enterprize* from 16 August 1825 to 13 October 1825, Science Museum, London.

H Campbell McMurray, paper on the conditions and employment of seamen.

H D P Cunningham, 'On the Rig and Sails of Steam Ships of War', paper read at the Institution of Naval Architects, 27 March 1862.

Samuel S Seaward, 'Memoirs on the Practicability of Shortening the Duration of Voyages, by the Adaption of Auxiliary Steam Power to Sailing Vessels', paper read 9 February 1841.

The Mercantile Marine Act, CAP 93 of 14 August 1850.
Copy of Patents obtained from The Patent Office, Nine Mile Point, Cwmfelinfach, Gwent NP1 7HZ. Reference – Bennet Woodcroft, *Alphabetical Index of Patentees of Inventions* (Evelyn Adams and Mackay, London)

Rigging

Patent No	Date	Person
5028	1824	Guppy
6332	1832	Heathorn
6743	1835	Smith
7261	1836	Smith
8009	1839	Smith
8223	1839	Todd
8594	1840	Newall
8762	1840	Newton
9656	1843	Newall
9811	1843	Greer
12835	1849	Wilson

Paddle Wheels

Patent No	Date	Person
4763	1823	Price
5253	1825	Palmer
5805	1829	Galloway
6212	1832	Galloway
6329	1832	Galloway
6359	1833	Hall
6631	1834	Symington
6887	1835	Galloway
6998	1836	Morton
8436	1840	Seaward
8671	1840	Wimshurst
8881	1841	Maudslay
8888	1841	Field
10349	1844	Hammond
10637	1845	Field and Maudslay

Index

All figures in **bold** refer to line drawings, plans and tables; all those in *italic* refer to general illustrations.